RETHINKING BROKEN

Childhood trauma didn't break you

it trained you

OWL CHRYSALIS MEDICINE

OWL MEDICINE
PUBLISHING

Dedicated to Adrianne Elsey

*& all the women who take it upon themselves
to nurture other people's children.*

Owl Medicine Publishing

Editor: Penelope Jackson

Cover Design: Owl C Medicine

Interior Design and layout: Jbookdesigns

Author Photo: Wren Morrow

Cover Design: Feat: The Kinstugi Porcelain Heart Vase, Concept by SELETTI S.p.A. Italy; Design by Marcantonio "Kintsugi-Love in bloom": Canva Pro, Shutterstock by Owl M.

CONTENTS

Section 4   Practices for the Path

PREFACE

I have no desire to add to the stack of literature that inspires its readers with poetic words and five steps to success promises that also inevitably lead them to a sputtering out. It's far too familiar, even among the best-intentioned books. There is one primary reason this happens. What's the reason?

People don't change according to what we <u>know</u>.
People change according to how we <u>feel</u>.

It's only after shifting our *mindset* about who we are and/or the context we find ourselves in that we can begin to *feel* differently about ourselves and make substantial, lasting changes. Only then can we let go of who we have thought ourselves to be to make room for who we *want* to become. The mindset shift allows us to see ourselves differently - so we can *feel* differently about ourselves, making room for becoming someone new.

Outcome does not follow skill set. It follows mindset.

If you teach someone a new set of skills, they're likely to stay relatively the same. They'll likely use their new skills to the same end they always have. Even if a person learns new skills but views themselves as more or less the same at the end of a book as they were at the beginning, what kind of decisions do you think they'll make? The same ones that they made before reading it.

If there's no mindset shift, no new and lasting worldview, there is no new vantage point from which to evaluate things, which means no new perspective. Even if the new information learned allows us to see the world in more detail, we see merely a more high-resolution version of the same, often crummy things. If we view ourselves and the world the same way we always have, how *could* we see anything new? How could we have a real lasting "Ah-ha!" moment? You can't.

That's why instead of simple 5-step promises to be healed, in this book, I have set out to establish one thing beyond any other.

THE MINDSET SHIFT

This book, though not a scientific text, uses multidisciplinary scientific information to provide you with the necessary mindset shift. Inside you'll find accurate, simplified scientific processes that are the all-important explanation of how a self-diagnosed "broken" person came to believe they're "broken." There are biological truths in developmental psychology and neurobiology that perfectly display why you are the way you are. And you're going to learn them.

This book seeks to provide readers with sufficient working knowledge of key subjects to recognize once and for all that none of us are broken. We never were.

We adapted appropriately to inappropriate circumstances.

The information in sections one and two is meant to serve as the functional framework for understanding how you and I came to be the way we actually are: *Chronic Stress Adapted.*

Once you understand how inevitably and perfectly you came to be the person you are, especially the bits you don't like, you will be free to use your newfound knowledge to build a better life for yourself.

Reading this book will not solve all of your problems. In fact, it seeks to solve exactly one of them. But that one problem is the single biggest problem a traumatized person can have. It's the one problem that guarantees living a miserable life.

Beyond resolving this fundamental root problem, the path you choose to walk is up to you. This may be the only book like this that you ever need or want to read. Or this may be the beginning of a lifelong pursuit of integration and wholeness. You can continue your life essentially the way it is going now, or you may decide to go live in an ashram for 40 years. It doesn't matter to me.

Whatever you choose to do after you address this one root problem is entirely up to you. No matter your path, you must first deal with this fundamental misunderstanding to avoid reentering old self-destructive patterns.

The primary problem that must be addressed
is the belief that you are "broken."

The reason believing "I'm broken" is a problem is, if that belief lives at one's core, when things get tough, it leads to one inevitable conclusion. *We are always at fault.*

Think about it for a second. When a real challenge comes your way, a person who believes they're broken has almost no chance to succeed. Why?

Anything worth doing is going to get hard at some point. When doing a hard thing, we inevitably come up against a challenge we don't readily have a solution for. Then, when we have to put our mind on solving these hard things, if we can't solve them relatively quickly and easily, we blame ourselves. We say, "It's because I'm broken." "I always do this." "This always happens to me." "Of course."

The excuse "I'm broken" is always sitting around, waiting, as our most convenient excuse. I'm broken makes you the scapegoat! No more of that.

This is just one of the reasons that childhood trauma causes those who survive it to begin life "behind the starting line." The lingering biological and neurological effects of childhood trauma create a lifelong, uphill battle. Luckily, the longer and more consistently we fight, the less steep the incline feels.

Whether your trauma was evident and acute, like the loss of a parent or fleeing a war-torn country, or whether yours was the more insidious death by a thousand cuts from a chronically dissatisfied caretaker, the results can be devastating.

Survivors of traumatic and chronically stressful childhoods have to work harder at nearly everything throughout their lives. It's not fair, it's bullshit, but it's real. Lastly, it's our *responsibility* to address it. After all, we are the only ones who are *able-to-respond* to the echoes of trauma living in our nervous systems.

It's time to regain control of your life by recognizing and using your innate skills.

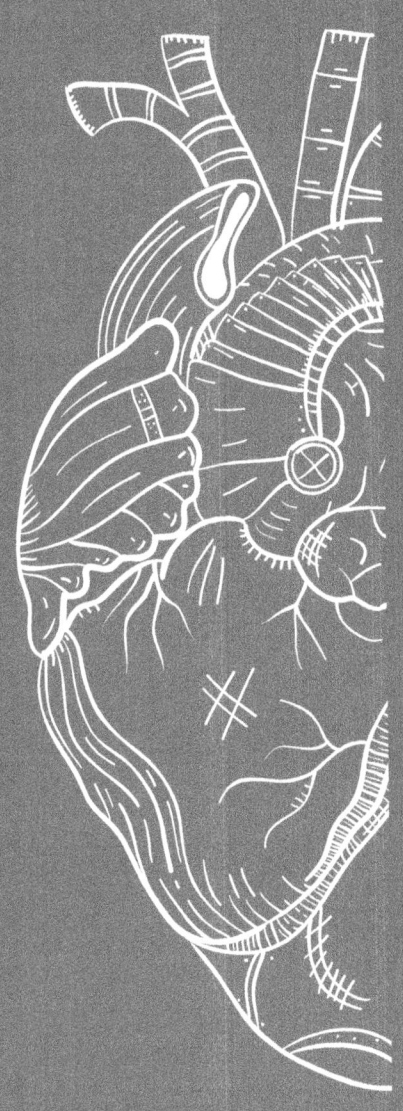

SECTION 1
Broken,
the Lens

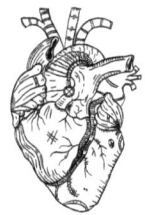

Welcome fam! In this section, we dig deep into the concept this book is about – brokenness. As a part of understanding what brokenness is and how screwed we are if we believe it - we are going to explore:

- Why people feel broken inside after trauma
- Establish the terms and definitions we'll use in our time together
- Explore what trauma really is - Chronic Stress Adaptation
- A brief introduction to your nervous system
- How trauma distorts our perception and therefore, our reality
- Establish a useful analogy to keep returning to for understanding conditioning

Each person's "healing" which I prefer to call integration journey is unique. What you choose to do with the freedom you gain from the insights in this book is entirely up to you. The interest of this section of the book is to encapsulate all the problems that come along with the belief that our trauma broke us.

Trauma is a sneaky and subtle creature. In this section, we set out to make trauma's subtle influences on our lives so obvious they become predictable. We will look at how the brokenness shows up in our adult lives.

By the end of this section, you will see how traumas you survived may be holding you back, screwing you over and generally preventing you from being the fully awesome person you are. Most importantly, you will understand why believing "I am broken" must forever be eradicated.

INTRODUCTION

We all got demons. Each and every person who has ever walked this earth has at least one true personal story that will break your heart. Each of us handles those demons differently. Some folks can pray them away. Some go to the gym or do yoga. Some shop, eat, gamble, and some sleep. Some drink, drug and try to fuck them away. And some of us tried every single way we could get our hands on, and it still wasn't enough. While some people seem to be able to successfully control their demons with these strategies, some of us can't. This book is for those people—the "broken" ones.

Eventually, the price of the bottle that can drown some memories is far too steep. For some of us, there comes a point where our strategies fail, and we can no longer eat our fear and loneliness into submission. Some of us will wake up one day halfway through our lives and realize we've slept through the best parts in hopes of missing the bad, but the bad came anyway. There even comes a point that a still greater emptiness follows the most satisfying sex, even with the most beautiful people.

Some of us just have too many demons to wrestle. And if we grow brave or stupid enough to spar a round? Our demons almost always seem to leave us feeling hopeless and broken under a dog-pile of self-loathing. If this sounds like your story, I'm sorry, me too. You are not alone. You are not broken. And although it's hard to see right now, I'll prove to you it's true.

Since you're reading this book, I assume that, like me, at some point in your life, you have believed one simple and detrimental lie. A lie you and I took to be our truths. A truth that you swear by even if you hate or consistently deny it. This lie is so powerful that if you agree to it, and believe it, you will become it. Hell, you probably already have.

Continuing to believe this lie creates many obstacles in life, this very minute. This lie has helped to form some portion of who you see yourself to be, just like it did for me. Recognizing this assumption as a lie is the most important thing I've done in my life, and helping *you* recognize it is the purpose of this book.

Since you're reading this book, it's safe to assume your childhood, like mine, was less than ideal. Although no one had a perfect childhood, some of us undoubtedly had it worse than others.

DIFFERENT TRAUMAS HAVE DIFFERENT EFFECTS

Those unfortunate enough to have faced sexual abuse from, say, an alcoholic father had to adapt differently to cope with their situation than, the child of a perfectionist mother. Both of which can be deeply damaging.

Those of us who faced physical or sexual violence, screaming matches or heavy objects flying across the room? We know that we are different. We have known it our whole lives. When other kids were afraid of the teacher or winding up in detention, we just laughed. And, of course, we did. We had already experienced real fear and real pain. Home was way worse than any detention or punishment a teacher could devise.

Experiencing violence from the one place you should feel the safest really screws with a child's head. The fear and helplessness experienced after that kind of situation leaves a child permanently changed. That change is why we feel broken.

Many, if not all of us, have always felt separate from, different than and not included. Something about us just didn't quite fit with the other kids.

It's not just the apparent adversities like violence or abuse that traumatize us. The less dramatic ones can sometimes be the most detrimental. Constantly being rebuked, corrected and rejected by those who are supposed to love us unconditionally hurts us profoundly. That perfectionist mother may not ever lift a violent hand. But her constant nitpicking can still wreck a person's sense of self so much they struggle profoundly and often silently, with physical and mental health problems.

People with less apparent adversities often have less apparent symptoms, making it difficult to overcome because they are harder to see. But that doesn't mean they're not deeply and profoundly hurt.

This type of broken person often *can* fit in, but only by playing pretend, which has left tens of thousands of people feeling that they can only be loved if they're pretending to be something or someone they're not. Is that you? This type of person feels hyper-self-conscious and is often obsessive about how others perceive them. They blend in like a chameleon wherever they go but never feel part of the group.

These people may find themselves pulling away from or altogether avoiding any chances at real, meaningful intimacy and may not know why. These are the "my childhood was fine" and "other people had it worse" people. That narrative, though probably true, eliminates any chance of living a purpose-driven, meaningful life. It denies the biological realities. So, it's time you challenge that narrative and take a second look.

SELF SABOTAGE

Some childhood trauma survivors sabotage themselves. When we get upset about something, we are much more likely to react strongly, tell somebody about themselves and get fired. If you're like me, you probably feel justified when doing it, too!

For example, we may have an idea or set a goal, and if it's important, subconsciously, we make sure that goal is all but impossible, except under miraculous circumstances. We stack a thousand things on top of the one thing that we actually need to do, making it impossible to achieve. We are seldom consciously aware while we are sabotaging ourselves.

In hindsight, we can sometimes see our meddling. But during it? We feel entirely justified in making decisions that totally derail our goals. Then, we interpret our sabotaged attempts as more evidence of our brokenness.

NO TRAUMA IS THE SAME.

Trauma affects each of us a little differently, and different situations require different strategies to survive. Some people tend to take on the blame for the whole world, while some of us blame the entire world itself. Some, if not all, feel guilty when we have no reason to. We can't seem to let blame and shame go. We love them.

Even while we hate them and deny it, our actions expose our truth. We crave these things. The evidence is clear. Under certain circumstances, we subject ourselves to punishments we don't deserve and justify it with something like "I know I can take it" or "I deserve it." Fortunately, I no longer believe that lie. But not by accident and not without help. I want to help you feel the same.

Like all heroes and fools starting on their journey, I found help. My help came in the form of a close friendship with a wise older woman named Kaya. She became the friend I didn't know I needed, and that changed my life forever.

My healing and integration path began when I met her. I met a friend who didn't judge me like everyone else seemed to. She saw the good in me. She saw me as lovable. I wasn't used to that. It was experiencing her, experiencing me as lovable, that allowed me to see myself that way. Her friendship was what allowed me, for the first time, to feel truly worthy of love. Although I learned many things due to my friendship with Kaya, the most significant and most subtle lesson took 10+ years to figure out. That lesson is:

To know one's self, one must first be known.

Through my friendship with Kaya, I got to see myself through the eyes of someone other than my messed-up family. When she saw me, I saw me. I saw myself from her perspective, and as a result, for the first time, I could see myself with some clarity. And to my surprise, I wasn't evil, a burden or broken.

Kaya gave me my first perspective shift. I want to do the same for you.

Kaya provided a safe place to explore my extremely fuzzy early-life memories. Because I was exposed to her thoughts, perspectives, and experiences, I became aware of my thoughts about myself and others for the first time.

I got the chance to observe and think about my tendencies and how they might affect other people, as well as how those tendencies affect my daily life. This friendship allowed and encouraged me to explore perspectives besides the ones I was raised with.

PERSPECTIVE IS OUR TOOL.

It is my desire that this book helps you in a similar way to how Kaya helped me. I want you to see yourself as a whole and unbroken person. The world *needs* you to see yourself as not broken.

There is no suitable replacement for a real live person who is physically and empathetically present; there's also no substitute for a good therapist. I have done my best to be as good a mirror and empathetic presence as this format allows. But I still highly suggest you get a good therapist if you can.

I hope this book becomes a judgment-free place for you to explore your thoughts, past actions and tendencies with curiosity. So you can have a shift similar to what I had with Kaya.

I encourage you to look at what happened to you without downplaying it. Look at what you have done and thought due to your experiences. There's no judgment here, only curiosity, reflection and occasionally a little sass.

THE GOOD NEWS

The good news is, for most folks who call themselves broken, the worst part of life is probably over. Whatever crap you have lived through, seen, survived, or would rather forget, the worst is most likely behind you.

In my experience, the worst feeling in the world for any human being is the feeling of helplessness. Barring some terrible accident, {Knocks on wood} you will likely never be as helpless as you were as a young child. That makes me hopeful. I hope it does fo you too.

You can take control of the narrative of your life using those perspective shifts. When we control the story we tell about our own lives, we have the power. What power isr that you ask? The power to see yourself for what you are: a skilled survivor and a badass.

To follow this path, you must become your own hero.

You have to embark on *your* life's journey. Your past is over. Starting right now, it's over. From this moment forward, you get to write, narrate and choose the ending of your story – no matter how it started.

Trauma is ubiquitous in our culture, and trauma comes in all shapes and sizes and from all kinds of places. Though the focus of this book was initially intended for those with what one might call extreme trauma, the purview of this book provides a perspective that's broad enough to have practical information applicable to anyone of any level of chronic stress and trauma in their past. A goal of the early part of this book is to help you see your experiences and yourself from angles you may have never considered before.

During our time together, I'm going to present to you a few perspectives for you to try on, like sunglasses. Viewing things through a variety of lenses allows you some understanding without judgment. Consider this book as your safe place when you start feeling crazy. It's meant to be an anchor you return to when you feel like you have lost your way.

Think of *Rethinking Broken* as your friend and field guide
for getting the most out of *life after trauma.*

What to look forward to

Rethinking Broken is a process, not a destination. It's a long path with no end. But being on this path makes incredible changes in your life, relationships, and, **most importantly, your relationship with yourself.**

I'm far from perfect, but I also know *I'm closer to perfect than I am to broken.* So are you. Since embarking on this journey for many years, I know I'm finally in charge of who I am. I know who I am and what I'm capable of. Which, as it turns out, is a hell of a lot.

I know what I like and what I don't like. I can finally ask for the things I need. And I quickly walk away from anything less than what I feel I deserve. I'm even beginning to get that down in my romantic relationships, which is always the most challenging part for folks like us.

I'm proud to say I've gotten a few truly challenging goals under my belt now, thanks to no longer believing that one detrimental lie. I'm very kind, and still, I take shit from no one. I love to try new things, and I live my life on my own terms. I feel fulfilled and complete all by myself. I have bad days and screw up like anyone does. And it's all thanks to knowing my trauma didn't break me.

I know for a person who sees themselves as broken, it's impossible to imagine right now. But there really is no better feeling than the feeling of wholeness. In this book, I have done everything I can to help you *feel* that wholeness, possibly for the first time. You are whole. You just need to experience it to believe it.

Being prepared for the work.

This is a long, cyclical and challenging path. It's challenging because, throughout this process, you will face big questions like "If I'm not broken, then what am I?" "How *do* I feel about *myself*?" "How do I feel about my parents or abusers?" "Did I deserve the mistreatment I survived?" all of these are big questions whose answers often have massive ripple effects in our lives.

You may outgrow certain relationships, which can be extremely painful. You may have to switch up parts of your environment regularly. Establishing new daily habits will help you move through sticky situations with more ease.

Walking this path means making slow changes until, eventually, you have performed a series of complete diagnostics on everything you think you know about yourself. That much work requires an equivalent amount of energy and drive to complete it.

Are you ready to be the person you've always wished you could be? Are you ready to change your *perspective*, *feel* your uncomfortable *feelings*, increase your *self-worth*, improve your *relationships* and upgrade your entire life? Good, then keep reading.

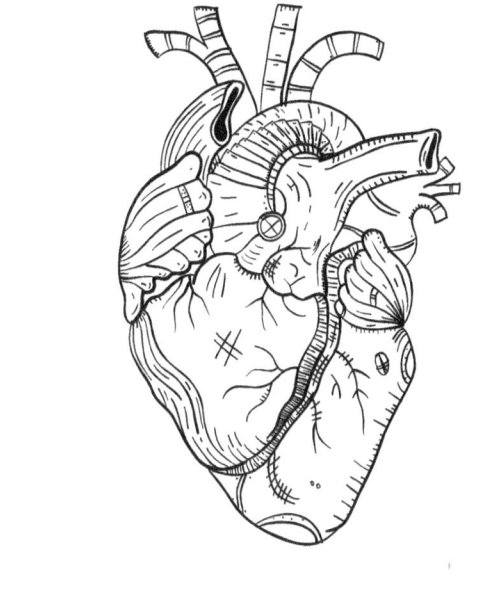

CHAPTER 1
MY STORY

Okay, so why listen to me? What do I know?

I'm just a human who, like you, once believed that I was broken and not just average run-of-the-mill broken either. I believed I was one of the most broken people on the planet. If not *the* most broken. And, like you, I had proof. I felt I could prove my brokenness in a court of law.

Life dealt me a pretty trauma-filled life. But that wasn't really anything unique where I come from. Like many people from working-poor families, I got dealt a crappy hand in life, but I've learned to make the best of it. Using my experiences and some scientific points, I've come up with a system for people to use to make the best of their crappy hands. Hopefully, it helps you too.

In this section, I'll share the general ark of my story so you have an idea of what my life has been like. More pertinent details come later in the book as examples to make specific points clear. My story may speak to you. It may not matter to you at all. It may remind you of your own story in ways. Some people might find that parts seem unbelievable. But I assure you that all the stories I share are true to the best of my knowledge.

I've had a wild life, and probably like you, there are too many stories to share them all. I've included only a few snapshots of what I consider to be more pivotal moments - to give you a general idea of the intense weirdness and awesomeness of my life. If my story doesn't matter to you, or you want to get straight to the work, feel free to skip this section and go straight to Section One.

In my life so far, I've slept under bridges, behind bushes and in dumpsters. As an adolescent, self-harm in a variety of forms was common for me. I attempted suicide in my early twenties. I was using alcohol, opiates and marijuana by 13. I was drinking almost daily by the time I was 16. In my early twenties, I was stabbed by an ex-boyfriend and continued in that relationship for years. To find sanity and heal, I didn't speak to either of my parents for over a decade. I've drank myself into oblivion more times than I could count.

HOME LIFE

I grew up the middle child of a single mother in a small town in Indiana. My parents got a divorce when I was about six years old. For most of my adult life, my mother lived as a closeted lesbian, even to her kids. I was teased and bullied daily over rumors of my mom's sexuality, which was the cause of an overwhelming number of fights I was in. Then, the rumors became about me. So, I had to defend myself in countless fistfights for being a "faggot" before I had any idea what the word even meant.

The exception that proved the rule was a fight over a girl ironically, which I lost. Naturally, my mom sent me back down the street to fight the kid again. Because, in my family, we didn't start fights, but we were damn sure expected to *end* them. My mother had primary custody of me and my two siblings. So, she mostly raised us.

My father has an associate's degree in bible doctrine and theology, and nothing matters to him like his religion, not even his kids or his sins. Thanks to my religious zealot and serial cheater father, I spent my later teenage years genuinely believing that if I fasted - starved myself until I proved penance for being gay and prayed hard enough, I could pray the gay away, which would save my soul from burning in a lake of fiery damnation. I actually believed that once I successfully prayed the gay way, I could lead a global charge that praying the gay away could be done. I failed at that too. Sorry Bruce, still gay!

Both my parents were the "You don't have to like me - but you will respect me" type. We were a spare the rod, spoil the child home. When I was young, she used a cutting board as a paddle. She used to spank me and my brother using that cutting board, which she eventually broke while using it on my older brother. So, we were all physically terrified of her.

My mother's wife has two children. My siblings and I were raised in the same house with her kids under two completely different sets of rules. My siblings and I had to toe the line, while her wife's kids got to bend and break the rules, stay out later, talk back, and, from my perspective, do whatever they wanted. I hated that more than words can express. But there was nothing I could do about it. That's most likely why I'm obsessed with fair application of rules as an adult.

I hated being at home. As a kid, I would rather be anywhere than at my mom's house. So, my senior year in high school, I had four jobs. I worked 39.5 hours a week at an all-you-can-eat steakhouse and buffet. I also worked at a greenhouse, a telemarketing center, and from midnight to noon at the same factory as my mother on weekends.

Between school, a full-time job and two part-time jobs, at 17, I was so exhausted I repeatedly fell asleep while standing up on my shift at the same factory my mother still works at. I almost lost my fingers more than once from it. Like I said, I did *anything* to not be at home.

While in high school, one of my coworkers and close friends died of an overdose. We had worked together the night before he died. Like most nights, he and I stood in the parking lot after close to drink. It was a small town, so my mom knew what happened too. In fact, she coached my late friend's little sister in softball. So, she knew what was going on when she came into my room and asked me what I wanted for dinner, and I said, "I don't care." Probably with some attitude because, you know, a really close friend of mine that I was just hanging out the night before had died. To which she responded, "Don't get mad at me. I'm not the one who killed him!" Empathy or sympathy were not family values when I was young.

VAN LIFE BEFORE IT WAS COOL

By the time I was 17, I had become sick of the daily screaming matches with my mother. It didn't matter if we only saw each other for 45 seconds. We fought in those seconds. After a fight one day, I decided I needed to move out. There was only one place I could go. I didn't want to live with *him* either, but at the time I felt it couldn't be worse than mom's house. So, I did the unthinkable and moved in with my father.

I tolerated living with him for less than a month for some genuinely ridiculous reasons. He had just married his 3rd wife. They met on January 1st and married 24 days later. Because, you know, *this* marriage was appointed by God. Apparently, unlike his previous two and her previous five marriages.

During this 3-week stint of living with him, things came to a head when he asked me if I could *see* the demons that my new 15-year-old aunt said she saw in the house. The demons, according to her, were apparently, *literally* crawling out of the television.

When I said no, I couldn't see literal demons; I was told I needed to "check my salvation." I'll never forget the seriousness in his eyes. Every truly *saved* person my father knew could *literally see* demons... I know this probably sounds like a joke to most people. It wasn't for me.

That was the end of me playing either of my parents' games. While my father was at work one day, I packed up some of my wardrobe and a few belongings, bought a clothes rack from Walmart, and moved into my red '98 Ford Windstar, which I finished high school living out of.

About this time, my older brother, Caleb, a Marine, was about to leave for his second deployment to the Middle East. I wanted to see him before he left, not knowing it would be my last chance to do so. So, I did. After high school graduation, while waiting for my MEPS date to join the Air Force, I drove to Camp Lejeune, North Carolina, to visit him.

I had no income anymore, just what I left Indiana with after quitting all four jobs. So, I ended up singing and testifying in a few churches, which gave me the gas money to make it back to Indiana in time for my cousin's wedding and my date to leave for basic training.

BURYING MY BROTHER

My brother died not long after that second deployment; He was 22. One day, he didn't show up for roll call. He was found dead, hanging by the neck in his off-base housing. I was 19 at the time, fresh in the military. Not just the military though, it gets better. I was in the United States Air Force Honor Guard. My job was performing military honors funerals, mostly in Arlington National Cemetery, for other fallen soldiers, where I performed the 21-gun salute five days a week.

So, of course, when Caleb died, I performed honors at his funeral too. With all of the stoicism I could muster and in honor of my dead brother's service, only days after Christmas, on one knee, I handed the flag to my own mother, just like was done for my grandmother six weeks prior, just before Thanksgiving. That wasn't all 2007 had in store for me either. There was a cherry on top of it all.

The cherry was while I was home performing in and attending my grandfather's and then brother's funerals, there was an investigation launched on my sexuality in the military. This was still the time of Don't Ask, Don't Tell. Which meant I was facing federal felony charges for being gay in the military.

During my time in the Honor Guard, I got to be a part of President Barrack Obama's first inauguration and the forced retirement of a general who managed to lose a nuclear warhead. I was handpicked to perform ceremonies for Queen Elizabeth, The Pope and more foreign dignitaries than I care to count. My favorite events were escorting the drunk wives of retired generals to fancy events.

After four years in Washington D.C. performing all those high-profile ceremonies and over 1000 military funerals, including my brother's, the Air Force said I had to switch jobs. So, I cross-trained into medicine. And as it turned out, I fell in love with it.

MEDICAL TRAINING

Technical school, which is what the Air Force calls its job training, is unsurprisingly fast-paced. What is usually a 6–12-month national EMT program is completed in 6 weeks. If you lagged, you were left behind. We were expected to learn an entire biological system per day. And I did. I had to learn FAST! Luckily, one of the gifts of my "brokenness," one of my *strengthnesses,* more on that soon, is the ability to integrate a lot of information quickly.

Unknown to me at the time, my trauma helped me learn the entire cardiovascular system in one day. Same with endocrine, respiratory and the rest. That meant we had to learn everything from how blood flows through every major artery and vein to the anatomy and physiology of the heart, its chambers and the vessels in a day.

We had lectures on one day and a final exam first thing the next day, Followed by lectures on an entirely new system. Rinse and repeat. Out of the 27 people in my class for this program, 7 of us graduated on time. Because after all that, there was still a national board exam to pass. So, if your brain dumped the info after each test, you failed the board anyway.

It was then I began to notice that it's fast-paced and intense environments in which I thrive. Not that it was all sunshine and rainbows. I lived on black coffee and Crown Royal every night. The coffee kept me alert enough to focus on studying late, and the Crown kept me calm under the pressure.

When I finished my training, I got stationed in West Texas. When I arrived there, my new clinic was the #1 worst-staffed clinic in the *entire* Air Force.

I took to medicine like a duck to water. I enjoyed the mystery and the problem-solving. Because of my traumatic past, it was nearly effortless for me to separate myself from the emotional experiences of my patients. I was famously cold-hearted in my clinic but also famously good at my job.

Two of the doctors I worked with trained me specifically to perform on them the same treatments they performed on their patients as doctors of osteopathy. One of whom was also an acupuncturist and trained me in that as well.

Then, there was the court martial in which I had to testify against the medical provider who took me under his wing. Unfortunately, this nurse practitioner who trained me was so amicable that it occasionally got in the way of him providing quality care for some patients, which put a few of them at risk on multiple occasions. He was brought up on multiple serious charges, and I had to testify in court against the man who trained me, trusted me, and made me fall in love with medicine, and whom I genuinely cared for as a person.

There are so many incredible and ridiculous stories from each chapter of my life. I could easily fill another book or three. I'm only trying to display the intensity and randomness of my life so you know I'm not just making this stuff up. Suffice it to say that by the time I separated from the Air Force, I knew two things for sure.

- I knew I was deeply screwed up
- I knew I wanted to pursue medicine.

But I also began to understand that my extra thick skin, developed by years of trauma and chronic stress during my childhood, thickened from burying people for a living, was then hardened further by Western medicine.

I had skin like concrete. And I knew from my osteopathic doctor friends and especially from the principles I learned about acupuncture that if I wanted to pursue medicine, especially acupuncture, I needed to shed some of that concrete skin.

So, after six years, two months, and one day, I got out of the military, and I set out to do just that. I threw myself into Buddhism, which saved my life, frankly. I started to drink less and spent hours a day learning to meditate. There's a whole chapter on that later in Section Four. I read the texts and went to Sanghas - Buddhist gatherings similar to church in my local area, Eugene, OR.

HOMELESS LIFE

This is when I met a guy who traveled, hitchhiking and hopping freight trains from city to city. He lived on the streets and played music for his money. Coming from small-town Indiana straight to six years in the Air Force, I had never heard of such a thing. I was planning on going to acupuncture school that fall, but I knew I still needed to de-militarize.

So rather than attend school acupuncture school immediately, I gave away basically everything I owned and hit the road. I lived life with him, traveling on the streets and playing music for enough money for food, cigarettes, and booze.

This is when all the sleeping under bridges and behind bushes happened. I spent almost three years as a homeless transient musician. Here, I learned many of the *most* painful and important things I've ever learned. I learned about equivalent exchange and generosity. I experienced first-hand what the Buddhist texts talked about interdependence.

One day, a few years in, I was walking down the street, backpack on my shoulders, dog and guitar in hand, and something incredible but straightforward struck me. Having come from poor midwestern factory workers, I believed I "did it on my own." I didn't speak to my mother or my father for nearly ten years of my life. I never asked for help from anyone. I was the definition of independent in my head. If I needed something, I would go out with my guitar and earn it.

The lesson I learned that shocked me was that *I did not earn* any of what I thought I did. Whether I was playing music or not, each dollar I had made and each piece of food I had put in my mouth for years was given to me out of the goodness and generosity of complete strangers. This was my first awakening to the reality of interdependence.

Of course, being a traveling homeless musician has its drawbacks, too. Being constantly harassed by the Police and tweakers was honestly the worst part. The guy I was with who brought me on the streets had been on them since he was a teenager. He punched me in the face almost as soon as we were far away from anyone I knew, traveling together. I never thought I would be in a relationship with someone who was physically abusive, but here I was.

After a few years, a few dozen fistfights, and eventually being stabbed twice by my "love," I realized that I needed to do something different, or I would end up dead like so many of my traveler friends. In section three, we talk about why people like us need more pain to change than the average person.

My alcohol use, which started before high school and got worse in the military, had turned into full-blown alcoholism by this point. So, I backed my plans up. I might be screwed up, but that insight about generosity and interdependence told me I had successfully de-militarized, at least a little.

Enter Acupuncture School

While attending acupuncture school, I again excelled in integrating the information, already having a foundation from a few years of exposure in the military. But I struggled *hard* to stay focused on the school work because the school itself was so screwed up.

I was like a dog with a bone. I was determined to fix the inequities in the school. Now I look back and see that it sounds a lot like trying to fix the unfair double standards I couldn't fix in my childhood.

While I was in school, native American water protectors in North Dakota were being tear gassed and shot at by the United States government for protesting a massive pipeline. My professors were kind enough to allow me to move up my finals a few weeks so that I could self-deploy against my own government to support the natives at the Standing Rock North Dakota Pipeline protest.

That was, by far, the most sacred place and time of my life. There, I learned what I really wanted. I wanted to help real people in real pain under real and present threats.

Since then, I've used that experience as a blueprint. I've set up care clinics at other protests, like an occupied protest in Seattle. There was a nationwide police brutality movement during which Seattle residents reclaimed an entire police station and the public spaces around it. That turned into a month-long occupation during which I provided care. I've continued this theme by working with international disaster relief organizations to provide medical care to refugees seeking asylum in places like Mexico.

My life has been one of intensity. It's been *"a lot,"* which you'll hear more about later, as it has been a theme of my life. But I like it that way. I'm good in a crisis, like damn good. If I hadn't been, I wouldn't have kept finding myself performing so well in those types of environments.

When normal people reflect on the highlights of their lives, they usually think of home with their families, watching their favorite TV shows, and playing with their kids. Or they think of that one beautiful vacation they had, their honeymoon or the epic touchdown that won the championship in high school.

When I think of the greatest moments of *my* life, I think of Standing Rock. I think of Tech School and providing medical care in war zones. I think of the incredible conversations about particle physics with a refugee in a squat house in Tijuana.

WHAT MY STORY TAUGHT ME.

The point I'm trying to make is I'm built different, just like you are built different. You and I are not built the same, but we're both different from many of our less traumatized peers in the world and thank goodness. I love being me.

I would rather carve my own eyes out with a melon baller than sit in a cubicle and answer phones from 9-5. This is true for many trauma survivors. Technology, to me, is boring and frustrating. So, when it doesn't work perfectly, it makes me want to nuke and salt the whole earth. Which means I need customer care often. Customer care folks usually live that 9-5 life. Maybe they just don't own melon ballers, but it seems to me it's more likely their jobs fit their build the same way mine fits me.

I have no problem with the 9-5 world. I need it. It's just not the environment for me. I'm pretty sure tech support folks are happy to let me set up medical clinics in combat zones or for refugees, and I'm more than happy to let them solve whatever technological issue I'm having. They have their skill sets, and I have mine. Both work best in a particular environment – which is a major theme of this book.

Repeatedly being in one particular type of environment, high pressure, high stakes, and somewhat dangerous environments, showed me that my adaptations to my childhood crap were not just useful *but damn near a superpower* in the right circumstance. Seeing how naturally good I am at something gave me a foothold for my sanity, my sense of purpose, and my calling.

You have probably found yourself in a situation or two in your life in which you were the perfect person for the job. You were in the right place, at the right time, with the right skills. Do you remember how that felt inside? If you just remembered an example, keep it in mind to put it on your list later on in Section 3.

We all have a subconscious intelligence inside us that occasionally guides us to situations where we're the perfect person for the job. That subconscious intelligence becomes a powerful tool when we make it conscious and use it toward our goals.

Once we tap into and begin to understand that subconscious drive, the brokenness we feel dissipates profoundly. It doesn't go away completely. But we aren't shooting for perfect. We are shooting for better. We're shooting for building *a life we want to live.*

So, to answer the question at the beginning of the chapter, who am I? Why should you listen to me? I'm a peer, friend and fellow fumbler who believes you have some serious power already bubbling inside you, waiting to be used. I've found it in myself and literally every other person who had a rough start to life.

What I and my story hope to offer is this: the perspective that you are "good enough" at this very moment today. To know it for yourself, all you need to do is find and lean into what you are already good at in a place where it's needed. When you do, you'll see yourself change, from broken to badass…

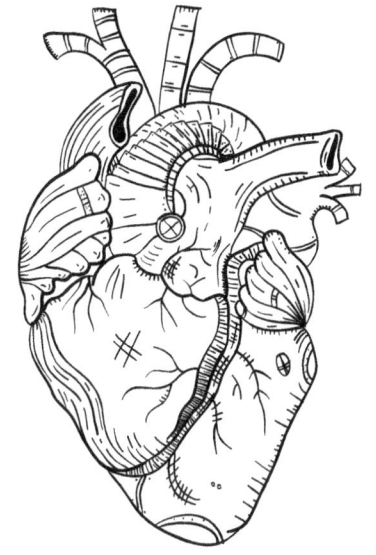

CHAPTER 2
DEFINING TERMS

Much of the information and concepts we will cover throughout this book is already a conversation being had in pop culture to one degree or another. Mostly, it's happening in bits and pieces, in short-form content all over the internet. The fact that this conversation is happening is a beautiful, necessary and timely thing. But some things could be improved.

One issue I see is that each person who has taken it upon themselves to talk about their trauma, chronic stress, and healing seems to have different definitions for the same terms. Since trauma is a profoundly individual experience, that makes total sense. Still, for the consumer of this information, it can become confusing to hear so many voices using the same terms in ways that frequently contradict each other. Let's define some of those terms for this book.

WHAT IS STRESS?

All trauma is stressful, but not all stress is traumatic.

Before we can talk about trauma, we need to talk about what causes trauma. We have to understand the physiological processes behind trauma. That thing we call *stress*. In biological terms, what we experience when we experience stress is a *stress response*. Stress is a word we are all familiar with. Still, the implications and associations of stress have changed a lot in recent years. So, let's start by getting on the same page.

Stress is *"any kind of change that brings on a physiological emotional or psychological strain."* (World Health Organization)

We all know that the only thing consistent in this world *is* change. The WHO's definition makes it clear that stress is "any kind of change... that brings strain." This means *stress* is a constant and inescapable reality of all our lives. That has been true long before the World Health Organization created that definition. So, over the millennia, our bodies have adapted themselves to be great at dealing with stress. It's everywhere all the time, so how could we not?

STRESS RESPONSES

Since stress is everywhere, our body naturally had to develop strategies to protect us from the types of stress we faced most often in our evolutionary history. Modern civilization has removed most of the stresses our species expected and is therefore designed to handle.

Those species expected life-and-death, short-term intense physiological stresses have been replaced by low-grade, long-lived forms of stress our bodies were not designed for. The only predators we have to worry about anymore are other humans. So, we are instead worried about climate change and how we will pay our bills. Modern forms of stress are so long-lived we never get to escape them. Which puts a new type of stress we aren't equipped for on our bodies and especially our brains.

As far as the body is concerned, the update on stress can be simplified into the following:

Short-lived stress = Good stress
Long-lived stress = Bad stress

WHAT IS TRAUMA?

Trauma is the Greek word for wound. (Websters) The kind we discuss can be physical at first, but the lingering effects are psychological. For us, traumas are psychological wounds that continue with us long after experiencing a traumatic event.

Wounds of a physical nature are tender when fresh. If you touch a fresh wound even gently, it will cause a person to flinch. Depending on the size of the wound and the healing ability of the person, that wound might become a scar.

A scar is usually an improvement over a wound. It isn't tender anymore. It's much tougher than real skin too. But it's also thicker, less pliant and elastic. It reduces flexibility and sensitivity as well. Our psychological traumas go through a very similar process.

Like physical wounds, all psychological traumas are especially tender at first. Some of our wounds heal quickly and some fester. Some wounds keloid, becoming extra thick and fibrous, which protects but also limits us. While others eventually fade to a pale line or disappear entirely.

What makes something a trauma instead of a stressful event is that the physiological and psychological effects of the stressful event stick around longer than they ought to.

Trauma for the person living with it shows up as a constellation of issues that are triggerable at any moment. And it's not just the conscious recollection of a stressful event that triggers it either. We may be triggered by the color of a room or a certain smell. These triggers often won't register consciously, making us reactionary, often not knowing why.

It always comes with unresolved emotions that, unless we become aware of our programming, predetermine our behaviors and reactions. Trauma keeps us vigilant, constantly protecting our wounds long after the scar tissue is formed and the tenderness is gone. Because of that, it resists healing. Scar tissue is preferable to a raw wound but has drawbacks, too.

WHAT KINDS OF TRAUMA ARE THERE?

There are a lot of kinds of traumas out there. There's generational or inherited trauma, childhood trauma, trauma from war, and primary and secondary trauma. The National Child Trauma Stress Network breaks trauma into 13 categories.

- Bullying
- Community Violence
- Complex Trauma
- Disasters
- Early Childhood Trauma
- Intimate Partner Violence
- Medical Trauma
- Physical Abuse
- Refugee trauma
- Sexual abuse
- Sex trafficking
- Terrorism violence
- Traumatic grief

But really, I view their list more as ways we can become traumatized or things that can be traumatizing. Each of these has unique lingering effects.

Other places break trauma into three categories: acute (short-lived singular events), chronic (long-term exposure to stressful situations), and complex (repeated exposure to multiple types of traumatic incidents). This, to me, is a fairer representation of categories of trauma.

BIG T & LITTLE T - TRAUMA

For our purposes, trauma types are best viewed as a sliding scale. The traumas at one end of the scale are acute and often violent. These kinds of trauma are what most people think of when they think of trauma. This has been referred to by some as Big T trauma. That's what we will call it too. Most trauma research focuses on this type.

Big T trauma includes events like rape, molestation, violence in the household, war, famine or the loss of a parent - that sort of thing. But this is only one type of trauma, and it's arguably not even the worst type. It is the most salient in our minds, partly because these traumas are "made for TV."

Big T traumas are terrible and highly memorable, having obvious long-lasting negative impacts on those who survive. We see this type of trauma making money hand over fist in Hollywood every year. But what about the other end of the spectrum? What kind of trauma lives there? And is it even trauma?

If Big T trauma is on one side, little t trauma occupies the other end of the spectrum. Little t traumas are the less memorable but deeply hurtful and far more common form of trauma. Children, especially highly sensitive children, can be injured in many ways. Little t traumas occur for everyone during childhood.

This could be bullying by siblings and/or peers. It can also come from relentless comments from a well-meaning parent. Not feeling seen by our parents can potentially leave any child traumatized, especially a highly sensitive one. It's the repeated exposure to the stress that causes an issue more than the event itself.

This type of trauma doesn't need the flashy memorable distress of a Big T trauma to leave a person permanently crippled, even if they don't see the crippling connection. We will use the term little t trauma to refer to this as well. Some of this type of trauma could be thought of as something not happening when something positive should have, like not getting our emotional needs met as infants. That may sound minor or inconsequential to you now. Still, by the end of section 2, you'll understand just how traumatizing it can be.

Little "t" traumas are less evident, making them harder to remember. Making these the sneakiest, most insidious types of traumas. These are hardest to solve because they parade around under the guise of "My childhood was fine." Because the survivors can't remember a singular Big T event, it's hard for them to call what they experienced traumatic. But it absolutely can be.

Big T trauma has been known about for a long time. We used to call it battle fatigue. Later, it was known as shell shock. Now it's known as PTSD. Unfortunately, PTSD symptoms are often a hallmark of Big T traumas. Only now, after decades of research, is PTSD beginning to get the traction it deserves in the medical and psychiatric communities. This means all those much more common little t traumas go *almost entirely unrecognized,* even though they do just as much damage.

IS EVERYONE TRAUMATIZED?

The short answer is yes. The reality I observe is that our culture fosters trauma. Trauma happens when parts of us are no longer connected. There is a fracturing of the self in all trauma, no matter the size of the T. *The fracturing or loss of connection to ourselves is the heart of all trauma.*

As that loss of connection to ourselves concretizes over time, it affects *every* aspect of our lives. It affects how we think about ourselves, what we expect from the world, and how we think we deserve to be treated. It's also tough to recognize the changes it causes because it happens slowly. It gradually takes over our subconscious and creates our view of reality.

> *Trauma isn't what happens to us, but what happens inside us in the absence of an empathetic witness. Gabor Mate" MD, Trauma researcher*

We will unpack this concept a lot in the chapter on resiliency. For now, keep it in the back of your mind. One of the primary ways our culture fosters trauma is because our culture is not one of empathy. Trauma is only possible if there is no empathy present for the wounded parts of us. When any piece of us gets hurt, and that hurt is not seen, validated or empathized with, that pain becomes traumatic. It is exactly a lack of empathy that turns a stressful situation into a traumatic one.

DON'T COMPARE TRAUMAS

It does no good to compare Big T to little t traumas or vice versa. It does no good to compare any trauma to another at all. Trauma, *again,* is *not* from what happened to you; it's the wound you still carry, caused by *your perception of your experience.*

We need a blueprint out of the hellhole we can get trapped in, thanks to the stacks of adversity some of us face in young life. Some people identify with being profoundly traumatized, and some less so. Some remember in detail past experiences of beatings, profound neglect or rape.

Some struggle to justify their immense struggle and do not know why. But the bottom line is we all struggle together. Even without the variability of our personalities, our parents, and the region of our birth, the issue remains that our culture is a culture whose social norms have created a toxic environment in which to raise a child. Much less be one.

Whether you have Big T or little t traumas, or if, like me, you have both, the wound we still carry is the thing that matters. It unites us and the thing that makes us different, even after it's been dealt with and integrated. Just because "other people had it worse" does not mean that you were not affected by your struggles, no matter how trivial they may seem.

The fact someone went through something horrible doesn't mean someone else who didn't experience the same trauma isn't also a victim or isn't also struggling. It means that their story and their struggle are *different* from yours. That's all.

STRESS, TRAUMA AND TRIGGERS

I said it before, and I'll repeat it because it's essential. *All trauma is stressful, but not all stress is traumatic.* An event is traumatizing if it leaves a person psychologically or physically limited in some way that persists beyond the event. There's a lot of stuff in our everyday world that is stressful and even traumatic. Unless experiencing those things left a person somehow permanently restricted, they were *not* traumatized by it.

DISSOCIATION

Dissociation is what we call the phenomenon that occurs when related processes become uncoupled or unrelated. It's when things intended to operate simultaneously or in relationship to each other operate separately. This is the psychiatric definition.

Another equally illuminating but more hopeful definition is chemistry's definition of dissociation. In chemistry, when something is dissociated, something large, like a molecule, is broken down into smaller constituent parts, i.e., when a large molecule dissociates, it becomes a smaller molecule; a small molecule dissociates to become an atom and atoms into ions. Importantly, it's almost always viewed as a reversible process!

Many people who identify as broken do so in part because they dissociate regularly. It's a very real struggle for many people today. When we dissociate, we are separating things that were designed to work together as a complete system. By separating or removing one or more facets of a system, there is a significant disruption in the organism's functioning.

Dissociation is an extreme form of compartmentalization that creates a gap between one part of you and another with no door between them. It's easy to see with this information how and why a widespread response for many "broken" people early on is "it doesn't affect me."

But really, what they are saying is that they have divorced themselves from the feelings and experiences of their physical body. That compartment they don't open but dissociate into served them as kids; I know it did me. Unfortunately, the sensations in our bodies are the only things that can communicate to us if something is amiss.

Our body houses our sensations, emotions, and our intuition. When we divorce ourselves from our bodies, we lose the ability to know what we are feeling while still being able to write books about what we think.

We become hyper-intellectual because we no longer have access to the wisdom of intuition that originates in our physical body. This means we have no choice but to rely on cognition to guide us through life, often affecting our ability to be empathetic.

Denial can and will look different for each of us according to which strategy was most helpful in the past. Sometimes, a high level of numbness or disassociation leads to naivety. Some of these people, for whom the bulk of their trauma occurred before conscious memory was formed, may go through the world with their heads in the clouds, wearing rose-colored glasses. They can do so because they are on an autopilot program that has dissociated them from the stresses their bodies experienced. Their program, based on what they need to do to survive their household, tells them to repeat over and over, "Everything's fine."

While folks on the other end of the disassociation spectrum move through the world harshly and are all but entirely calloused, they see the world as a harsh place that must be conquered and interpret most of life as exclusively life or death scenarios. They have dissociated themselves from the feedback of their body for so long that they genuinely can't tell if they are safe or not. So, they assume that a threat is eternally present, and they "keep it moving." Their autopilot program sounds like "If no one is dying, there isn't a problem."

These people are also ignoring the realities of their experience, just in a different way. In this case, it affects them and the positive things in their life. Saying, *"It doesn't affect me."* is one of the surest signs that a person might be suffering from trauma.

The hopeful part of the chemical definition of dissociation is that when we disassociate from our whole self, we become a smaller part of ourselves. This explains why when we get stressed out, some of us revert to a more basic or childlike form of ourselves. We are reverting to our smaller parts. The parts of us that were separated or dissociated for safety and simultaneously aren't a threat.

Since these events are considered reversible in chemistry, even if you have spent your life dissociating, which is often viewed as one of the more extreme stress response strategies, *you still aren't broken.*

STRENGTHNESSES

Lastly, I need to introduce you to a term I coined for this book. It's a core concept of this system, and all traumatized people have at least one. A strengthnesses is an attribute that is a strength and a weakness simultaneously. It is an attribute that gets successfully relied on during stress responses that that strategy becomes overgrown and is no longer under our control as an attribute should be.

When this happens, the automated coping strategies that got programmed into us in our traumatic childhoods predetermine our behaviors whether we want them to or not. This seeming unpredictability is what makes a strengthness both a strength and a weakness. The determining factor as to whether it is a strength or a weakness is the environment we are in at the time. We dive into this topic fully in chapter 13.

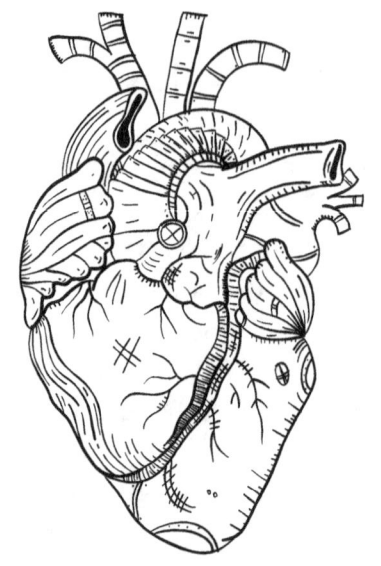

CHAPTER 3
YOUR NERVOUS SYSTEM ON STRESS

We have established trauma is a wound, a fracturing of ourselves, that received insufficient empathy. We have also established that all trauma results from a stressful situation. So, let's quickly look at what happens in our bodies when responding to stressful stimuli. This will make clear what makes for stress and what makes for trauma.

DEFAULT MODES – THE 5 FS

Our nervous system has two parts: the autonomic nervous system and the voluntary nervous system. The voluntary nervous system refers to the things we have conscious control over, like walking or cartwheels.

The autonomic nervous system is involuntary, subconscious and has a much bigger job than its conscious counterpart. It runs the millions of complex hidden functions the human body does every second.

The autonomic nervous system has a few default modes to choose from when triggered by stress. They are often called the 5 F's: fight, flight, freeze, fawn and sex. For what I hope are obvious reasons, we will primarily deal with fight, flight, freeze and fawn in this book. Other folks that study other (non-human) mammals sometimes call it approach, retreat and panic responses – with panic accounting for fawn and freeze.

As a child, we didn't have the opportunity to fight or flee our traumatic situations. Fighting dad or running away from mom, especially at a young age, is not an option, so what do we do? In this case, our bodies go with the only other option, plan C. We freeze or fawn.

At first glance, freezing seems like a bad idea, especially to us as adults. But that's an inappropriately narrow perspective when we look closer, and we must look closer. Throughout this book, when you think of what happened to and around you as a child, it is paramount that you remember the mind that made the decisions. Or, more accurately, the nervous system, which is so young *that it's on autopilot*, is what makes decisions for us at that age.

Emotions are at their heart *somatic* experiences. *Soma* means the physical aspect of an organism separate from the mind or spirit. All emotions and feelings are physical sensations meant to keep our organism alive.

According to our nervous system, its job is to help us survive using one of the first two primary strategies, fight and flight and if both fail or are determined not to be an option, we go with the third. We freeze. Freezing in the face of a traumatic event or chronic stress as a child is what we do when it is deemed the least bad option.

If the most successful strategy we can find during stressful events is to fight, our trauma, like that scar, will make us inflexible, and we will almost always default to wanting to fight. (Raises hand sheepishly)

If fleeing was the most helpful strategy, we would most often default to a desire to flee any stressful situation we find ourselves in, even if it's a bad idea, even as adults. In many instances of childhood trauma, the most successful coping strategy is freezing. So, when we get stressed, our most common response might be to freeze.

In the case of childhood trauma, if the stress we are exposed to is chronic (and it almost always is), we never get the chance to learn how to unfreeze. Fighters may never learn how to calm down and stop looking for a fight, while runners never stop looking for exits. The scars left by trauma leave us stuck on autopilot, unable to launch a survival strategy different than our default, even when it would be appropriate.

Having only one automatic coping strategy when stressed is how we get ourselves into trouble. That's why you think you are broken. Freezing and fawning are probably the most essential strategies to understand when evaluating childhood trauma. Its dependability as the primary strategy to get a person through a rough childhood, in which we often can't fight or flee, makes fawning the most common strategy for many of us.

In severe chronic childhood stress, because we can't fight or escape, we freeze to keep ourselves safe. Then, over time, we stop registering the signals from our body meant to mobilize us to safety. Eventually, that makes us numb.

This is why one of the single most common outlooks I've seen among "broken" people, big T and little t alike, especially those with little t trauma or those with big T trauma very early in childhood, is *"It doesn't affect me."* To which I say, "Cool bro, glad you made it this far with that story, but I still call BS."

DYSREGULATION

Dysregulation is a term you will hear over and over in this book. It's a term I use daily for a common state that people with trauma enter when triggered. It's not precisely the stress response but an escalated version of it. It's like the cherry on top of the trauma sundae.

Unfortunately, for people like us, our stress responses can be like a stress response *plus*. That stress response plus is what I call dysregulation. Oxford describes dysregulation as - an abnormality or impairment in regulating a metabolic, physiological, or psychological process. For us, this usually is the result of a stress response being triggered in a person who has chronically been exposed to chronic, unpredictable stress.

Essentially, the stressful experiences we survived were hard enough on our nervous systems that they now scream "OH FUCK NO!" at any little reminder of the events.

WHAT DYSREGULATION FEELS LIKE

Everyone experiences dysregulation a little differently. My body starts to feel like it's vibrating inside a giant and high-pitched bowl. I feel it through my whole body, like deep bass in a song, except unlike booming bass notes, it's decidedly unpleasant.

It starts low and ramps up in both frequency and magnitude. Meaning the waves of displeasure come faster and become more prominent. That's what the beginning of dysregulation feels like for me. Next in line, if I don't catch it early, is breath holding followed by hand and jaw clenching. It almost feels like I'm hunting or being hunted.

I often use the term dysregulated because frankly it's handy, as well as accurate and non-judgmental. I cannot regulate myself when I'm in that state. None of us can. When dysregulated, I tend to want to overreact to things, read too much into things, and totally dismiss important things. It's the state that most of us spend most of our time in, and we often don't know it. It's in this state of dysregulation that we most often shoot ourselves in the foot.

In this state, terrible ideas seem great, while the good ones are never good enough. If you remember nothing else about dysregulation from this section, remember to NOT make decisions if you can help it while dysregulated. It always ends *less* than ideal.

REPRESSION V SUPPRESSION.

Another important term to define to prevent confusion is suppression v repression. They are often used interchangeably in pop psychology. But they are *not* the same.

Suppression is when we actively, consciously ignore or restrict a feeling, thought, or sensation. Suppression is a conscious act. Meaning we consciously suppress it. We are aware of our effort to avoid experiencing whatever we are suppressing. But if we suppress something long enough it habituates. Then we move into *repression territory.*

Repression is subconscious suppression. It happens automatically by our biology due to repeated suppression of an undesired thought, feeling, emotion or memory. It's repression when our subconscious mind takes over our suppression for us.

Certain events can be so stressful that our central nervous system represses them for us without any effort on our part. Some big T events can be so terrible that the admission or conscious recollection of their occurrence could break the mind of a small child.

This makes accessing some traumatic memories from early life difficult and sometimes impossible, which makes understanding our reactions to the things that trigger that repressed memory complicated to say the least.

Some repressed memories feel like a shadow of a dream. Some are black holes. But those blocked-out memories still need to be honored. Even if we may not know the details of what happened, we ought to understand that our mind created that hole to protect us.

So, if parts of your childhood are fuzzy like mine, don't worry. You don't need to remember an event to know something happened. The fact that your body responds in the way it does is enough proof that an invisible piece of you needs empathy and protection. Please give it to them.

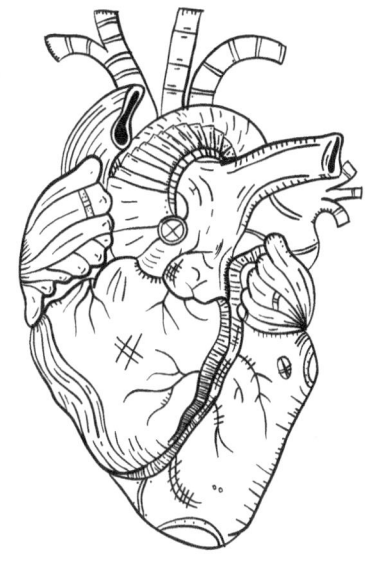

CHAPTER 4
CHRONIC STRESS ADAPTATION

We must cover one more definition before heading deeper into our journey together. I keep telling you that you aren't broken. We've also established that people like you and me are, in fact, different. So, if we are, in fact, different from others but are not broken, what exactly are we? What is it that makes us different from everyone else while we have so much in common with each other?

Labeling ourselves broken sometimes acts as a calling card to others like us. But it remains a judgmental, lazy and loaded way to describe a whole subculture of genuinely incredible people. "Broken" people find and cling to other broken people.

We are a tribe unified by surviving neglect, abuse, stress and trauma. "Broken" is often our calling card. It's a very real vibe we easily read off another person, letting us know they are a kindred spirit. People who identify as broken are often extremely talented drifters and creatives. We are explorers and lovers of authenticity and togetherness.

There is undeniably a thread that ties all this awesomeness together. But if it's not "brokenness," what is it? In writing this book, I needed a simple way to describe this group of badasses in a way that was accurate *and* not loaded with preconceived notions or judgments.

I racked my brain until one day, it dawned on me. I thought of a way to describe us all. It was perfect. I scribbled it onto a fluorescent yellow post-it, and the concept was born! The thing that formed us and unifies these kindred beautiful misfits and queirdos is being what I call:

CHRONIC STRESS ADAPTED

For some folks reading this, this term might sound like a "Well DUH!" When I thought of it, I immediately said, "There is no way that I'm the first to think of this." But a quick Google came up with no scholarly or otherwise article that contained the phrase "chronic stress adapted."

But there was one and only one article called *Neuro control of chronic stress adaptation.* (Herman) Since then, there have been a few more with other variations of the phrase. This article was excelent. I wish I had found it sooner. It could have saved me a lot of time, effort and research.

It was the first and only scientific discussion I found about the lingering effects of chronic stress during development. It describes the mechanisms that chronic stress affects in a developing body.

Essentially, all I've done with this is turn this newly explored phenomenon, which had only been used as a verb, into a noun to describe a category of people living with the effects. What unifies the fantastic artists, creatives, thinkers, and changers *is* the changes in our bodies and minds that result from adapting to chronic stress.

In Herman's paper, he beautifully describes what happens in the brain and body as a result of chronic stress. Pointing out that a stress response must include some specific few things. He says:

Autonomic, endocrine, and immune systems produce an integrated stress response. While initially adaptive, prolonged activation of molecular pathways engaged by these systems can cause pronounced changes in physiology and behavior that have long-term deleterious implications for survival and well-being.

WHAT IT MEANS BEING CHRONIC STRESS ADAPTED.

Okay, so what does all that science lingo mean?

The second bit means that the adaptations to chronic stress work great to keep us alive in the short term but cause a host of issues in the long term.

The first sentence means that a stress response, by definition, must include the autonomic (automatic) and, therefore, the subconscious nervous system, hormones, and immune systems together. Stress then directly affects every system in the human body!

This means that long-term detrimental changes will happen in all these systems. This piece of info is vital to grasp. It goes a long way to explaining the negative health effects of ACEs or adverse childhood experiences, which we cover in the next chapter.

So, Chronic Stress Adapted- from here on out, will be abbreviated to CSA. It is the best term for what we are. Because it *is* precisely what we are. It describes the process we survived that created the only sometimes useful defaults in our neurological patterns.

PERSPECTIVE SHIFT #1

That's why CSA is the lens from which we ought to view ourselves as adults trying to make changes in our lives. It was chronic stress during development that caused the underdevelopment and micro-malformations of the substructures of our brains, which we know cause things like dyslexia (Martin Kronbichler), ADHD (Amy L Krain), developmental dyscalculia (Ursina McCaskey) and even epilepsy (A. James Barkovich)

It is interesting to me that dyslexia, dyscalculia, and even epilepsy, along with ADHD and especially Complex PTSD, have so much data behind them, linking them quite closely with being CSA. The correlations between these and developmental trauma are well documented. To me, the overlap is much more important than the differences.

YOU ARE NOT BROKEN. YOU ARE CSA

This is the first and single most important perspective I have for you. If you aren't convinced and want more details than the quick down and dirty you get here, check out the bibliography for McEwen's or Herman's work. They do a marvelous job of breaking down every step of the way.

I highly suggest you also read *Behave, The Biology of Humans at our Best and Worst*, by Robert Sapolsky. That book formed much of my scientific understanding of behavioral biology. It is an excellent introduction for the uninitiated and still thorough. If you are at all curious about the biological underpinnings of human behavior, there's no better book. Dr Sapolsky is my Bio-Bae.

The definition of CSA in this book is

Chronic stress Adapted- describes an individual or group whose exposure to chronic stress created long-term pathological changes to their psychology, physiology, immunity and neurology, which is continually and/or presently experienced.

Little t trauma is usually chronic and is the most obviously correlated to CSA. If your mother nit-picked you to death, body shamed you in church or was always riding you about your weight, it's easy to see how the constant correction becomes chronic stress. You start nit-picking yourself before she can, so when she does it, it hurts less—the classic you can't hurt me if I hurt me first mentality.

Big T trauma takes just one additional step to understand the chronic effects of a stressful event. So, let's consider an example of big T trauma to make the correlation between a singular traumatic event and chronic stress clear.

Your Brain and the Bear Analogy.

If you take a psychology class anywhere in the U.S. there is a story you're all but guaranteed to hear in the first week of class. It's usually called something like "your brain and the bear." It's a cute little story used to illustrate how stress affects the human body. From the example, it's easy to conceptualize the effects of chronic stress on the human body intuitively, and it goes something like this.

> *You're in the forest, and you see a bear. Uh-oh! That bear represents a danger to your safety. Your body releases a flood of stress hormones, among other things, so you can either fight that bear or run away. Your heart will start racing. Your blood vessels dilate, cortisol and other stress hormones are released to make you more sensitive. Your eyes focus, and you're ready to fight or run away from the bear. That's a pretty darn helpful system!* **If** *you're in the woods and* **if** *there is a bear.*

That's the normal or "adaptive" stress response. It's short-lived; therefore, we're good because we're designed for it. This is the response designed by millions of years of evolution to help keep us soft, squishy humans alive in the presence of a threat in our big bad jungle world. But what happens when our "bear" comes home every night? This normally helpful adaptive system becomes (mal)adaptive or not helpful.

Let's say that Dad came home drunk and assaulted the crap out of you. Let's say it only happens once. It would be a big T trauma. So how does a one-off event like that become chronic stress?

Well, for days, weeks, months, or years, depending on how bad the assault was, the child will be stressed out any time they're expecting dad to come home. That is chronic

stress.

The biology of that child will still be bracing their body in case it happens a second, third, or 40th time.

The bracing we do is, biologically speaking, a ramping up of the sympathetic nervous system, a branch of the autonomic nervous system. Using Herman's definition for a stress response, it's automatically a ramping up of the endocrine and immune systems too. That automatic bracing is the beginning of the stress response. If it happens a lot because you are not sure what kind of mood dad will come home in, that stress response is now chronic due to a singular event. That's how big T trauma leads to being CSA too.

So there you have it. What you are, what I am, is Chronic Stress Adapted. Now, each time you think, "why am I the way I am?" "why am I like this?" "why am I broken?" Whether your trauma was big or little, you have an answer. From here on out, your job is when you have those thoughts automatically, you automatically respond to them with, "well it's because I'm chronic stress adapted." And you move on with your day.

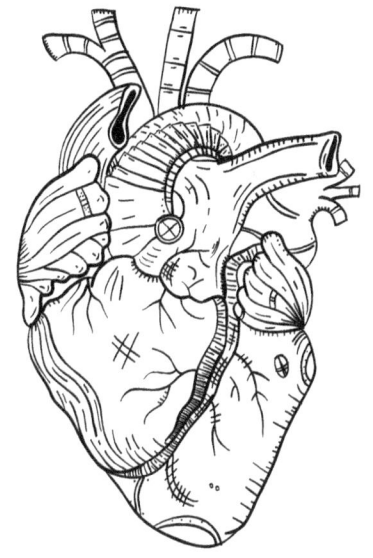

CHAPTER 5
TRAUMA DISTORTS OUR PERSPECTIVE

The world we believe in becomes the world we live in. Though this is true, what this leaves out is the fact that the world itself is what creates our minds when we are young. Not the other way around. Trauma, especially severe trauma, can determine our view of how all things are. The numbness created to survive a stressful childhood extends far beyond the original wound. It can often extend to the whole of our personhood. This is especially true for big T trauma survivors.

For those who have survived things like physical or sexual abuse or war—especially if it was repeated, say by ongoing molestation by family members or neighbors—that numbness will likely extend to the whole being of that person. This is especially true for survivors of sexual trauma.

Sexual trauma virtually obliterates the concept of self in the victim. When someone else exerts their physical power over a young child, the child develops a sense that their body is not their own. If their body *had* belonged to them, the abuse wouldn't have happened. So, it's common for sexual trauma survivors to become not just numbed but utterly detached from their bodies. This is part of how many sexual assault survivors- an estimated 31% or more become morbidly obese.

CHRONIC STRESS ADAPTATION AFFECTS OUR EXPERIENCE OF LOVE

It's time to examine the most personal subject covered in this book. It's a big question with even bigger consequences. So, let's get straight into it. How do chronic stress and trauma in early life affect our experience of love for the rest of our lives? It's no secret that CSA people have a hard time in relationships. We often have some of the more extreme attachment issues, but have you ever stopped to ask yourself why?

Some of us notice sooner, while others notice later that we tend to gravitate toward people, especially lovers, who remind us of our parents. I don't mean in a creepy, incestuous Freudian way but a more innocuous yet awkward and very annoying way. Over time, many people notice little parallels between our parents and our partners.

It could be the way our partner breathes obnoxiously when they get a piece of distressing news. It could be the dismissal of a particular type of emotional expression. Stand-up comedians for ages have been cracking people up on stage with jokes about how their husband or wife acts just like their mom or dad, making them want to murder each other. But have you stopped to wonder why? What is it that makes this weird little quirk so comically common? The answer is all about familiarity.

FAMILIARITY: LOVE AND TRAUMA

When we are born, our first experience of love comes from our mothers, fathers, aunts, uncles and grandparents if we are lucky. This familial love sustains us - literally. This love for helpless babies keeps our exhausted parents feeding us and working long hours. When young, our caregivers' love and attention ensure our survival. This is why neglect is so incredibly detrimental and leaves many of us desperate for attention from our partners.

As we grow, we slowly become less dependent upon our parents, but we continue to mirror their behaviors. We quickly gain the ability to do some basic survival things like regulate our body temperature and latch on to our mothers' breast or a bottle.

As we grow, we gain independence and learn more complex skills from modeling our parents. Whatever they do the most, we will do too. This is when our parents' adaptations begin to appear in us.

That's when things can and usually do begin to get messy. No parent wants to see the most challenging aspects of themselves in their children, but it happens invariably. And they don't often treat those aspects kindly.

The most challenging aspects of all people are nearly always related to how they give and receive love. That's why acquaintanceships are easy, and romantic relationships are always much, *much* harder.

Here lies the heart of many of our *relationship issues* as CSA people.

Our experience of love is mixed up with our experiences of pain because they came from the same place.

Our first experiences of love and mistreatment came from the same people. My earliest experiences of love from my mom are also mixed up with unpleasant feelings of abandonment and exclusion.

My mom and dad got divorced when I was about six years old. That's one factor. Another factor comes from after the divorce, my mother was forced to work swing shifts. She worked shifts that rotated every few weeks from days to evenings and nights - at a local factory. So, to provide for us, my mother had to pass my siblings and me off to our grandparents' extended family and sometimes neighbors when she had to work.

She loved me and my siblings, even if I didn't always feel that love. That love drove her to keep a roof over our heads, clothes on our backs and food in our mouths. That meant rotating - day shift, then evening shift, then night shifts - at that factory making tiny glass bottles. This also meant that as a kid, I was with my mom for a while, then grandma, then at my father's, and then Aunt Bert's house.

Kids being passed around to extended family is not uncommon, especially in poorer rural and immigrant families in the US. But that doesn't mean it's not damaging to the kids getting passed around. Infants are wired to get all their safety and security from one place. When that isn't possible, the security of the child feels threatened. The concept of stranger danger in young kids displays this.

My entire life changed when my mom had to work a different shift. My siblings and I would stay on the other side of town with Mammaw and Papaw and ride a different bus to get to school on those days.

To my little 6-year-old brain, my mom abandoned me every few months when her schedule switched. Some months, I would barely see her because she was forced to work or sleep during my after-school hours. The effect was a complex blend of feeling abandoned and neglected by the very person keeping me alive.

This is the power of a child's perception. Children aged 3-7 spend almost that entire time in the Theta brain states. You probably know or have heard that everything in the universe has a vibration or frequency. As kids, that frequency their brain creates is called Theta. Which is also the brain waves leveraged during hypnosis. So when people say kids are sponges, they might not know how accurate that statement is. During that time, whatever assumption our nervous system makes remains our truth until we challenge it.

So even though I know and recognize now that my mother was busting her butt to take care of me, circumstances were such that essentially it didn't matter. The habits in my nervous system had been established.

Because the love and the abandonment I experienced came from the same person, I have a neurological and biological expectation that all of my love interests will abandon and neglect me.

Compounding this, whenever I feel neglected or abandoned by a partner, my biology automatically assumes it's "necessary." Being neglected still feels like *a jagged little pill I must swallow because my needs and desires being ignored is simply necessary.* When my needs aren't being met, I assume it's because they can't be, just because my first-ever experience of love happened that way. My mother needed to work swing shifts to maintain custody and keep us kids fed. It was a necessity. I know many CSA people who have similar experiences. I call it "living on scraps" when we do it into adulthood.

Even though I recognize this pattern consciously, as an adult, I still have the same fear embedded in my psyche that anyone who loves me will eventually leave. They'd HAVE to, and they would be right to do so. This obviously causes a problem for me because long-term relationships count on the ability to depend on each other. If I can't depend on my partner because I'm afraid they'll leave, what's the point in having a long-term committed relationship? To me, there isn't one.

If I expect whoever I'm with to leave me because they love me, I'm in for a rough ride. I can't plan anything big or important that I might need or want help with because I can't count on them being around for it. I also don't like this trait about myself. I don't want it to be true, so sometimes my subconscious tries to hide it from myself!

But wait, there's more! To add another layer of Tom-fuckery, we've discussed the self-centeredness of all children's thoughts. We know children's thoughts will always circle back to themselves as a necessary part of development.

Even though I had a little bit of brain at 6, I didn't have much. So, when my mom was gone for weeks to months at a time, guess how my brain interpreted the experience? Yes, a piece of me understood that it was necessary because my mother was good enough to explain it to us at some point.

But the rest of me, a significant portion of me, turned the blame back to myself as any child – driven by biology - does. I adopted the most straightforward explanation to a typical self-centered 6-year-old about why mom isn't around. It was my fault. I knew it deep down inside. The thing I did wrong was have needs. That's the biology of a child. We always think everything is our fault, which is at least part of why, to this day, I can always find a way to blame myself. How about you?

So, do you see how when a child experiences love and pain from the same person, the brain's automatic habituation can get the two jumbled up together?

Love is something we develop a sense of very early. It might even be the first thing we develop a concept of. Most moms and dads tell us they love us. Our church tells us Jesus or Allah or the Goddess loves us. Hollywood makes love the star of nearly every film, regardless of genre. So, we understand love enough to have an idea as to what it is and means.

How love is displayed around us and toward us becomes how we give and receive love to everyone, including ourselves. If someone's parents were constantly arguing and always mad at each other but never broke up or got divorced, often, a child who saw this type of love displayed will find themselves always mad at their partner. Sometimes it will be for something reasonable, while others will be less reasonable.

As an adult, that child will have a powerful tendency to find something wrong, something to pick at in their partner. Not because they don't love each other, although that can happen if the picking lasts too long. But because, in their experience, that is what love does - It picks. To this person, love never leaves a relationship but is never satisfied. This person then will have a loving but slightly unsatisfying marriage.

Again, this isn't because they are bad or have "no idea what love is." It's because, to her, this **is** what love is. *Love is a universal concept, but individuals express it in individual ways.*

Since all people are inevitably flawed, their expressions of love are also inevitably flawed. Since there is no master download or guidebook for life - *our earliest experiences of love become our <u>default.</u>*

This is also why cross-cultural relationships take a lot of effort, time and patience to work out. Love is very different from culture to culture in its expressions. It's not a failure to love differently than someone else. It's inevitable. Whoever you marry will have a different way of giving and receiving love than you do, and you will spend time learning to navigate those differences.

My father was a person who, with all his flaws, pursued excellence according to his life path. Which meant everything had room for improvement. So, any interaction with him also left me and my siblings feeling like whatever we did wasn't good enough. In his head, he was always helping us get better and better. In my experience, he was a morally superior, if sub-clinical, narcissistic perfectionist.

So now, in a relationship, I regularly feel I'm doing something wrong. I'm playing the part of myself as a child in that father-son dynamic. I also respect his pursuit of excellence even though I fundamentally differ in my path choice and definition of excellence. So, now I occasionally play the part of him too.

I simultaneously nitpick myself and if I'm not careful, those around me too. Not on purpose, of course, but because my mind has the habit already installed as a part of its algorithms, thanks to my father's influence. That algorithm appreciates the steps taken, but I believe the most important step I can always take is the next one.

I have a tendency to forget to celebrate or even acknowledge the work that I did to get me where I am. My mind is predisposed to discount the work it took to arrive out of a desire to be even better next time.

Sometimes, I play out aspects of my childhood's son and father dynamics simultaneously. I have repeatedly been romantically attracted to people who are perpetually unsatisfied with life and with me—people who don't celebrate their wins. Let alone mine. *Sound familiar?*

For CSA people, our adult romantic relationships are predicated on changing the outcomes of our childhood relationship dynamics. *If you were beaten, you've probably fallen for people who beat you*. If you were *ignored?... ditto*.

Familiarity with a type of expression of love draws us to people who embody that type. But that doesn't mean you are broken. It's a natural phenomenon. I had an aunt who would say, "You're fine honey, it's just your picker is busted."

What she meant by this is that the part of you drawn to another person, your person "picker" was not picking healthy partners. But if you come from a toxic family environment like me, you will always pick a person with familiar toxic traits. All so the little kid inside you can change the ending to the traumatic events and dynamics of their life. Unfortunately, the story's beginning has to be the same to change the ending. *Toxic*. This is why...

TOXIC ATTRACTS TOXIC

"Why do I keep falling for these toxic ones?!" - every CSA person ever.

The most significant difficulty we experience trying to change that ending of our childhood relational dynamics is our algorithms are predicated on surviving the circumstances we experienced, not thriving in those circumstances.

I deserved better treatment than my mother and father gave me, and so did you. But like you, I kept finding and loving people who injured me in such familiar ways until it became undeniable that these relationships have that familial karma motivating them.

Karma is a Sanskrit word that translates directly as "action." In India, there is a phrase I was introduced to by Sadguru that says, "Your karma is your life." Meaning your actions are your life. Said differently, your life **is** the actions you take. Love and relationship karma is about changing the ending or those toxic dynamics. So that we finally get the treatment we ought to have had in our childhood.

So, I have had to learn to overcome my biological predisposition to survive and choose to take the action that's needed to thrive, which means *choosing discomfort now over resentment later*.

It means asking for what we ought to have had when we needed it most, especially when we are afraid to. It means not allowing ourselves to play a role in a dynamic that will not get us any closer to the life we want.

Romantic relationships for CSA people are all about finding someone with *compatible & complimentary core wounds* and then helping each other change the ending of the story that wounded us.

So, who do you find yourself with? For years now, I have used a phrase that encompasses this phenomenon. I used to see my friends picking guys over and over again who were basically the same dude. I called it the "same dude different dick" phenomenon.

I'm very sure that you know people who have experienced this phenomenon over and over again. And now you know why.

When your "friend" does this, what's happening is their (your) picker is picking people with toxic traits similar to our original wounding. We do this so the beginning of the story is the same. The beginning has to be the same if we're going to change the ending. Otherwise, it's a different story altogether.

If we are unaware of the pattern or do not take the necessary action to change the ending, we simply rinse and repeat. We leave the story to end the same way again - toxic. When you take the actions necessary to change the ending of your story, you change your karma. When you change your karma, you change your life.

So please don't judge yourself for having or having had a "busted picker"; you didn't pick your picker, just like you didn't pick your distorted perspectives on life.

The reason love is harder for the CSA person than for a less traumatized peer is that we have to pick a person who injures us in the same familiar way. After all, that injury is so tied to our experience of love that we don't actually *feel* loved without it. Love without the injury, especially early on our healing path, often feels boring. It's why everyone loves a bad boy... at first.

It works out that it happens this way because we will always be attracted to people with whom our dynamics allow us to change the ending and finally complete that chronic stress response. It sets us up to practice fighting this uphill battle against our biology that has been programmed to make us survive. If we continue to make survival-based, easy, biological decisions, we can never change the ending of our painful experiences of love & program ourselves to thrive automatically.

Regarding love and relationships, as CSA people, we all got the short end of the proverbial stick. But we can improve our relationships by having good boundaries, some well-placed non-negotiables, and staying in touch with our inner truth, no matter what.

Having a busted picker is as old as trauma is. So, you're not alone, and if you find yourself picking the "wrong guy or gal or they," your picker is fine. It's your **karma** that needs to change. Your **actions** must change. So, in your next attempt at love, try doing something different to make the ending different.

That means your next romantic pursuit will be flawed, and your job is to make sure you don't fall into the same default actions, that saved you then but screw you now.

If changing that ending ends the relationship? GOOD! That's progress. Kick 'em to the curb and on to the next one. It's not the dustbowl era anymore. Because of this, dating, especially for CSA people, as bad as it may sound to some, is a bit of a numbers game. It was for me.

With all my trauma, I had a lot of endings that needed changing. I also needed a lot of practice to get proficient at changing the ending. This meant I needed many stories for there to be enough endings to change. Some call it being a hoe. I call it being thorough.

HOW THE STORY STILL SHOWS UP

Maybe your father hit you. Maybe your mother was obsessed with keeping up appearances. Maybe she loved you very much, but in her attempt to keep the family name immaculate, you were consistently told to be quiet and not to speak up. Do as you're told, and do not ask questions. Don't have needs.

Whatever self-blaming story your little 7-year-old brain imagined at the time has continued as your subconscious reality. It imprinted on you, confusing and conflating love and repression.

Rather than thinking someone will leave you just because they love you, you believe you are unlovable unless you pretend to be someone else. That was part of my damage, for sure. It did make me a great performer on stage though! (*Another strengthness of mine*)

Maybe you can be anything to anyone except yourself because if you let your authentic self out to be seen and interacted with, you constantly expect mom's voice to chastise you for your "inappropriate outbursts." Except by now, it's not usually Mom's voice; it's yours.

These are no longer straightforward one-to-one correlations your body has with love. The original wound has been stimulated and re-stimulated so many times in so many ways over the years that it's nearly impossible to see these connections plainly for ourselves.

We almost always need someone else, like a therapist, a Kaya, or a system like Rethinking Broken, to point out these trends for us. By this point in life, the pain and precedent set by the original dynamic have been watered down by a thousand similar but not identical situations, making it impossible for us to see for ourselves.

We must understand the dynamic setup from our "original wound." This does not mean you need to dig into forgotten or buried memories. This doesn't mean you need to dredge up the terrible experiences from your past. You just need to see your tendencies clearly.

Often, people who were molested, beaten, or cruelly abused have locked up those experiences tight. They keep them in a tiny lead-and-steel reinforced concrete box. Nothing gets in, and nothing gets out.

I don't know what happened to you. Some experiences are buried for damn good reasons. If I asked you to explore them, I might be asking you to relive a rape, terrifying physical violence, witnessing a death, fleeing a war-torn country, neglect, or the horror of a helpless child in real, immediate danger. To do that would be irresponsible and cruel.

That's why I won't ask you to uncover or dig into your darkest wounds. You don't need to relive it through your memory. For this work, in this book at least, you only need to understand the patterns that were created. I guarantee those patterns are still playing out in your life, just like they are in mine.

Most of my early life is blank. It used to be even more blank. It took years of self-work and therapy before I knew that having less than five memories before 4th grade was not normal. When I started writing this book, I talked to my little sister about her childhood memories; her memory is just as blank as mine.

We will get into memory and how the memory system works in chapter 11, but for now, all you need to know is that memory is a highly unreliable record keeper. It's even less reliable for CSA people.

"Hold on Owl, if you can't remember big chunks of your childhood then how in the world did you figure out what is wrong with you?"

Well, I'm glad you asked. The dynamics from early life are so deeply ingrained they appear in nearly all aspects of our lives. Some might even call those aspects and dynamics our *personality*, and I'd be hard-pressed to argue against it.

The bottom line is you don't need to uncover the original wound because the programming it created keeps showing up whenever you think, "God, I'm so broken." All you need to do is recognize the pattern and place yourself in an environment where your conditioning is helpful. We do that together in Section 3.

If we use an appropriate lens, every instance we see as evidence of our brokenness can be seen as a clue, giving us more information about that original dynamic. The things we hold in our minds to be our biggest failures are often our biggest clues as to how those core wounds shape us without having to tell a soul about the wound.

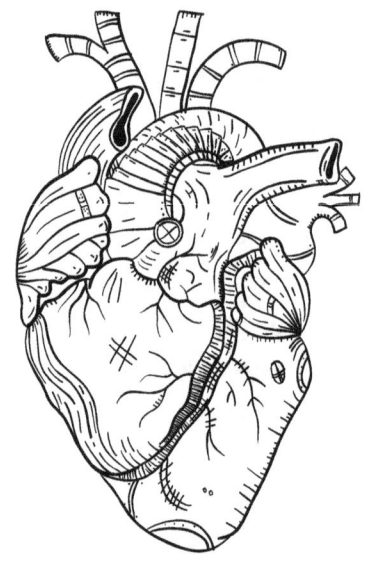

CHAPTER 6
THE WET COMPUTER

We've already talked about the algorithms in our brains that led us to the conclusion we were broken. In this chapter, I want to expand on that concept because it's a helpful analogy for how things get imprinted to become a part of our algorithms. Humans, especially the human brain, can be described as a wet computer.

If you imagine our brains as a wet computer, our nerves and each physical part of our brain are the hardware. And it's our thoughts and emotions that are the software. Programming and developing the hardware is a chicken-and-egg situation. It's a closed loop, so it doesn't matter which we cover first. I'll start with programming.

PROGRAMMING THE HARDWARE

What happens inside us as we develop is our software becomes the hardware over time, especially right after birth. Infants' brains are a jumbled mess of wires. At birth, an infant has about 100 billion brain cells but few connections called synapses. (Government of Wales n.d.) Initially, this may seem like a neat factoid, but it has massive implications.

As wet computers ourselves, we are born infinitely programmable! We have all the potential to adapt to nearly anything at birth. Your child will make 700 new connections per second from birth to age two! By age three, 90% of the brain is developed!

So, when I say your software becomes your hardware, I'm talking about this. Each experience stimulates the development of our physical brains. This is especially true because it's the purpose and concept behind *developmental windows*.

A baby born blind will adapt to that blindness by repurposing the parts of the brain that are usually reserved for vision and using it for other senses like hearing. That doesn't happen by magic. It happens by *mechanics*. It happens this way because there is no stimulus to the retinas to create connections that would create the need to build a visual center. If no photons enter the retina to engage the vision parts of the brain, those parts won't develop. Use it or lose it.

HOW HARDWARE DEVELOPS

Each part of our brain is made to do different things, and we build our brains from the ground up. I also mean that literally. The first parts of a newborn's brain to develop are the lower and central aspects. Brains grow bottom up and from back to front. The lower portion of the brain controls things like breathing, feeding, and movement. Babies learn to breathe, suckle, and wiggle pretty quickly.

The middle portion of the brain develops next. It governs emotions like bonding, fear, joy and anger. Which also makes some intuitive sense. After breathing, suckling, and wiggling, the next thing we do is bond, and it's pretty immediate. That happens through sharing emotional experiences with our caregivers. This is called *attunement*.

- Attunement can be defined as the reactiveness we have to another person. It is the process by which relationships are built, the foundation of empathy.

Attunement is an essential process.

Dr. Dan Siegel says, "When we attune with others, we allow our own internal state to shift, to come to resonate with the inner world of another." Attunement is how bonds are created between a mother and an infant. Ideally, a mother is attuned to her baby to know when the baby needs to be fed, cuddled, or changed. But attunement goes both ways.

An infant may cry because they see their mother crying. Infants are wired for attunement because we are wired to need a caretaker. The bond established through attunement keeps an infant safe, biologically speaking.

If a baby cries because it's hungry, no problem. Just feed the baby. If it does so when hiding from a threat? Everyone could end up as lion food. So, it makes sense for a mother or caregiver to have the ability to drop into the emotions of an infant and soothe that infant. You know, so they don't get eaten.

If attunement from mother to child doesn't happen for any reason, whether physical separation, anxiety or postpartum depression, the child will attune or - tune in - automatically to the mother. They are mimicking the mother's emotional state. Any mother who can't figure out how to get their baby to stop crying is undoubtedly stressed, either before or because of the crying. This sets up that baby's nervous system to be freaked out, stressed out, self-deprecating, or whatever mom is. Sound familiar?

The "higher" brain is the last to develop and is responsible for our self-awareness, decision-making, empathy and situational awareness. That part of our brain is only considered complete decades later.

After the foundations have been laid in those first three years, 90% of our little brains have been developed. The prefrontal cortex is the last part of our brain to develop and is only considered complete by our mid-twenties to early thirties. So, once we are adults, are we just stuck with who life made us out to be? Are we just stuck with whatever hardware was created by our stressful or shitty childhoods?

Of course not! It's not only possible to change your hardware. It is each of our **jobs** as CSA people to do so. Socrates said the unexamined life is not worth living. Harsh, but

I agree. It's especially true for CSA people. They say hurt people hurt people, and CSA people have definitely been hurt.

Reprogramming ourselves is *how we hurt those we care about less.*

But we were getting a little ahead of ourselves. We pick up this conversation again in section 3 about unleashing our superpowers. We detail how to break through the stress and use focus to change our hardware then.

BRAINS CAN'T DEVELOP APPROPRIATELY UNDER CHRONIC STRESS.

When stress grows prolonged or becomes constant, it causes serious problems. We've already established that short-term stress is fine, biologically speaking. Even if it's life-threatening, we have systems that are built for short-term stress, passed down through the millennia from our ancestors. Our nervous systems simply weren't designed to withstand long-lived or chronic stress, even if it's not life-threatening and, therefore, seems less stressful.

When the body is in its parasympathetic mode, its "down time," which is to say times of low stress and sufficient nutrients, the body smartly uses the opportunity to repair and rebuild all the different structures of our brain and body. That is part of the genius of the human design. It's designed to *always* be doing something.

In times of high stress, our bodies and brains must respond to the stressor to keep us safe, like running away from a bear. So naturally, it cannot perform restorative functions in those moments, having a life to save and all.

If chronic stress is a regular part of life during development, when we are supposed to build literal brain structures, guess what happens to the structures? Imagine an apartment complex designed by Ikea. It'll work, but not well and not for long. They'll have to do some major renovations sooner rather than later to make it livable. The same is true in the CSA brain. Our brains were built hastily in rare moments of peace and rest. So, it functions about as well as Ikea furniture does. It does the job well enough to fake it for a little while.

Biologically, childhood is intended to be the most stress-free time of our lives. The importance cannot be overstated. Not only are our bodies meant to rest, restore, and repair from the wear and tear of regular use during this downtime. During childhood, the physical structures of the brain and nervous system are literally, physically being built and programmed simultaneously.

When a child's body and mind cannot enter states of physiological and psychological safety with sufficient nutrients, their bodies cannot build and properly develop the regions, subregions, and organelles they ought to develop at the time they are supposed to develop them.

In child development, there are "windows" of time in which the development of certain physical and/or psychological events is intended to occur. (S G Selevan) If, during the time that window is open, the child cannot spend enough time in that downtime, sometimes called rest and digest mode. They are unable to reach those development milestones on time. And when those windows close, they are mighty hard to open again. (S G Selevan)

~ PHYSIOLOGICAL SIGH EXERCISE ~

In the next chapter, you will be asked a series of possibly uncomfortable questions about your childhood. You may get through them with no issues. Or you may have some reaction. If you do start to have some unpleasant reactions while you are answering these questions, there is a trick I'd like to share with you that I use for getting through a challenging moment. It's called a physiological sigh.

In whatever position you are in now, take a huge breath. Fill your lungs as much as you can, and then at the top, hold that breath for a few seconds. Notice how the pressure seems to subside a little? Now, take an additional breath on top of that one! It'll be a small breath. That's fine. As soon as you've packed as much air as possible with the second breath, exhale slowly. I mean really slowly – slower! Slower still!! Exhale as slowly as you possibly can - Annoyingly slow. Make an "f" sound during the exhale for best results.

That's how you do a *physiological sigh*. It's straightforward and very effective. Please memorize this sensation. Remember the physical sensations you had before compared to the physical sensations after. It only takes doing this once to experience effectiveness for yourself. It's evolutionary; it works every time.

As you read the challenging questions on the next page, remember to breathe this way, and you ought to get through it more easily. As you move through this work, it will help you to remember this technique. This subject is a difficult one. Breathing like this will serve you well.

For best results, use it as your first line of defense when you start to feel dysregulated before becoming overwhelmed. Continue to use it throughout the rest of this work and the rest of your life. I mean it.

Genetically engineered mice who were bred not to be able to sigh always die of a lung disease. Suggesting that sighs are not just natural; they are necessary for survival. (Ramirez) Yet, most people often feel too self-conscious to sigh where someone else might see because it might be perceived as rude or bad etiquette– le' sigh.

During the polio outbreak in the US, the first iron lungs killed the patients that were meant to be saved by it because they didn't include regular sighs. The patients slowly suffocated to death. Once large capacity sighs were added to the ventilation, the problem was solved. People stopped dying from the machines meant to save them. So yeah, sighing is essential. Give it a try if you start to feel strange.

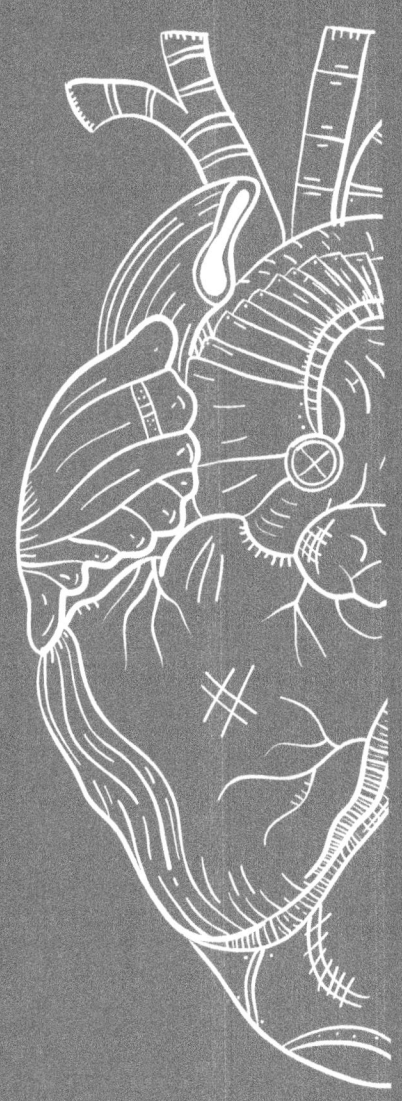

SECTION 2

THE BIOLOGY OF BROKENNESS

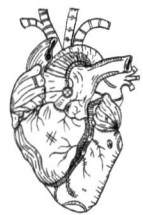

You made it to section two! Congratulations! It's time to switch gears. As a recap, you now understand a few key things that should help motivate you on your journey. You understand:

- The ways trauma shows up as an adult reinforces the belief that we are broken.
- The differences between stress and trauma.
- You understand what your body's pre-programmed stress response systems are (5 F's)
- You know you are not broken. You are Chronic Stress Adapted.

Now it's time to dive into the nuts-and-bolts biology behind human behavior. This section is denser with scientific information. But don't worry if you aren't a science- or biology-loving person. The only jargon information in this chapter remains as simplified as I could make it and still be accurate.

The point is to prove to you once and for all that you aren't broken. This section describes exactly how you came to be the way you are. We look at:

- Your ACE and Resiliency scores.
- Conditioning
- How you adopted negative beliefs to adapt to your trauma
- The Reticular Activating System
- The effects of chronic stress on specific brain structures
- All so I can prove to you that, in fact, Emotions are Logical - shameless plug for my ebook.

By the end of this section, you will have been presented with an airtight biological argument as to why you are not broken, and how **you adapted appropriately to inappropriate circumstances.** Only once that piece truly sinks in can the real journey begin. You will know the immutable biological realities that govern all human behaviors. Let's get into it.

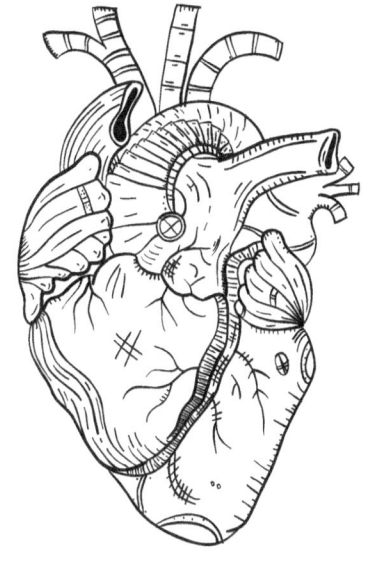

CHAPTER 7
ACES AND RESILIENCE

I spent the last section giving you an overview of the book and the basic mechanisms of how we came to believe we are broken. But if you're like me, the cliff notes version wasn't good enough. My trust issues demand to know details, or I'm not convinced. So, let's get into the nitty gritty for a bit. The perspectives I am presenting you with are sound, scientifically rigorous information that I have often used to <u>gut-check</u> myself in tough times.

We will explore facts that provide us with a different story we can narrate our lives with. This section is about understanding what happens to the developing brain and body when exposed to chronic stress during development.

Note: all brains, especially CSA brains, need repetition, so I'm going to repeat important information a few times so it will stick. Take breaks as you need to, and if you need to, remember to use the sighing exercise you learned at the end of the last section!

ADVERSE CHILDHOOD EXPERIENCES

I come from a Western medical "evidence-informed" background. Additionally, as a Midwesterner, it is in my DNA to discount the importance and impact of psychology. I needed more evidence to understand how my "brokenness" was not my fault. It was just too easy for me to dismiss all psychological failings as a weakness or flaw in my character.

To prove once and for all the powerful effect that chronic stress has on a developing child, we will look at one of the most groundbreaking and paradigm-shifting studies ever.

One of the most potent pieces of information that helped me discover where I was on that scale was learning about the Adverse Childhood Experiences study (ACE study.)

The study's goal was to see if there was any correlation between childhood adversity and health outcomes later in life, and oh boy, there was. Health outcomes are just medical science jargon for if a person acquires some type of disease or diagnosis during their life.

The study was conducted by the CDC and Kaiser Permanente in 1997. It was the first ever of its kind, and the study itself was massive, with almost 20 thousand participants. The results of this study changed the game by looking for root causes of diseases outside the lens of pure biochemistry.

They asked 10 questions about 10 categories of adversity in the study. Each participant got a 1-10 score for each yes, representing the adversity they faced as children. Then, they took those scores and compared them to their medical records.

What they found shocked everyone involved; the field has never been the same. Not only was childhood adversity much more common than they thought, with 1 out of 8 Americans having at least one ACE. The correlation between childhood adversity (which causes chronic stress) and health outcomes was undeniable.

What the ACE's study did for me, although it feels silly to admit now, was very important. Much of my early life is blank. I have only a handful of memories before middle school. This has always made me feel a little crazy. Sometimes, a lot crazy.

My memories were so few and so fuzzy that I didn't and still don't trust most of them. If you've ever studied how memory works, you know how faulty all human memory is—some I denied as bad dreams. I was told over and over as a child that I was extra sensitive and I had an "overactive imagination," so I always wondered if I was just overly sensitive or if my perceptions were real.

To be fair, I believe I *was* a highly sensitive child. Another fantastic book worth reading is The Highly Sensitive Person by Elaine Aron, Ph.D. She spent a lifetime researching and discovered that many species have a percentage of their population that is naturally highly sensitive. The increased sensitivity among HSPs is thought to be an evolutionary adaptation that benefits the group. This relates to CSA people because HSPs or highly sensitive people are that much more easily injured as children. So, even though I was sensitive, I also believe I was not making things up. Taking the ACE questionnaire allowed me, for the first time in 30 years, to finally accept that I wasn't "just a big baby." I indeed faced challenges that made me different, and they indeed had lasting effects on my mind and body.

Seeing that 8/10 score of mine made me feel so damn vindicated. Then I cried, a lot. Because finally, by some official objective measure, I found I indeed had a rough start to my life. I couldn't deny it anymore. Answering these questions brought solace to me.

Whether your experience with ACEs is earth-shattering and eye-opening or not. I hope that some of your uncertainty is relieved after answering these questions. Whatever your experiences, to complete this process, you must accept your adversities and the effects of those adversities, even if you don't understand them fully. And you might never fully understand them.

Have you heard of *Radical Acceptance*? This is exactly that. Accepting that shit happened. It doesn't mean you like it, approve of it, deserve it, or anything else. It just means you accept that it happened.

The ACE questionnaire is here to eliminate any uncertainty about the adversity you face by providing a quantified 1-10 score. My evidence-informed brain liked that. I think yours might too.

I would also like to note that the questions on the ACE questionnaire are not comprehensive. These are only 10 categories of adversity, among many others. Many people have faced challenges other than the things included on this list.

Things like immigration at an early age, constantly moving and having to make new friends in foster care can be hard on a child. Adoption is another. There's war and natural disasters, being raised in a cult or having a religious zealot for a caregiver or in the home like I had.

I don't believe the study's authors thought that these ten questions were by any means exhaustive. It is not only possible but likely that you went through things that are not on this list that deserve to be. Keep that in mind as you answer these questions.

Below are the 10 questions in the ACE study that they then correlated with health outcomes. I've included it here so you can take this questionnaire and see where you lie on this spectrum. Fill out the questions by marking a 1 or a checkmark. On the blank at the end of each question.

ACE QUESTIONNAIRE

From birth until the age of 18…

1. Did a parent or other adult in the household often swear at you, insult you, put you down, or humiliate you? Or act in a way that made you afraid that you might be physically hurt?

   If Yes, enter 1 ____

2. Did a parent or other adult in the household often push, grab, slap, or throw something at you? Or ever hit you so hard that you had marks or were injured?

   Yes No If Yes, enter 1 ____

3. Did an adult or person at least 5 years older than you ever touch or fondle you, or have you touched their body in a sexual way? Or attempt or actually have oral, anal, or vaginal intercourse with you?

   if Yes, enter 1 ____

4. Did you often feel that no one in your family loved you or thought you were important or special? Your family didn't look out for each other, feel close to each other, or support each other?

   If Yes, enter 1 ____

5. Did you often feel that you didn't have enough to eat, had to wear dirty clothes, and had no one to protect you? Or your parents were too drunk or high to take care of you or take you to the doctor if you needed it?

   If Yes, enter 1 ____

6. Were your parents ever separated or divorced?

   If Yes, enter 1 _____

7. Were any of your parents or other adult caregivers often pushed, grabbed, slapped or had something thrown at them? Or sometimes or often kicked, bitten, hit with a fist, or hit with something hard? Or ever repeatedly hit over at least a few minutes or threatened with a gun or knife?

   If Yes, enter 1 _____

8. Did you live with anyone who was a problem drinker or alcoholic or who used street drugs?

   If Yes, enter 1 _____

9. Was a household member depressed or mentally ill, or did a household member attempt suicide?

   If Yes, enter 1 _____

10. Did a household member go to prison?

    If Yes, enter 1 _____

#

ACE SCORE (Total "Yes" Answers): _____

(theannainstitute)

Take a minute to breathe....

Breathe some more......

Breathe again....

I know reading about these kinds of things can be uncomfortable and triggering. I hope you remembered to use your physiological sigh if that got hairy.

I have read these questions out loud for presentations and podcasts and had to start over 2, 3, 4, even 5 times to get through them without stumbling. In addition to the physical symptoms I described in section one, another sign of my dysregulation is it gets hard for me to read more than a few words at a time, especially if they're out loud and especially if they're on a screen.

If you are stumbling while trying to read this or feel uneasy in this moment, pause. Take a few more breaths. In and out. In and out. In and out. One more breath.

Now, let's look at the results of the study...

Let's break down your likelihood of physical diseases as an adult according to how much adversity you faced as a child.

Folks with four or more ACEs are...

- two and a half times more likely to develop COPD and hepatitis.
- Four and a half times more likely to develop depression,
- and twelve times more likely to consider or attempt suicide.

Those with Seven or more ACEs

- have triple the lifetime risk of lung cancer
- are three and a half times more likely to get ischemic heart disease. The number one killer in the US.

Before your inner critic responds with, "Of course, a rough childhood makes you more likely to engage in health-damaging behavior like drinking, smoking and drugs," there's a rebuttal to this, too. The study also controlled for that exact argument and found that even if you don't engage in any high-risk behaviors, you are ***still*** *more likely to develop heart disease and cancer!*

So, as you can see, early adversity in life significantly affects physical health, even if you do everything right, but this book isn't on physical health. I'm not here to teach you how to prevent heart disease or cancer. I included it here because the ACE study beautifully displays the immense impact that childhood adversity has on our physical bodies.

It may seem like I am beating a dead horse here. Still, it's imperative to understand and believe the connection between early childhood experiences and your psychological and medical reality as an adult. Our physical body and brain are what give rise to our mind.

Since 1997, many more ACE studies have been done in states across the US. All that I'm aware of, as of this writing, have had similar and often higher incidents of both ACEs and their associated health problems.

Your physical and psychological realities and reactions right now while you read these words are *directly linked to your early life experiences.*

Right now, your body is using a set of programs created to keep you alive in the environment you were in during your childhood. I need you to hear me when I say this. You must understand and believe this to progress further. You need to understand that it's not you failing or being broken. You're programmed for an environment you don't live in anymore. That programming is so profound it affects far more than our psychology. You react the way you do physically and psychologically because little you thought you would have to endure the same environment forever. So, little you was programmed with alarm bells on high alert and created one or two default responses to deal with a multitude of situations.

I want to absolutely and irrevocably take away, for all time, the thought and excuse of "It's all in my head." It's not. The ACE study proves that the stresses we experience not only have obvious but still not well-understood psychological and physiological effects.

GET -IT'S ALL IN MY HEAD-
OUT OF YOUR HEAD

At first, the results of the ACE study can be depressing. But here's the good news. *It's not just in your head!* It's in your damn medical records too!! So many CSA people know other CSA people who had it worse. We have become strong through adversity, and sometimes, denying that adversity or its impacts has allowed us to get through our lives.

Even for me, as a midwestern, allopathic medicine-trained son of ex-military factory workers, the impacts of *Adverse Childhood Experiences*, which are forms of stress that may become traumatic, are undeniable.

Even when I couldn't consciously see the results clearly in myself, seeing these medical outcomes was and remains the final nail in the coffin of my self-diagnosed brokenness—no more. There is no way adverse experiences have that much impact on physical health, and they do not also profoundly affect mental health.

"It's all in my head." "I should be fine." "I should be able to handle this."

We use these phrases to beat ourselves up. Sometimes, we beat ourselves into having a pity party so we can throw in the towel on our work for a while.

While resting is important, it is best accomplished purposefully and on a regular schedule, not after a temper tantrum or pity party. This section about ACEs is included for one reason: to rid you forever of the excuse "it's all in my head."

As I mentioned, the question will eventually arise as you go about your daily life: "Why am I like this?" As part of this journey, you can no longer say two phrases.

"I'm broken" and "It's all in my head" **are officially banned phrases.**

Both of these excuses are lame, inaccurate and off-limits. The best answer to "Why am I like this?" is… "I'm Chronic Stress Adapted." But even then, as chronic stress-adapted people, we are still left with faulty default programming, so the next question is what matters from here on out.

You're Chronic Stress Adapted. What are you going to do about it?

ACEs are not the end of the story. So, what we are going to do is get a better picture! The ACE study makes clear all humans are heavily influenced by adversity and chronic stress in early life. Still, there is a lot of *variability* in the manifestations and magnitude of our adaptations, even in people with identical overall ACE scores. Why? The answer to that question will help us fill a few more gaps in our new perspectives.

RESILIENCE

We all know stories of people who overcame unbelievable odds to rise like a phoenix from the hell that was their abusive young lives. Why can some people rally and do well while others with the same ACE score struggle? Where does the variability come from? If we are all stress-adapted, shouldn't we all think and react the same, especially if our ACE scores are the same?

By this point, you can probably guess the answer is no. Each person reacts differently, obviously. The circumstances we experience, both pleasant and unpleasant, condition us. This creates variability in ACE score outcomes.

Getting granular can be beneficial when it comes to understanding the effects of early life trauma—but we don't need to dive deep into your traumatic experiences. We will instead look a little closer at the more pleasant details.

ACEs let us know that our challenges negatively affect our health for a long time. Even if we do everything right and don't smoke, drink, or engage in high-risk behaviors. But how negatively varies.

You just learned about all the detrimental health effects of childhood adversity, especially for people with four or more ACES. A logical question to ask next might be. What makes one 9/10 ACE score a heroin addict or crackhead, while another 9/10 score grows up to be a social worker? Some folks seem able to rise above their challenges, while others struggle hard and never come out on top. Why? Are some people just stronger? Were they born with more willpower? There are a few significant factors that are rarely discussed, namely the availability of heroin and crack to a person as a young adult. That's the largest factor and one driving force that keeps poor CSA families, poor and CSA. Without a supply, it's hard to get addicted. But beyond circumstances like that, resiliency is the term we use to explain the difference in paths.

In this chapter, we are going to look at resiliency. What is it, what is it good for, and most importantly, *where does resiliency come from*? Going into this topic, it is important to understand upfront that a person's resiliency is not set in stone. You'll soon be asked to answer a resiliency questionnaire. It'll give you a resiliency score to counterbalance your ACE score.

The ACE questions were to help us identify specific circumstances of early childhood that negatively impact health. The *resiliency questionnaire* was designed to identify those things that *positively* impact us in early life. It helps us identify *protective* factors contributing to the variability among people with ACEs.

The most important part of this chapter is not your score. It's not even the questions. It's what the questions tell us. The questions can teach us what contributes to a person's resiliency. But before we get there, you must complete the questionnaire yourself.

According to the American Psychological Association, *resilience - is the process and outcome of successfully adapting to difficult or challenging life experiences, especially through mental, emotional, and behavioral flexibility and adjustment to external and internal demands.*

There are a few important pieces of information to take away from this definition. First is that resilience is both the process and the outcome. That means only by being resilient can we become resilient. The second is successfully adapting to challenging experiences.

Remember, trauma takes away our ability to choose our adaptation strategy during high stress and dysregulation. Especially for those of us with high ACE scores, when some part of us gets triggered, those most heavily relied on strategies that we used as kids get launched automatically. But not for all of us. Resiliency allows one 9/10 to become a social worker while another becomes a heroin addict. The real question is how?

To answer this, we have to look closely at the Resiliency questionnaire. This questionnaire was specifically invented to answer these types of questions. So, the next thing I will have you do is answer the questionnaire yourself. It will help you evaluate your level of resiliency and, more importantly, learn what **builds** resiliency.

Answer the questions and score yourself 1-5 points for each question. Definitely true 5 points and definitely not true counts as 1 point.

RESILIENCY QUESTIONNAIRE

1. I believe that my mother loved me when I was little.

    Definitely true   Probably true   Not sure   Probably Not   True Definitely   Not True

2. I believe that my father loved me when I was little.

    Definitely true   Probably true   Not sure   Probably Not   True Definitely   Not True

3. When I was little, other people helped my mother and father take care of me and they seemed to love me.

    Definitely true   Probably true   Not sure   Probably Not   True Definitely   Not True

4. I've heard that when I was an infant, someone in my family enjoyed playing with me, and I enjoyed it, too.

    Definitely true   Probably true   Not sure   Probably Not   True Definitely   Not True

5. When I was a child, there were relatives in my family who made me feel better if I was sad or worried.

   Definitely true   Probably true   Not sure   Probably Not   True Definitely   Not True

6. When I was a child, neighbors or my friends' parents seemed to like me.

   Definitely true   Probably true   Not sure   Probably Not   True Definitely   Not True

7. When I was a child, teachers, coaches, youth leaders or ministers were there to help me.

   Definitely true   Probably true   Not sure   Probably Not   True Definitely   Not True

8. Someone in my family cared about how I was doing in school.

   Definitely true   Probably true   Not sure   Probably Not   True Definitely   Not True

9. My family, neighbors and friends talked often about making our lives better.

   Definitely true   Probably true   Not sure   Probably Not   True Definitely   Not True

10. We had rules in our house and were expected to keep them.

    Definitely true   Probably true   Not sure   Probably Not   True Definitely   Not True

11. When I felt really bad, I could almost always find someone I trusted to talk to.

    Definitely true   Probably true   Not sure   Probably Not   True Definitely   Not True

12. As a youth, people noticed that I was capable and could get things done.

    Definitely true   Probably true   Not sure   Probably Not   True Definitely   Not True

13. I was independent and a go-getter.

    Definitely true   Probably true   Not sure   Probably Not   True Definitely   Not True

14. I believe that life is what you make it.

    Definitely true   Probably true   Not sure   Probably Not   True Definitely   Not True

Total Resiliency points ___

Now you have your resiliency score. Your score aims to demonstrate opposing conditioning acting on your default programming. Your score isn't the important part. Your number may feel very important to you, and it may not. The most interesting and important thing about the resiliency questionnaire is the questions themselves. Did you notice a theme? Glance back at the questions and reread them. What do you notice?

When I took this questionnaire, I noticed a theme that became critical to my understanding of resiliency. _The questions are centered around people other than our primary caretakers and whether we believe ourselves to be liked, loved or lovable._

The story I got from these questions, regardless of the score, is that having people other than our caregivers, who see us as good, likeable and lovable, is what gives us resilience. This is so important. It tells me that resiliency is established by having people in our lives who care about us, take an interest in what we do and have a positive outlook, just like Kaya did for me. Most importantly, these people can offer us a compassionate narrative. There's a whole chapter on that in section 4.

This means resiliency can be increased! It can be trained. If I could say yes to more of the questions above, I would have more resilience. Right? So, it stands to reason that if I could have the answers to those questions be a yes now, I would increase my resiliency!

This section can feel weird. When I first found and took this questionnaire, I had to think long and hard about some of the questions. They were genuinely tricky for me to answer. I had mixed feelings about the questions and my answers to them. Maybe you did, too. If you did, don't worry too much.

It makes sense that we would have mixed feelings about some questions because our experience concerning the answers to those questions is mixed. At times the answer for me was definitely yes, and other times, definitely no. So, of course, when we try to choose just one answer, we feel a little twisted about the answer. That's ok. You can let that go too.

Like I said. It's not about your score. It's about what the questionnaire tells us. It tells us that it really does take a village...

IT TAKES A VILLAGE TO RAISE A CHILD

Much of this work toward the end of this book is about trying on perspectives. We will try them on like sunglasses. Try a perspective on for size. To do so, you pick a perspective and then act as if it is the only perspective for a little while. If that experience is pleasant or makes sense and helps us in some way, we can agree with a truth of that perspective.

This is how we choose our I am statements. In order to know ourselves, we must first be known. This is the way that we become known. First by our parents, then by our non-caregiver community. For me, by Kaya too. The strength of our relationship with our community is our resiliency.

This extends to our adult life. If we focus on fostering the relationships in our lives now, we increase our resiliency. Resiliency increases if we put time and energy into the relationships that build us up.

If you are unhappy with how your life is going now or feel isolated, alone or unworthy, I ask something of you. Please reach out to *one person* today in your life whom you know loves you, respects you and has your best interests at heart. Even if they don't agree with everything you do or vice versa, reach out to this person today. Foster that relationship, and you *will* increase your resiliency.

Resiliency *is successful adapting to challenging experiences*. By reaching out and fostering that one relationship, you automatically increase your ability to adapt successfully to challenging experiences. That is why you're reading this book, after all. So do it. Before you sleep tonight, send a letter, a text, an email, or a voicemail to someone who lights up when they see you coming. Then, watch your resiliency skyrocket. I'm rooting for you.

Suppose you were raised by a single mother. In that case, it's helpful to understand how genuinely screwed she was when it comes to meeting the emotional needs of her young children in the modern world.

When I evaluated these questions, I realized what each question is doing in a way is providing a different perspective than what would have been available to a Child with Adversity.

When a bear comes home every night, the chronic stress we experience prevents pieces of our brains from developing properly, let alone thinking clearly. Each person's opinions and perspectives that we encountered as kids exposed us to a new possibility for our reality that was different from what our childish, stressed-out minds came up with.

Our culture considers the nuclear family to be the standard family unit. However, the nuclear family has had some unintended adverse effects on our biology. One of the most significant ways it impacts health negatively is by removing elders from our family units.

Throughout our existence as a species, we have lived in intergenerational pods. Mom and Dad were there, but so were Grandma and Grandpa, aunts and uncles. I know this might seem like an odd thing to talk about in a self-help book, but think about it now with your new resilience perspective. For CSA people, context is everything.

Grandparents' aunts, and uncles' additional perspectives can be life-saving for a chronically stressed or abused child. For some of the people reading this, myself included, these relatives provided us with our resiliency cushion. It was Grandma who consoled us and told us that Mom loves us even when she is mad at us.

Maybe it was grandpa or the neighbor who asked after your school work or took an interest in your hobbies. Just think about how perfectly positioned grandma is to give us the perspective we need when mom is angry.

Grandma can tell us, "Don't tell her I said so, but your Mom did the same thing at your age. It's alright honey" That one perspective at the right moment can be the difference between a child believing they are a human being bumbling through life, like everyone else is, and believing they are fundamentally fucked up just for fucking up.

In our modern nuclear family, we have removed that crucial protective factor. In our modern "standard family unit," a child has only one option for a perspective: the perspective of the parent—the one who is angry and, therefore, dysregulated. The child not only has their dysregulation to deal with internally, it's then compounded by picking up on and usually amplifying Mom's dysregulation. Just like attunement!

In a dysregulated state, we will always choose a negative narrative. One that ends with "I am __" fill it in with whatever your favorite insult is.

It's the relationships we have and the way those relationships make us feel that condition us. Resilience pads the blows of high ACE scores. How we feel about ourselves despite how we are treated is the sign of resiliency. Often, the people we interact with outside our primary caregivers, especially extended family and our community, build resiliency. But how exactly? We know the perspective they provide us with as kids act as protective factors against ACEs. But how do the opinions of grandparents and community members become protective?

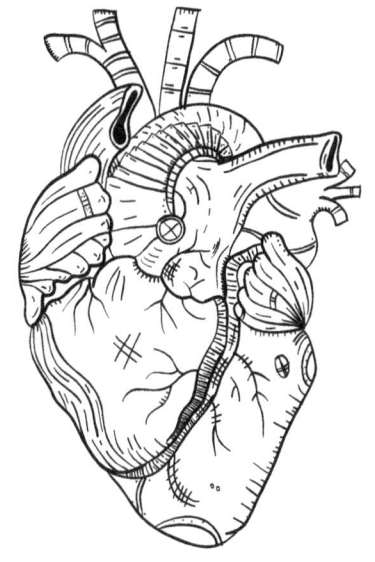

CHAPTER 8

CONDITIONING

H uman brains are designed to be customized in the early part of life. Then, we are meant to play out those customizations for the rest of our lives. – *Stanford Professor, Dr. Andrew Huberman*

In people, we call that customization conditioning. Conditioning is "a behavioral process whereby a response becomes more frequent or more predictable in a given environment as a result of reinforcement."

There's an important piece of this definition worth pointing out. Conditioning is **always** *context-dependent*. That's what the definition implies in the "in a given environment" part. The other aspect is reinforcement. Reinforcement can be automated from the environment or from a person or culture that wants us to behave in a certain way.

Many things condition us. Our cultures, parents, teachers and life events all teach us to expect things to be a certain way. The conditioning happens just by experiencing them.

Conditioning is how nature controls behavior. It gives rewards for desired behaviors and punishments for undesired behavior. It's an efficient system designed by evolution.

A great example of functional subconscious conditioning is that when we eat bad seafood and get sick, we no longer desire that food. If the feedback, the illness, was severe enough, we may feel sick just from looking at or seeing seafood. This is a natural adaptive process.

I still have a conditioned response like this from drinking way too much warm Jim Beam with Redbull. The smell of either of them causes me to remember the smell and taste of both warm together from a mason jar, and I feel nauseated. Can you relate? It's a pretty standard experience of conditioning. But conditioning begins long before we drink whiskey or eat imitation crab legs.

Humans learn all kinds of things at break-neck speed when we are little. We learn to walk, talk, and even speak English, French, or Swahili in just a few short years, all simply by watching, observing, and mimicking. In the same way, a baby's body visibly grows, strengthens, and solidifies over time, and so does the brain.

While we can mark external physical changes like height with simple chalk on a door frame, changes in the brain need a bit more fine-tuned of an instrument to measure with. Most rentals don't have a washer or dryer, let alone an fMRI machine -functional magnetic resonance imaging. So, how can we keep track of the growth of the brain?

During development, a baby must learn to do certain physical tasks in a specific order. Not because someone makes them but due to the interplay of the limiting effects of the laws of physics. Things like gravity, geometry, and lever systems combine with laws of biology, like "fire together wire together," to force certain things to be learned before others. These forces interact in ways that ensure "baby steps" during development, at least regarding physical competency skills.

As a baby, we must develop enough strength and coordination to do the little stuff first, like lifting our cute, fat, and surprisingly heavy little heads. After that, we learn to roll over, crawl, walk, and eventually run. Thanks to help from those previously listed external influences, physical competency skills like walking and running are invariably in one obvious, pre-ordained order. First crawl, then walk, then run.

Brain skills are a little different. Brain skills, for lack of a better word, are often conceptual. The concepts we learn in early life are especially compelling because they're meant to be permanent! The things we learn get integrated into the algorithms in our heads and are expected to be repeated for the rest of our lives.

Our DNA expects us to speak the same language and interact with people in a way appropriate for our environment. The order in which we learn things profoundly affects our psychological health for the rest of our lives. They become part of the framework tool kit and coping mechanisms we use to navigate the world. The principles we hold help us make decisions and guide our lives. Importantly, *it can be traumatic to learn certain things in the wrong order.*

An Example:

Children establish their fundamental sense of self, aka their identity, leading up to the age of 7 during those Theta years. Our opinions of ourselves form our sense of self. Our opinions of ourselves when young are always reflections of the opinions we think others have of us - namely, Mom and Dad or our primary caregivers. Our *interpretation* of the interactions we have as children becomes our concept of who we are.

If we are doted on and loved unconditionally, we will expect similar treatment from our interactions with all things. Our sense of self will reflect a general feeling of deservedness. Some might even say entitlement. Similarly, if interactions with caregivers are erratic or unpleasant, we will come to expect erratic and unpleasant interactions with all things in the future, which creates that constant anxious, foreboding feeling that limits so many of us as adults.

If a mother is too depressed or exhausted to attune to her child, it causes emotional problems. If it's for an afternoon? It's no big deal. The experience of the child is needing something and not receiving it. All is well if that happens only once, twice, or even a few times. But what if that happens repeatedly due to drug abuse, war, workaholism or postpartum depression?

If, as a kid, we have already learned through consistent experiences that mommy loves us because she usually meets our needs when they arise, then we can chalk it up to mom being busy or simply temporarily unavailable. If we haven't engrained that yet and we repeat the experience of not having our needs met, then we begin to wonder. "Why?"

As a tiny living organism, we start looking for explanations before we have words or a developed enough brain to think our explanations through. An assumption that is easy to make from this is when we really need something, we won't get it.

Enter the feeling of helplessness often accompanying strong desires in a chronic stress-adapted person. But then the all-important question comes up again. "Why?" As we grow, we ask why to better understand a situation in our desire to predict future scenarios. That is often where our sense of brokenness comes in.

In this case, the self-centered focus of broken -which is natural because kids have to be self-focused during this time as it is when they're supposed to be developing their sense of self - can easily lead to thoughts like "I don't get the attention I want or my needs met when I need them."

It's important to remember at sufficiently early stages of development, to us as very young children, our parents, for a short time, are basically Gods that keep us alive. So, blaming our mom/dad/God isn't an option, no matter how extreme or obvious the fault may be to an outsider.

If this happens often enough, a natural desire for something basic like a hug or food can twist and resemble something more like "I want more than I should get or deserve." The assumption about the interaction is "I'm too needy." You say that enough, and it can easily become "I must be broken." When you just wanted a hug.

One of the things that happened here is the child learned lessons in the wrong order. I believe that many early life traumas occur because we learn a life lesson when we aren't biologically prepared for it. If a person learns one or two lessons in the wrong order, it makes them quirky. When you learn a bunch of lessons in the wrong order, it makes you feel broken.

This is the mental equivalent of learning to run before you learn to walk. We've established that people can't learn to run before walking due to other external forces like gravity. But since the brain is less affected by gravity than the musculoskeletal system is, let's try a thought experiment.

NO BRAKES

What would happen if a person could run but couldn't walk? Once they start running, what happens to them? Once they started running, they could never slow down past a light jog. They would run and run and run, slowing down but never able to stop until they got so tired they eventually collapsed.

That's precisely what happens to CSA brains. Once our minds start running, they are unable to slow down. We don't have brake lines. We have on and off, and that's just about it. I mean this as literally as I do figuratively—more on that when we discuss the vagus nerve.

You weren't designed faulty. You were designed with an incomplete nervous system for a purpose. That purpose was so it could be customized. You were supposed to learn how to "ramp-down" at a specific point during your development, referred to as a *development window*.

However, if you were experiencing chronic stress during the ramp-down *development window*, the ramp-down was meant to act as your braking system wasn't experienced. So the skill wasn't imprinted. Although we were designed to have brakes, they weren't installed.

Braking is a metaphor for the activities of the parasympathetic nervous system. Our sympathetic nervous system is tied to the stress response we discussed earlier. The parasympathetic nervous system allows us to calm down after a stress -sympathetic-response. All trauma is centered around poor coordination of these two nervous system states. A healthy person, mentally and emotionally, has to be able to smoothly move from a sympathetic activated to a parasympathetic restful state and back.

Everything in the body is "use it or lose it," so our nervous system, in its attempt to keep us well prepared for our environment, formed itself in a way that doesn't include a calming down stage. All because we rarely experience an environment in which it is safe enough to stop evaluating threats.

So, when our minds start running, they keep running until they're so exhausted that we collapse either from fatigue or our favorite coping mechanisms, which we love so much because they are crutches that help us slow down or stop, like TV, social media, food, drugs or sex.

Identifying as CSA is a shorthand way to say that our default settings are different from everyone else's. But that doesn't have to be a bad thing. You want the default settings on your TV to be different from what you set your microwave with because it wouldn't work. It wouldn't be functional. If you have ever thought, "why am I so dysfunctional?" the answer is that some of your default programming has the wrong settings for your everyday world!

The biggest problem with feeling broken and believing you're broken? The real kicker is...

A person can <u>never</u> rise above their opinion of themselves.

If your opinion of yourself is that you are broken, wrong, stupid, over-reactive, or whatever awful thing you tell yourself when you're upset, you will never be able to stop being those things.

Some people reading this right now have never felt it was possible for them not to be broken. I know that some people reading these words have always believed in their heart of hearts. They have always been broken and always will be. They never believed they had a chance at peace or happiness. My brother might have been one of them.

I think many people who commit suicide or people who have attempted or considered suicide have this mindset. I know I did. I'm glad I was wrong. This mindset comes with a sense of irreparable damage - it'll never be better. They believe there is no way things could ever be or will ever be different.

We feel this way because we can't see things from any other perspective. Because of our conditioning, we get locked into one way of looking at ourselves and our world. We see ourselves as irreparably damaged, and in our internal logic, it's undeniably true.

If you are bold enough to change your opinion of yourself, you will finally be able to become better. That's the only way. We have to know, we may need to change some things, but we are not broken. We are *chronic stress adapted*.

You can never rise above your opinion of yourself, so watch what you say after "I am." It will get you into a whole mess of trouble.

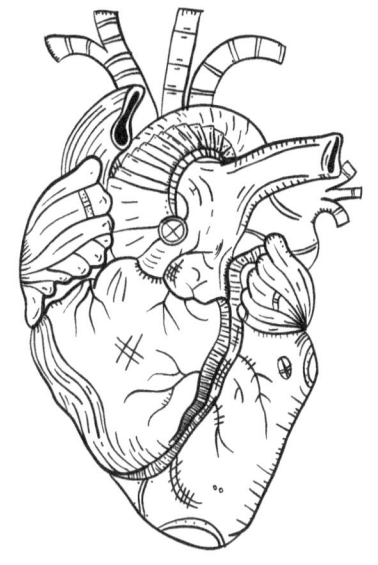

CHAPTER 9

ADOPT TO ADAPT

Okay, you just learned conditioning is a type of learning that happens by reinforcing specific behaviors. It can come from punishment for undesired behaviors or rewards for desired behaviors. But we know trauma isn't just about what happens to us. It's a living wound inside us, resulting from our narrative about a traumatic event.

So, on a deeper level, whatever our life situation may have been, no matter the extremity of them, it's the story we tell ourselves about it that makes an event traumatic or not. So, where do we get those stories? Are they pre-programmed? Do we make them up on the spot? That's what this chapter is going to look at.

There is a phrase I use that encapsulates the entire concept. Please remember this phrase, as it has become a cornerstone of my understanding. It allows me to remember why my brain always finds ways to blame myself and helps me figure out why I react inappropriately to certain situations.

ADOPT TO ADAPT

To <u>adapt</u> to circumstances, we <u>adopt</u> beliefs.

Adopting a belief is the primary way we adapt to the inappropriate circumstances we experience. Why? What does that belief do for us? Any belief that gets adopted during stress has one purpose. It helps us make sense of the pain because, remember, *all trauma is stressful, but not all stress is traumatic.*

The adopted belief must allow us to reduce the stress and cognitive dissonance we experience when chronically stressed. It also helps us act in a way that gets us closer to our goal. For a child, the goal is always belonging because belonging is the most fundamental survival aspect for any human who can't fend for themselves. Because children are developing their sense of self, all their thoughts are self-centered and are supposed to be, so the adopted belief is about ourselves.

OUR ORIGINAL "I AM" STATEMENTS

Most of the time, we don't adopt beliefs consciously and, therefore, don't consciously understand their impacts, nor are we usually aware we have them. They are most commonly expressed as "I am" statements.

Remember when I said you must be careful about what you say after the words "I am"? This is where we first get ourselves into trouble with I am statements. Remember when I said that we must first be known to know ourselves? This is the first way we get to know ourselves. Implicitly. We assume "I am <u>fill-in-the-blank</u>" based on how we are treated.

This phenomenon happens inside a child's mind, who initially doesn't know themselves. That's why the child's thoughts are self-centered: so that we *can* get to know ourselves. Our opinions are created by the way we interpret how we are treated. So, the assumed belief will be self-centered, like a developing child's always is. It will be childish as a child conceived it. If that child is only around mom and dad or has little input from others around them, guess whose narrative they'll agree with? Their caretakers'.

Since we make these subconscious decisions to accept beliefs about ourselves when we are stressed and feeling terrible, it's reasonable that the assumption we adopt allows us to reconcile our idea of who we are with how we are being treated is equally stressed and terrible. Expressed as an I am statement is often something like "I am terrible." or "I am needy." "I am whiny." "I am lazy." "I am broken."

The joy and utility of aunts, uncles, grandparents, teachers, and counselors is that they model a perspective and story that is neither ours nor our parents. These non-parental adults have more brain real estate to leverage, which they can use to present kids with another more logical, still true perspective, boosting the child's resiliency.

The young child then feels safe while co-regulating with grandma or grandpa. That time together also gives them a chance to hear what Grandma and Grandpa have to say about the situation before the narrative becomes concretized in biology. If we like the perspective they share? If it works for us? We adopt their perspective rather than the self-deprecating one our little stressed-out child brains come up with. We keep their sunglasses.

Grandparents relay old stories of their kids' antics as children, providing a sense of humanness to our parents. If you were lucky enough, like I was, to know at least some of your grandparents, you may remember how validating this can feel. I know it was relieving for me.

Do you remember a time when an aunt, uncle, or grandparent told you an embarrassing story about your parents? How was it to hear? How much did it change your reality when you were presented with a story that humanized your parents? This is another thing that may seem silly at first glance but can be significant.

As I said earlier, in our early development, there is a phase in which Mom is experienced essentially as God. That takes time to work its way out of our little baby heads. Grandma and Grandpa are great at letting us bend some rules just a little, and they (hopefully) tell us they love us and sneak us candy in church. That may seem insignificant, but it helped me.

Our relationships with our extended family, friends, and community foster resiliency. They teach us we are not alone. They give us other perspectives to look at a situation from. They teach us that our parents are human and flawed as well. This alone can be lifesaving for a child whose parent feels they must know what's right. These relationships teach us that even when we feel unloved or unwanted, someone around us loves and cares about us, fostering a stable sense of self. That is resiliency in action.

As an adult who understands this, it's up to us to use the knowledge. ***The ability to choose and change your narrative is the heart and soul of resiliency.***

Sometimes, we get a little help dealing with big early life stresses, which builds our resiliency. But some of us got fuck all from outside the home as well. Some of us were unfortunate enough to score high in ACEs and low in resiliency. But that's okay too.

If you are one of the people who, when answering those questions, felt worse and worse because as you went through these questions, you kept having to give 1s and 2s, Your story is NOT over.

Again, your score is not the critical piece. A person's total resiliency score can give them an idea of where they are on the resiliency scale now. But resiliency is not set in stone. You can increase it at any time. That's why we evaluated the questions themselves. We read between the lines and found the key takeaways.

The takeaway from this half of the chapter is that your resiliency is in your hands whether you scored high or low, whether big T or little t. All you need to do is foster the relationships that support you today. If you do this, your resiliency will rise. You can choose your reactions instead of having them chosen for you by a past you couldn't control.

With all of this information, you can choose your reactions to stress. You can choose the narrative that you leave a situation believing. These two things combine to grant freedom to CSA people when we halt our dysregulation early enough. The narrative we adopt to describe and recall a situation determines how we adapt to it.

We can't always choose the circumstances in which we find ourselves. When young, we couldn't choose how we reacted, what we believed about the stressful situation or our reaction to it. But now we can. Now we must.

Whatever your default adopted beliefs are, you can choose new ones. ***You can choose a narrative that gets you closer to your goal*** that isn't self-defeating and doesn't contribute to anything that might be described as brokenness. It's entirely up to you now.

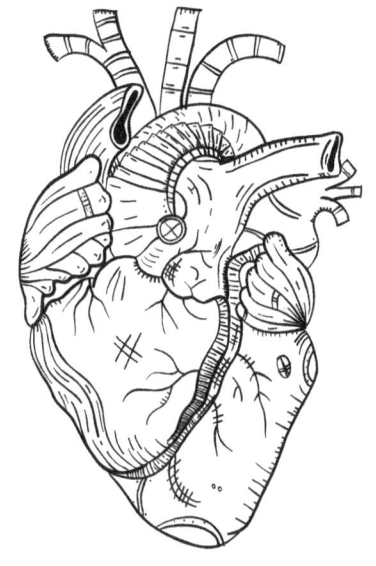

CHAPTER 10
RETICULAR ACTIVATING SYSTEM

This next piece of biology is pretty wild – like almost science fiction wild. It's also the final piece of evidence you'll need to remove any remaining doubt that you were ever broken. It's called the reticular activating system, or RAS for short. Just wait. The biological defense against brokenness is just too airtight. Once you understand what the RAS does, you'll have no choice but to admit defeat and abandon the "I'm broken" BS forever. All that evidence of your brokenness we talked about earlier? I told you it's all crap. Here is the truth about your so-called "evidence."

The RAS is a specialized network in the human brain that is in charge of filtering out everything in the environment that is more or less irrelevant to *you*. That's a big job because *a lot* is happening around us *all* the time. Most of it is irrelevant to us. So, our brains developed over time to not notice everything, just the things that affect us most.

It's not beneficial for humans to be able to count how many ants are in a colony quickly. Although beneficial to an anteater, that kind of observation skill has no real-world impact on us human folks. So, we don't notice the number of ants. *We don't <u>need</u> to notice it – so we <u>don't.</u>* The same is true for so many other things in our environment.

So, we need a filtration system: Enter the RAS...

So, if the RAS is a filter, the next question is, what does it let through? After all, that is what filters are for—not only to keep certain things out but also to let specific things in.

A few things almost always get through the RAS's filtration and into our conscious minds.

RAS thing 1: The first and most obvious one is our name. I'm sure you have had the experience of being lost in thought or engulfed in conversation with a friend until suddenly you hear your name. It breaks your concentration, and then you look for whoever was trying to get your attention. That's the RAS at work.

RAS thing 2: The next thing the RAS lets through is sexy. I'm sure you have had this experience as well. You're on your couch chilling, watching TV, playing video games, eating caramel & white cheddar popcorn when, out of the corner of your eye, you see your partner looking like a snack. Something about them is a little different. Maybe it's the way they are moving or standing, or it's the look in their eyes. Then you know. It's sexy time! This is the RAS at work as well. If we want to continue the species, it's wise to know when our person is "in the mood" to do so, or at least practice!

RAS thing 3: The last thing your RAS lets through are things it deems "important to you." You are probably familiar with a form of this called the new car phenomenon. Say you're in the market for a new car, and you see a green Miata that piques your interest. You have never seen a green Miata, so you buy it. What do you notice as soon as you drive it off the lot? Another green Miata, then another and another. That's the RAS at work too. Green Miatas were only important to *you* once you owned one. So now you notice them everywhere, when before they were non-existent in your world.

With the green Miata, it's fairly intuitive how the RAS picked up on its importance. When you buy a new car, you think about it a lot. It fills your thoughts for days to weeks or even months, depending on how long it takes to settle on a vehicle. We hem and haw for ages thinking and thinking and thinking about if it's exactly what we want or not.

Repetition of information is a big part of what informs the RAS of what is important to us. We think about the new car over and over and over again, our brain marks it as important to us and lets information about the new car into our heads without our even trying.

So, if you catch yourself repeating things like,

"God I'm so stupid."
"I'm too weak."
"Nothing ever works out for me."
"Why am I the one who always winds up holding the bag?"
"I don't get this shit."
"I never understand."
"I'm always too late."
"No one ever likes me."
"Everyone is always talking behind my back."

Guess what your RAS will deem important? Every single one of your self-deprecating beliefs. And it will do it with incredible speed and consistency.

If you say over and over to yourself that horrible crap always happens to you, guess what your RAS will focus on? Every negative thing that happens to you! Which again makes biological sense. Remembering negative and unpleasant things has helped our species survive for millions of years. But what happens if you switch the things that you say to yourself?

What do you think happens with the RAS when your belief is something like, "things might be crap now but they eventually work out for me?" You'll start noticing the things that work out in your life. The memories you recall will be memories of when things worked out!!

For each of our less-than-desirable experiences, no matter how bad they may have been, they eventually ended. We can focus on the fact that the bad crap happened, and our RAS will remind us of the horrors. Or we can focus on the fact that it did eventually end. That leads to the RAS focusing on resolutions instead of problems. Both are true, both happened. One is more functional and more pleasant than the other.

This is important because it's the way your brain works, whether you like it or not. You now understand a piece of the functioning of your brain in a specific enough way to leverage it to your benefit. Knowing this, you can change the things that your mind focuses on.

One more thing: *It's hard to lie to yourself.* Especially us CSA folks. We are walking lie detectors. We can feel in our bones whether a person is lying to us or not, sometimes even when that person is us. You can't be able to tell yourself "I'm the most beautiful person on the planet" and expect it to work if no part of you believes it's true. You will instantly reject it because it's something you flat-out don't believe.

So, if you can't lie to yourself and your RAS is programmed to constantly look for negative horrible things about yourself and the world? How in the world are you supposed to change your outlook? How are in the world am I supposed to learn to focus on the things that make life worth living? Rather than the things that make it hard? How do I change my RAS?!

REPROGRAMMING THE RAS: "I AM" MANTRA'S

Well, Reprogramming the RAS requires a few basic things. First is awareness – You are now aware of the RAS, it's profound role in all our lives and how it works. <u>That's step one – done.</u>

<u>Step two</u> is to create replacement things to focus on. You start with something that is true that you do believe…

For me, I used to believe I was *"too much."* I was told it from the time that I was a child and I believed it. I saw evidence everywhere that I was indeed too much. Too loud, too dramatic, too weird. I'm sure you have a similar experience or 20, where in childhood, you were told something awful about yourself, and then you believed it because after hearing it over and over, you eventually saw evidence of it in your life. Now you know why. It was just your RAS, not *the truth.*

This makes the RAS a large contributor to confirmation bias. Whatever you believe that's important to you becomes what you notice in the world. We tend to only find and see things that we agree with. This means those years of evidence that you had that you were indeed too whatever fill in the blank with your favorite poison, wasn't actually necessarily factual evidence. It was just the RAS doing its job based on what you repeat most often.

Is it any wonder we believed the things we were told over and over about ourselves? No matter how cruel or incorrect they were? Is it becoming clear now that after a rough childhood, the RAS takes over to provide you with evidence that you are indeed whatever messed up thing you had to agree with for survival?

I'm telling you all this to show how perfectly packaged this damage is. It's almost guaranteed that we believe these awful things about ourselves because of the combination of these two phenomena. The stars, or in our case biology, align perfectly to believe the brokenness crap.

But what else does this mean? It means that all the evidence you collected over the years was biased. Biased evidence is thrown out in court. You need to, and get to be, judge and juror of your life. You're an adult now, and no one else's opinion matters but your own. Now, you have the tools to change those beliefs that hold you back. Just like I did. To make clear how to reprogram your RAS, I'm going to tell you what I did to change mine.

Reprogramming my RAS fundamentally changed my life for the better. It allowed me to leave behind the baggage of the traumas in my life. The things you choose to replace and the replacement beliefs may be different, but the process will be similar. Reprogramming the RAS always starts the same though. Start with picking the repetitive belief that causes you trouble and needs replacing.

I used to believe I was "too much," and yes, just like you, my RAS showed me evidence of this every day. I never fit in. Since I'm an evidence-based kind of person, I believed it. Since lying to myself "I'm perfect just the way I am" failed miserably I had to come up with a new tac. The replacement was I'm just enough. But before I talk about that, I first want to talk about this failed mantra.

MY FAILED REPROGRAMMING ATTEMPT:

"I'm perfect the way that I am" was not something I could use to train my RAS out of looking for evidence of my "too much." It didn't work because too much of my identity thought it was a lie, even though it's something I have chosen to believe in my life.

I choose to believe that every person on the planet is perfectly imperfect, just the way they are. I hold this truth very near and dear to my heart. It helps me to have peace and to be kind to people when my biology doesn't want me to be. It gives me patience in trying situations. But at the end of the day, when it came to applying the "universal" belief to myself, the years of training that my RAS had received simply wouldn't let the evidence through.

This bit can be tricky. When you set out to change your RAS, you will have to choose new important self-concepts that will allow it to find evidence of your newly held belief.

I failed on my first attempt. I chose something that I wanted to believe about me but didn't; something I believed was true for everyone else, but I didn't believe about me.

It was simply too far from what I believed about myself to work at the time. This can happen to you if you are overzealous with the new positive replacement beliefs you repeat to yourself. But just like me, it's not a big deal if you don't get it right the first time. Do try again and aim a little lower.

On the next try, I chose something that resembled more closely my current beliefs and something I also had evidence for, even if it wasn't as much evidence. I chose to go with "I'm a lot." At first glance, this might not look much different. But the implications of this slight adjustment are HUGE.

You see, I never fit in anywhere if I am too much. No matter what the event or situation, having the self-concept - I'm too much - automatically puts me at odds with every situation I find myself in. It leaves me feeling separate, not included, and therefore unwanted. Which is painful and stressful 100% of the time.

I'm a lot is still a belief that maybe isn't the best self-concept to have, but again, our goal isn't perfect—it's progress. It was absolutely progress for me when I shifted my self-talk from "*I'm too much*" to "*I'm a lot.*"

It worked! And it worked because it's not absolute. It's not great, but it's a step in the right direction. It says that who I am is a lot, sure, but it doesn't automatically alienate me in every situation. With my new mantra, I at least had a chance.

So, "I'm a lot" became my mantra for a few years. It was a vast improvement over "I'm too much." With it, I could stay in situations and feel like even though I might be a bit uncomfortable, I'm at least not automatically incongruous – *too much* - in every situation.

Although it was an improvement over - I'm too much, I'm a lot - still left me constantly wary that I would be too much for someone at any moment. It left me anxious that I was always one step away from doing or saying something stupid.

Granted, one step from stupid is still better than stupid. It's better than being guaranteed that I will never fit into any situation, which is exactly what being "*too much*" equates to. But even the "I'm a lot." belief was eventually too tiring to maintain as well. That's when I upgraded my I am mantra yet again.

My personal RAS journey looked something like...

- I started life believing I was "too much." Which put me on the outs in any and all situations
- I tried replacing that with "I'm perfectly fine just the way I am," and that failed miserably.
- Then I changed that to "I'm a lot," which worked for a while. It was an improvement for sure, but it could have been better.
- But then I settled with "I'm just enough." And I think I'll stay here a while longer.

Everything changed again when I switched from saying "I'm a lot" to saying "I'm just enough. Even if I'm *"just"* barely appropriate for the situation. "I'm just enough" worked like a charm.

With this attitude toward myself, I've been able to travel Europe as a physio for circus acrobats. I fell madly in love in a foreign country with men I would have once thought were so far out of my league it's laughable. I've come into my own as a musician and performer. I started clinics for people without homes and transients. I even set up a treatment center in the middle of a war zone in Seattle Capitol Hill when the local community took over the police station to demand they stop murdering black people in the streets. I could do all these things because I switched my thinking by tweaking my automatic negative responses to something more functional. Changing my "I am" mantras changed my RAS, which changed my life.

You can do the same thing too. You can change your RAS. You can train it to find real-world evidence of the qualities you want to see more of in yourself. But you have to start with seeing some amount of good in yourself.

Maybe you were told you were "too emotional." That belief can be tweaked to "My emotions make me compassionate." Find some piece of yourself that you want to see more of - that you want to encourage and create a mantra out of that. That's exactly what negative self-talk is. They are self-deprecating mantras and core beliefs that you had no choice but to agree with until now. I hope you choose a better one.

Start with one of your not so kind I am statements. Write It out below:

Detrimental I am statements:

_____

_____

_____

_____

Then please come up with some replacements (4 or 5 total)

_____

_____

_____

_____

_____

_____

_____

Now, think about the implications of your replacements. And I want you to pick one you think is best. Don't worry if you can't tell which will be best. If it doesn't work, pick a new one in a few weeks. Think of the implications of these replacement statements.

Think about the implications in the same way that I framed how being too much made me feel – and how trying -I'm perfect just the way I am - failed because of my biases. I'm a lot was not perfect, but it was progress that dramatically improved my life for years before I felt I wanted or needed to replace it.

Which of your replacement statements (above) is a believable (for you) improvement to the negative statement you want to replace?

Write a new believable - I am statement - for your RAS to start looking for in your life in the line below.

_____

_____

_____

_____

_____

_____

_____

CSA CAN BE A LITTLE STOCKHOLM"Y."

This may sound like a stretch to some, but give me a chance. I'll show you just how perfectly everything we have covered in this section adds up to be a very similar phenomenon to Stockholm syndrome when you add the effects of *conditioning* in a child with the effects of the *Reticular Activating System*, especially when viewed through the *adopt-to-adapt principle*. Starting life as a CSA person with abusive or violent caretakers is a nearly perfect parallel to Stockholm syndrome for more reasons than one.

This is one of the more apparent chapters to those of us whose defaults are deeply screwy. Those of us who knew we were being abused. Those who know that their childhood was shit and that it fucked them in the long run - for us, this chapter will hit home in a major way, while those with fewer wounds might be confused.

According to WebMD, Stockholm syndrome *isn't* a diagnosis as much as it is an emotional response. Miriam Webster defines it as - *a psychological tendency of a hostage to bond with, identify with, or sympathize with his other captor.*

The term Stockholm Syndrome originated from a bank robbery gone wrong in Stockholm in 1973. Some bank robbers took hostage four bank employees. They stayed in the bank vault for six days together. During that time, the hostages formed an incongruous bond with the robbers that held them captive. The syndrome is considered rare, occurring in only around 8% of hostage victims.

Since then, there has been a lot of controversy around Stockholm syndrome, with many people saying it's not real, not a diagnosis or doesn't exist at all. Some even say the whole concept is sexist because the original victims were female. When I looked into all these arguments, I was pleasantly surprised to find that the thing that unifies most of the counterpoints to Stockholm syndrome is precisely the point I'm making here. Aligning oneself with one's captors, especially when they treat you well most of the time, is an obvious biological decision for preserving one's life.

One hugely interesting thing to me here is that almost 10% of adults with presumably fully functioning brains form an irrational emotional bond with a person who is a real threat to them in less than a week.

How much more likely is it that children without the benefit of a pre-frontal cortex might form bonds with someone who has not only been there since birth but has also fed them, clothed them and sheltered them their whole lives?

If these irrational emotional bonds are formed under extreme stress to approximate some form of safety in a matter of days, imagine what living with an abusive captor for 18 years would do. Just imagine the confusing emotional and logical schisms.

This might make some of you reading this confused or uncomfortable, while others who read this will go, "Well no fucking shit." If you were ever a child, whether you view it this way or not, you were captive to your parents.

It's mostly a good thing too. Left on our own as children, most of us would almost certainly be dead or worse off than we are. In this situation, our captors feed, clothe, and shelter us. If we're lucky, they love and adore us and make us feel accepted and whole.

If we are less lucky and mom or dad has a drug problem or an alcohol problem, a gambling problem or a temper problem, a mental health problem, or maybe mom is depressed, or dad disassociates. Or maybe you don't know your parents at all, and you were shipped from house to house month after month for years on end in foster care. For these people, my earlier statement was a "Well, duh!" Because they lived it in a very direct way. For the rest, let me explain.

When you are "captive" to parents, if your feelings, thoughts and reactions are validated, meaning self-expression is allowed, it's easy to see why Stockholm syndrome seems like a reach. This is because the defining piece of the syndrome is the captivity part.

A child doesn't have a concept of captivity because they never *feel* trapped. If they feel fully loved and accepted for who they are, the majority of the time, Stockholm syndrome cannot and does not occur. This is because the captive member must be aware of their captivity. A well-taken-care-of child tends to feel taken care of rather than taken captive.

So, the definition of Stockholm syndrome should include perceived captivity. This is why this chapter is more obvious to those who lived through lots of trauma, especially Big T trauma - while feeling like a stretch for those without. We consciously perceived our captivity.

To drive this point home, let's say you are captured and locked in a basement for years with no perceived chance of escape. What type of interpersonal dynamic is going to keep you safe? What perspective might you adopt in order to adapt and protect yourself since fighting and fleeing are not options?

The safest opinion a captive can have is one that agrees with the captor.

Seeing the world through their eyes can and likely will ingratiate a person with their captor. *If I spend all my energy pleasing my captor, I am doing everything I can to make my futile and dangerous situation as safe as it can be.*

That's what we do automatically with abusive, even accidentally abusive parents. Think about it. You had no chance of leaving. You couldn't fight them; they were bigger and stronger than you. You couldn't get a job to be fully independent because you were a child.

The things that make it into our heads during this time are what we hear the most often. Suppose you hear Mom constantly worrying about the bills or Dad always complaining. What do you think you, as a child, will pick up as a pass-time?

Could any of the things we say to kids that seem innocuous on the surface have accidental, more profound, long-lasting effects? Any parent reading this will, without a doubt, say, "Duh!" because they've lived it.

So, let's look at a super common one. What happens if we tell our kids over and over again that they are too loud? To exist harmoniously with our captors, we have to listen and eventually agree. So, there's a good chance they learn that to receive love and be accepted, they must remain quiet. But what if they want to get loud when they get excited? Maybe mom works 12-hour shifts and doesn't have the energy to notice or care that the loudness that grates on her nerves stems from excitement or joy. What then?

That kid will learn that the expression of joy or excitement is unsafe. Through repeated suppression of the expression of those emotions, the body takes the hint. It represses those things, making for a flat, dull person who finds joy and excitement anywhere from unimportant to irritating. No matter how they look at it, it will be viewed negatively.

If a child is told enough times to be quiet when experiencing joy, their body eventually learns NOT to experience joy at all! The energy that was present and intended for expressing joy is now working much harder to suppress that joy.

If you grew up in an unstable environment, which to a child who can't fend for themselves means an unsafe environment, then you, my friend, have a perfect storm of fuckery that locks you into this pattern for the rest of your life. Until you actively seek out ways to change it. Luckily, you have done exactly that.

When we look honestly at how *conditioning* happens and then add to that the functions of the *reticular activating system*, it's no wonder we blame ourselves for everything. It's a perfect storm.

CSA people, especially those who experienced abuse as a child, whether we realize it or not, are experiencing a version of Stockholm syndrome. We still, as adults, many CSA people do everything we can to explain why a person is cruel to us rather than walking away from it. We always turn that blame onto ourselves. In the end, we will almost unerringly tend toward the shame and self-blame that kept us safe while captive.

Conceptualizing constant correction as a form of love is so ridiculous for a child. It's virtually impossible. That kind of mental gymnastics is the kind of delusional crap only an adult brain living in a toxic society could come up with - let alone find appropriate.

I know for me, it's incredibly tempting and sometimes even functional to blame myself. I take pride in calling it *accountability*. Because at the end of the day, **when the blame falls on me, there might be something I can do about it.**

That's the same narrative we had as a child, even if we were unaware of it. The *reality* was that our entire lives were out of our control. But even though that's a fact, <u>believing that fact was more stressful for our bodies than admitting the truth of our helplessness</u>. So, we believed and continue to believe that lie.

Remember what I said at the very beginning of this book about CSA people? I said one of the things that unites us is that we "take on the blame of the whole world" even when it's not ours to bear. Our CSA version of Stockholm syndrome is where that started.

But now, as CSA adults, we must recognize what is our responsibility and what is not. *Justifying the opinion of abusers is **not** within my purview anymore.* It shouldn't be in yours either.

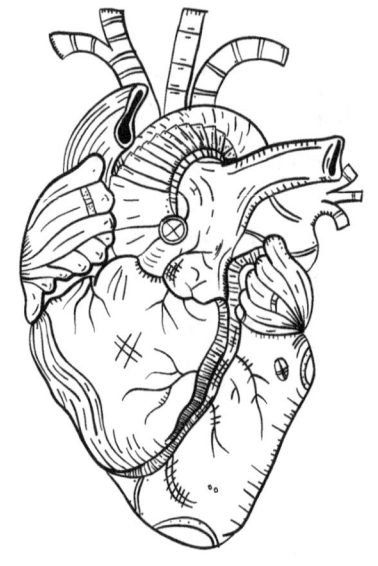

CHAPTER 11

EFFECTS OF CHRONIC STRESS ON THE DEVELOPING BRAIN

Chronic stress during development affects every single part of our brains and bodies, and there are a few brain regions that are of particular interest to us CSA people.

This chapter will examine how certain parts of our brains with specific intended functions become malformed. And get their programming cross-wired due to that early life stress. We'll look at how they fail to develop the proper shape and size and how that affects our lives today.

We will look more closely at the part of our brains in charge of conscious rational thought and executive function: the prefrontal cortex (PFC), the threat-response center, the amygdala, and the memory facilitator, the hippocampus.

It's important to understand that when we are stressed or feel threatened, most information we take in and operate off is below conscious awareness.

Except for the PFC, the rest of these brain regions are deep inside the brain. This means these parts of the brain are older and less subject to our conscious input, and it takes longer to change them. Our bodies house our subconscious. Most of what we aren't aware of that affects us is affecting our bodies without our awareness.

SPECIFIC BRAIN CHANGES CAUSED BY CHRONIC STRESS IN EARLY LIFE

Our developing brains undergo dramatic changes due to chronic stress. Becoming an "evidence-informed person" is a common strategy to cope with the dramatic physical sensations we feel, especially when we are young.

This is why we focused on ACEs earlier. That study is a piece of cold, hard, undeniable evidence to convince us evidence-based folks that the reality is that you and I and every single other person, especially with four or more ACES, are undeniably different from our counterparts with less stressed childhoods.

If you dissect and measure us, you will see *significant* differences in our physical anatomy. We aren't built like everyone else. Parts of our physiology developed differently. Many people now call these differences *neurodivergence*. CSA people are absolutely *neurodivergent* people.

The three systems in the brain that are altered by chronic stress during development *are the memory system, the threat system, and the reward system*. After that, we will look at the effects of chronic stress on the nervous system as a whole.

MEMORY SYSTEM- HIPPOCAMPUS

The hippocampus is a small region in the brain that controls memory. People who experience chronic stress in childhood often have a shrunken hippocampus. There are also notable changes in the autobiographical memory system, which controls how you think about yourself.

As we mentioned early on, what we think about ourselves determines not just who we believe ourselves to be but also the kind of treatment we believe we deserve and, therefore, the amount of mistreatment we will subject ourselves to.

We are literally built in a way that predisposes us to forget the good and focus on the bad, even more so than a non-CSA person's negative bias does. This locks our RAS into looking for proof of it.

These changes are tough to deal with for a few reasons. Negative memories become more salient after trauma, meaning we think negatively more often to avoid repeating similar traumatic situations.

Combining that with the fact that, due to a shrunken hippocampus, everyday memories become less detailed, making them harder to put into long-term storage, it causes real problems as grown-ups. For other folks, that happens automatically. For CSA, it doesn't.

As CSA people, we need to consciously and consistently draw on recent positive experiences to use as evidence to teach our bodies and threat centers how to react appropriately to the situations we face.

If we can't remember the good things we experience, how are we supposed to convince our body - Which keeps score. And yes, please read *The Body Keeps the Score* by Bessel Van Der Kolk if you haven't already - that it is safe.

Without remembering details of life, even our most positive memories become less potent because of their vagueness. So, our hippocampus does not have a compelling enough story to update the threat centers of our brains to tell it to calm down.

THE AMYGDALA, THREAT ASSESSMENT AND RESPONSE CONTROL CENTER.

The amygdala used to be known as the fear center. Although it certainly plays a role in fear, it's better understood as the threat control center. It's not just about fear. Its job is to evaluate all neuroceptive sensory input above and below RAS detection for threats.

If it senses a threat, it sends signals to the parts of the brain that produce the stress response that it's time to respond. Then the neurotransmitters and hormones are released to help us launch one of those stress response strategies we discussed earlier – the 5 F's - *fight, flight, freeze, fawn and sex.*

The amygdala lives in the ancient and deep part of the brain that is designed to always be in survival mode. His job is life or death, so he's the serious type. He's stubborn too. The amygdala requires compelling hard evidence to change his mind, and lots of it.

It takes more than a few blurry memories of vaguely positive moments to change his feelings about the world. Whatever your amygdala believes about the world is what *you* believe about the world – especially when dysregulated.

However safe or unsafe the amygdala thinks you are is, is how safe or unsafe you think you are. Even if you're busy finding rational explanations for why you are safe, if the amygdala feels things are unsafe? *You* will feel and, therefore, behave like you are threatened.

And yes, you've probably guessed that our trend of chronic stress affecting the development and, therefore, the physical structure of our biology continues here. Like all organelles of the brain, the amygdala is just a bundle of nerves.

The problem is that since his job is threat evaluation and response, the amygdala gets constantly stimulated under chronic stress. That constant stimulation prevents it from growing to its full size. You might think that smaller is better. But in biology, especially the brain, it's not. Smaller is not better because, especially in the brain, smaller is harder to regulate.

The crux of the issues with the amygdala is what's called *fear conditioning.* We covered conditioning earlier. We can be conditioned into almost anything. The amygdala's job is to teach us exactly what to be afraid of. What will the amygdala find threatening if it develops under chronic stress - *basically everything.*

Anything that happened to us just before something threatening will be remembered and categorized as a threat or threat precursor. In either case, we become sensitized to it.

A part of the amygdala's job is to help us learn how to avoid threats. The way it does this is by talking with the hippocampus to recall the context of the threat. In the rats studied to glean much of this information, the threat context would be the cage in which some form of conditioning was done. For people, it would be more akin to the house we were in. But it also includes anything we experienced just before the threat.

If things were peaceful until mom came home, because mom was the bear in our lives, the amygdala associates the calm with the storm to come. Since this is how we survived before, it's how we automatically function now. Which you can see now causes issues.

Through threat conditioning, the amygdala eventually becomes the boy who cried wolf, at least consciously. CSA people are often frustrated at how threatened we feel on the inside by minimally threatening situations. But it makes sense from a biological lens. If your amygdala yells, "WOLF!" your body pays attention. It has no choice.

The threat evaluation part of brains is at least as old in evolutionary terms as lizards. And his job has stayed more or less the same for millions of years. Years in which his primary considerations exclusively revolved around life and death.

There are lots of ways people have learned to cope with this. Some people eat those feelings when emotionally distressed, while others do heroin, shop or work 12 hours a day, seven days a week. All of which work in the short term, or we wouldn't use them but also have long-term complications to consider.

THE REWARD SYSTEM

Another part of the brain that's structurally affected is the reward system. It is intrinsically tied to our learning and memory as well. This also makes sense from an evolutionary standpoint because if our ancestors get a big reward, say they find a berry patch or honey hive, they would want to remember what the reward is and how they found it, so they'd have a better chance of getting the reward again in the future.

From the brain programming perspective, when it comes to reward conditioning, there is a trigger, a behavior, and a reward. They run like a relay race, one after another. Everything starts with a trigger.

The trigger nowadays could be that you see a piece of candy; the behavior is you eat that candy. The reward is the sugar but also, the brain dumping a flood of neurotransmitters to remember the candy and where you got it because it tastes so good! That's how it's supposed to work.

Unfortunately, as a result of abuse or neglect in early life, things that should have positive associations and rewards attached to them don't. Things like social contact or intimate relationships.

As a child, if you got insufficient meaningful attention from your mother, father, or caregiver, you might have been trained that *intimate relationships are not rewarding*. You may even grow over time and with repeated stressful experiences, to be wary of relationships entirely. Or even find them pointless.

This is profoundly damaging because, for human beings, ***the quality of our lives is determined by the quality of our relationships.*** Suppose the quality of our relationships has been pretty crap or even just been an unpredictable mixed bag. In that case, you probably won't have much impetus to invest in relationships. Why would you? So far, they've been taxing in one way or another. *Unfortunately, that means by not investing in your relationships, even if for understandable reasons, you're not investing in your quality of life!*

Effects of Abuse on the Reward Circuit

Abuse and neglect in early life adapt a kid's entire brain and nervous system to become less damaged by that abuse. Meaning we're neurologically what my mom would call "a glutton for punishment." We learn painful lessons slower than others. Through abuse, we experience pain; through standard conditioning processes, our biology adapts so we feel that painless. Eventually, since we experience less pain from painful things, we learn painful lessons more slowly.

You know that phrase that says change happens when the pain of staying the same becomes more than the pain of change? CSA folks *literally need more pain to change.* Our rock bottom is genuinely lower.

This manifests in many ways unique to our experiences and the narratives we use to describe and understand them. This is also why so many of us struggle with addiction. If there was physical or sexual abuse, there may be an even more substantial repellent effect with intimate relationships.

Not only would they not feel rewarding, just the thought of them may feel taxing or threatening. Complicating it more, all of this is happening below the surface, below our conscious reasoning. All humans act out when they feel threatened, even if they have no conscious idea why.

That's the power of a too-small, underdeveloped and therefore hyper-reactive amygdala. It can prevent intimacy and meaningful relationships. It makes us view every future possibility with paralyzing anxiety and makes us treat everyone as a threat, which is a great way to make enemies.

EFFECTS OF INCONSISTENCY ON REWARD CIRCUITS

The developmental response to inconsistency may be the most challenging adaptation to manage. Especially if inconsistency is experienced in combination with other adversities, which it usually is.

Inconsistency trains the body to expect that its everyday world will be one in which, even if we feel safe in one moment, we must remain constantly on guard for the "other shoe to drop."

This is hard to overcome because the general process we are designed to use to overcome the previous lessons we learned depends on providing consistent proof to our nervous system (PFC & amygdala) that its programming needs an update.

It gets even more complicated when you think of the effect of that person being the one who is meant to keep you alive and safe. When you are told, "I love you," but are treated like, "I am sick and tired of you," or "I don't have time for you," how might a child's body respond?

THE VAGUS NERVE - THE MIND-BODY CONNECTION- OUR FAULTY BRAKES

The Vagus nerve is the last thing I want to cover in this section. The vagus is a big nerve with a big job. The vagus nerve connects your organs and sensory equipment with your brain and manages the famous "fight or flight" response we've been talking about. You've heard of the mind-body connection. Well, folks, this is it, literally. It's the vagus nerve that connects them.

This nerve, cranial nerve 10, is not just one nerve. It's actually comprised of 100 billion nerve cells. It allows for two-way communication from our body to our mind and vice-versa. It controls the millions of involuntary processes constantly happening behind the scenes in our bodies. It's in charge of nearly everything automated, like

- breathing
- speech
- swallowing
- heartbeat
- blood pressure
- hearing

- taste
- bladder control
- orgasms
- fertility

Without a healthy and well-regulated vagus nerve, we cannot access certain brain functions, like self-regulation. Without it functioning correctly, we can't access our innate creativity, problem-solving, higher cognition and complex decision-making. If it's dysfunctional or damaged, we can only access the more primal parts of our brain, like fear and the fight or flight responses.

You can think of the vagus as an internal email system. It communicates sensory information from the body to the brain for the brain to process and decide what to do and then sends the decisions back to the body to respond appropriately. It's our senses that inform us about the world around us. As living biological beings, our prime biological directive is survival, so our senses are always helping us evaluate safety and threats. A poorly developed vagus nerve then causes errors in our internal communication system because it too, never got to know safety.

A healthy vagus nerve allows for a smooth transition from an activated state -fight & flight response - to an inactive state - rest & digest and back. A smooth transition between these two states is the primary goal we are after, for better lives. But for CSA people, we are often stuck in this limbo where we never actually get to rest fully because we never experience safety fully.

This is particularly important and impactful for those of us whose trauma happened before we were old enough to develop a memory of the event. As a primary driver of the sympathetic nervous system, the vagus nerve responds to the memory of past traumatic events even when we don't have a conscious recallable memory. The vagus nerve responding to a subconscious perceived threat causes us to launch a strengthness strategy for seemingly no reason.

Maybe you've had an experience where, for some reason unknown to you, you have a severe visceral response in which you felt threatened, and you had no idea why. This is the result of chronic stress on a developing vagus nerve.

The vagus nerve is supposed to act as the brakes for your autonomic nervous system. When you go into fight or flight, it's up to the vagus to move you back into rest and digest. That's the braking system many of us CSA folks don't have. With childhood chronic stress, the vagus doesn't get a chance to develop fully.

Any biological system under chronic stress will not develop the way it would in a less stressed (ideal) environment. In the same way, a tree that's planted and survives in the desert will grow but will be stunted in its growth. The same is true for our brains.

PUTTING IT TOGETHER

As you can see, chronic stress affects these fundamental systems in the brain in ways that create a kind of perfect storm. We get conditioned to fear anything our memory has associated with traumatic and stressful events. For many of us, it seems like just about everything.

Our memory systems get conditioned to focus more on the negative stuff for our survival, making it harder to convince our threat systems that we are safe now. The reward system also gets hijacked to focus on surviving life rather than enjoying it.

So, we are less interested in the things that feel good and more interested in those that don't. While simultaneously being worse at learning from our painful experiences. It's a serious mess.

Feeling broken is an obvious conclusion if you only see the results of these processes. CSA people shun relationships; we constantly dismiss any positivity about ourselves. It makes sense why we've seen ourselves as broken.

But now you know the processes that lead us to those ends. We adapted appropriately to inappropriate circumstances. It's what we do.

So, what now? Now you know the primary mechanisms that led you to believe you were broken. You know the processes that made you Chronic Stress Adapted.

So, stop blaming yourself for the way you are. You are not a failure. You are not a screw-up. You are not broken. And you never have been. You are a god-damned miracle. Deal with it.

I want you to hold this information close to your heart. Come back and revisit this section from time to time if you start to become too hard on yourself again. You deserve compassion. Especially the parts you dislike. In times when you can't muster the self-compassion you deserve. Please call a CSA friend or revisit these pages. Remind yourself of the rational biological processes at play during development.

The bottom line is that there is no room for self-blame when decades of neuroscience have concluded **it's not your fault**. It's never been your fault.

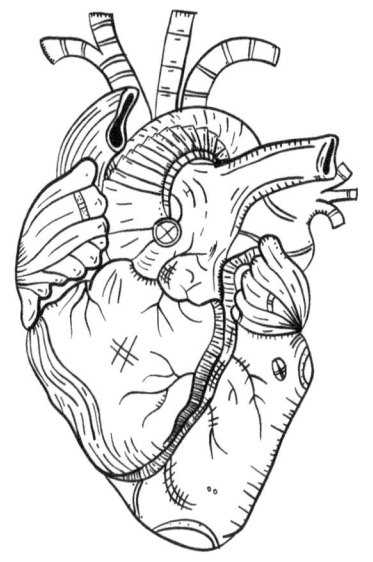

CHAPTER 12

EMOTIONS ARE LOGICAL!

"Even the stupid ones."

W hen we put all these pieces of neurobiology, developmental biology, conditioning and chronic stress adaptation together, it makes sense that our reactions as CSA people may not always be the most appropriate.

That's all I'm trying to do here. I'm trying to get you to see that no matter how ridiculous, stupid or annoying your reactions and emotions might sometimes feel or how inappropriate they are, they still make perfect sense! Which means they're predictable!

With all of this biological data, it's now possible to convince you of the title of this chapter. It takes a while to lay the foundations and the framework of it all. But now it's done! You know everything you need to know to understand that emotions are logical. They are biological.

Still, making this claim because it's so polar opposite to what we have been told our entire lives needs a little more time to sink in. That's what this section is for. Let the reality of everything you learned so far sink in!

You've got the bones. The theory holds water. Now, let's make it pretty.

Anyone who believed they were broken came to believe so through repeated experiences in which something inside them made them behave in a way they weren't proud of. Understandably, this makes us feel broken. It's easy to see. But that doesn't make it true. Enter the next fundamental perspective shift.

PERSPECTIVE SHIFT #2
EMOTIONS ARE LOGICAL

Emotions *seem* illogical upon reflection with our rational brain. But that's because emotions use a different set of data to function.

Emotions are a biological process in the body, and bodies are very wise. Your body performs countless important life-sustaining stuff behind the scenes 24/7. We don't think about it often, so dismissing or forgetting is easy. But what can't be seen is nearly impossible to truly appreciate.

So, I will continue to put on display that emotions are not only logical. They are biological. And we are going to uncover the deeper meaning. By the end, this will feel more normal than it sounds. Looking at the body's wisdom in other realms of decision-making, it becomes painfully apparent that our emotions are logical.

If you stop and think about what you've learned so far, you can see dimly that conditioning, captivity during conditioning and the RAS creates an airtight case against your evidence of brokenness. That was *almost* enough for me.

This section will put the cherry on top of this anti-brokenness hot-fudge sundae. At the risk of repeating myself an annoying amount, I will walk you through how *all emotions, even the stupid ones, are logical.* Then, we will break down why this matters that much more to CSA people.

HOW IN THE WORLD ARE EMOTIONS CONSIDERED LOGICAL?

When I say emotions are logical, the automatic response for most sane people is "Bullshit." And for good reason. We have all experienced times when our emotions get the better of us. Every person alive has had an experience in which their emotional reactions got them into trouble in one way or another.

We are doomed to fail when we pit logic against emotions because they are two sides of the same coin. Most people intuitively feel that there is a logical aspect to them and an emotional aspect.

Since childhood, we've been told that we need to control our emotions to favor our logical minds, with the implied understanding that our logical minds will do a better job when it comes to making decisions for us. And in today's world, it's pretty easy to believe that's true, which is why it is so easy to dismiss emotions simply as distracting, complicating factors in our lives.

But emotions make our lives worth living. The sense of joy we feel when our children score their first soccer goal, the sense of awe we have on a mountaintop looking at the beauty of the Earth, and the excitement and joy when we see a long-lost friend are what make life worth living.

These powerful emotional moments are what every person reflects on, in their death-bed. It's the sensations and emotions that we experience when we remember these moments that determine for us whether we lived a life worth living or not. *Emotions are that important.*

"Nothing in biology can be understood except through the lens of evolution."
Ukrainian-American geneticist Theodosius Dobzhansky

Evolutionarily, emotions are a part of the limbic system, an older system than conscious processing. Does it make sense to you that emotions - a part of the limbic system - are irrational? If they were irrational, do you think complex life on Earth would have survived?

The limbic system is intricately tied to our reflexes. We depend on our reflexes to keep us alive in threatening situations. If there's a snake by your foot about to bite you, isn't it a rational biological adaptation to feel fear and react quickly to the threat?

Reflexes are quicker than conscious thought. Reflexes kept all living things alive long before our highly rational frontal lobes developed. Guess what the limbic system uses as data? The data that doesn't make it through the RAS into our conscious minds!

So, the question has never been whether emotions are logical. We know they have preserved the lives of our ancestors for millions of years. It makes no sense that they are irrational. There must be rationality in there somewhere, but where is it? It kept our ancestors alive, so something was right about it. The first clue for where it lies is in where it functions.

The official theory I'm describing is called the *cognitive reflex hypothesis.* (1) The idea is what I've explained to you. There is a stimulus in the environment that causes a reflex. The reflex then causes cognition, and then an emotion follows.

For CSA people whose baseline stress levels are higher, certain stimuli can remind us subconsciously of a traumatic incident in our past, which can cause us to react immediately before having a chance to think. Then we react to that subconscious narrative. That reaction immediately fills in all the gaps in our heads about what might be happening and auto-chooses the story laid out by our previous traumas. That is what I call a biological decision.

Emotions create biological decisions.

Our emotions are logical because they are biological. The root of *bio* means life. *Logic*-al means pertaining to logic. Logic is *the distinction of true and false reasoning.* Emotions begin as sensations in the body. They are affected by what we think but are even more strongly affected by what we experience. So, it makes sense that our subconscious logic is built from our past experiences, just like those social media algorithms.

Every experience you've had up to this moment lives in the past. But each also lives in your body. Each of those experiences was imprinted, cataloged, and stored in the form of memories by our biology.

Most of us don't want to spend all day thinking about the terrible things that have happened to us. It's hard to function that way, and it's beneficial not to, so cognitively at least, we consciously forget many extraneous details of traumatizing experiences.

So, when a stimulus comes along that reminds our biology of a past trauma —like the smell of cologne or the color of a room—is it a surprise that we react quickly? Emotions are reflexes that have informed us about the sub-cognitive aspects of the world around us for millions of years.

If a stimulus is strong enough and similar to traumatic events from our past, it's perfectly reasonable and *logical* that the part of us designed to register and keep track of the subconscious and sub-cognitive cues of the environment would launch a protective reflex to prevent further trauma.

It's our evolutionarily older limbic and emotional systems that we depend on to pull our hands back from a hot burner before they get burned. When your hand gets close enough to feel the heat, your hand reflexively yanks back before you can cognitively register what's happening. Only in the milli-seconds after our hand pulls back do we put the whole story together into a conscious rational narrative. "Don't touch a hot stove!"

You may not have realized it as such, but you've always known there was rationality to your emotions because rationality was built into your reflex system. That's the key to understanding that your emotions are logical. Even the ones that screw you over occasionally.

If you hadn't experienced irrational experiences, you wouldn't have *seemingly* irrational biological responses to them. It really is that simple. Not to be glib, but if your mustached uncle never molested you, you probably wouldn't be irrationally afraid of mustaches. Your fear isn't what's irrational. Molestation is.

Emotions really *are* logical. They are biological.

THE WISDOM IN OUR BIOLOGY.

Our biology does fantastic things to keep us alive every moment of every day and night. We don't have to worry about making our lungs breathe or our heart beat. Our livers and kidneys are always functioning in the background. Our biology is constantly working to keep us alive.

The prime directive for all living things is to continue living. Either living our own lives or creating smaller versions of ourselves to hopefully outlive us. Our body is all about survival. Many CSA people are also all about survival. Specifically, many big T CSA people have an outlook on life based almost entirely on surviving.

Unfortunately, decisions based on survival are not the same as decisions that would help us thrive. Survival decisions are always based out of fear of the loss of life. This creates many fear-based decisions in a CSA person's life. Surviving is about what's wrong and what's missing. Thriving is about what we have and what we seek. It's based on hope and surplus.

But if our decisions are being made for us by our biology and biology is about survival, we will never do anything but survive. I don't know about you, but *I'm over just surviving.* I survived long enough. Which is why, years ago, *I set out to live my best life.* That's what we all deserve.

I'm biased, but in my world, CSA people deserve their best life even more than the rest. We survived hell, and we came out the other side. We endured more, and as a result, we can offer more. But only if we get our programmed responses under our control. That means turning biological decisions into logical ones over and over and over again until they happen automatically.

BIOLOGICAL V LOGICAL DECISIONS.

CSA people have adapted appropriately to inappropriate circumstances.

Those inappropriate and usually irrational circumstances inform and imprint on the biology of CSA people that the world is and always will be inappropriate and irrational. Therefore, its automated responses can often feel the same way, at least to our cognitive brains.

What we are trying to do as CSA people is to move our decision-making from a biological subconscious process to a conscious, logical process. Your emotional reactions and reflexes to stuff are just your body trying to protect you from the world that's been imprinted in your biology.

You can't go back and undo the traumas you survived. The experiences you had are already imprinted in your biology. And those experiences created the algorithms you use to think and understand life. The memory of those experiences is always being considered subconsciously. If the threat is similar enough to an unconscious memory, the decision to respond in a certain way is made for us by our biology. Or, said another way, our biological memory of events makes decisions for us instead of our conscious, logical, rational brains, which most of us prefer.

A CSA person's strengthnesses are the overgrown strategies we launched with the most success to get us to survive an irrational, inappropriate and traumatic incident or environment. The work that we are embarking on is this.

MAKE BIOLOGICAL DECISIONS
BECOME LOGICAL ONES.

We are consciously aware we aren't the scared, helpless child we once were. In a way, it's that child or the residual memories on our body of what that child experienced that make those troublesome decisions. So, we have to focus on how our reactions were logical, even if they were also seemingly stupid. That's all the stuff we cover in this section up to this chapter.

When we do that, we find compassion for ourselves. We recognize that our reactions aren't because we are stupid but because we survived a stupid world as kids. And now our body expects a stupid fucking world all the time.

We cannot blame ourselves if we want any chance to change lives. By tuning into our body and our subconscious more and more, we begin to erode the invisible cliff that we accidentally and automatically throw ourselves off with our reactions. By tuning in to our body, we tune in to our subconscious. That's how we make the subconscious conscious. And that's the goal we must have to gain leverage over our conditioned reactions.

All CSA people **must** turn subconscious processes into conscious ones to improve our lives. Observing our physiological sensations allows us to tune into our body's wisdom and watch the patterns. When our sympathetic nervous system begins to ramp us up, it's our responsibility to notice that!

When we notice something is off early, even if we can't put our finger on exactly what it is, we stand a chance or put on the brakes. Focusing on our body as dysregulation and discomfort increase makes the subconscious conscious. The result is we don't screw ourselves over as readily.

By paying attention to the sensations in our bodies – things like warmth, coolness, heat, agitation, or just feeling "stuck," (which I believe is a version of the fawn strategy) we undermine our trauma's ability to undermine us. Our subconscious can only undermine us if it remains subconscious. We can only self-sabotage if what drives the sabotage is subconscious.

The goal is to help you eliminate those reflexive automatic behaviors and assumptions that get you into trouble. The goal is to move the subconscious to the conscious. But we can't do better if the two are pitted against each other through this false dichotomy. My goal for myself, as well as for you, is to make as many of our biological decisions become logical as is helpful.

We need accurate explanations of the physiological processes occurring during trauma—the universal processes of trauma lead to some commonalities among the broken and traumatized. But over time, even those shared traits change through further experiences, leading to more differentiation, which creates your unique brand of adaptation.

For these reasons, it is up to you to use your own best judgment as we move through the rest of the topics in this book to figure out what traits, thoughts, assumptions, and values are something you want to change or keep. Many of the ways you have learned to cope with life *will be* common trauma responses. While some of it will feel more like the "Real me," but that's misleading. That's why this work is not linear. It is cyclical, complicated, and subtle. So, let's get this out of the way now.

WHAT'S THE REAL ME? AND WHAT'S MY TRAUMA?

The short answer is, **"It's all you baby."** The common trauma survival strategies that you employ are just as much the real "you" as anything else is. I wasted years and years of my life trying to separate what was "me" and what was "my trauma." I spent years digging, worrying and thinking. I often made myself miserable trying to "heal" myself by eliminating any common behaviors in the trauma literature.

I thought that to heal, I needed to return to some pure version of me that existed before the world got to me. I wanted so badly to uncover little 7-year-old me and tell him that he's safe and he's all I need.

That's what I kept hearing from the self-help world. I kept hearing about healing your inner child. I kept hearing about getting back to the *wholeness* that's supposedly a part of the childhood experience. But I can't live life as a 7-year-old. Neither can you. Never mind the fact I was already screwed up even as a child.

I wanted to erase the habits that I was acting out due to my trauma. So, I studied all the common trauma responses. I evaluated where they came from. I found a narrative that explains their adoption. I sought to understand who I was at that moment. I thought that this is what healing from trauma was. *I thought it was returning to a true or pure self that existed before all the trauma happened.* It's not.

Unfortunately, my trauma started months before I was born, which is true for all of us. It turns out that even a father's mental and emotional states two months before *conception* influence the child! Not to mention sensitivity to everything happening to our mothers during the nine months they carried us.

All of these things affect us. Chinese Medicine and Yogic traditions have known this for thousands of years. Western science is notoriously slow to update itself, but even Western science has conducted studies that validate it.

There are just so many factors at play in creating a human. As a species whose global survival strategy is adaptation, we were designed to adapt to and survive anything the world throws at us, including trauma. So please don't do what I did. Don't fracture yourself more by trying to jigsaw yourself into something that can't exist.

I believed there was a pure, unadulterated version of me somewhere deep inside. I thought I would be free from the automation of my trauma if I could somehow reach that part of me and live as that person again. I tried to find the me who existed before all the trauma. But that person doesn't exist.

It's a radical stance, but it's what I have found to be the truth. Since things like a mothers' stress levels as well as dad's mood affect a developing fetus. I was never unadulterated. <u>There is no pure, perfect, or unadulterated anyone, not even our inner child.</u>

CSA people have to come to terms with the fact that we were designed to be programmed by every single experience we have. ***The person you are today is the only person you could be.*** Whatever habits you have are from the experiences you've had, good and bad. Traumatic and supportive.

You mustn't shun any part of yourself. Don't even shun your trauma responses. The unpleasant parts of us we don't like, have often done as much, if not more for us than the pleasant bits. They became strengthnesses.

This is why I have tried to avoid relying on the term *healing* throughout this book. To me, *healing* from trauma is the process of *integration*. If we shun any part of ourselves, we are creating a chasm between the pieces of us. We create a separation. In a closed integrated system, if you remember from chapter two, that separation is called trauma.

By shunning any part of yourself, even your unwanted trauma responses, *you are actively perpetuating and compounding your own trauma!* Don't do that.

Although it can be lovely and even healing to re-explore what interested us as kids, whether that be music, math, or farming, do not look for some pure version of yourself there. That person is a fantasy.

Each of us is born more or less the same and still unique. We have tendencies and innate interests that we are meant to explore and deepen in childhood. Those parts of us are what some might refer to as the real you. But the badass who takes shit from nobody and sometimes shoots herself in the foot with her protectiveness is equally the "real you." Don't throw the baby out with the bath water. She's a badass too. She is probably a *strengthness!*

I'm not interested in creating hierarchies or pushing one perspective over another. The heart of any matter to me is its practicality. So, from that pragmatic standpoint, the things you were interested in as a child might be you, or they might have changed.

You might be interested in different things after 20 years of life experience. Just because you used to love to draw and you don't now doesn't mean your creativity is stolen or ruined. _The interests you take up in your 30s, 40s, and 80s are just as much the "real you" as what you were into as a kid._

The way that you respond to a threatening situation, even after conditioning, is equally you. I can't give you the perfect step for you to take for your growth because all this trauma stuff is so individualized. But if you want, you can change those biological reactions with this framework.

GET PERSONAL GOALS

You have the power to change your brain right here, right now. Which of your automations to change first is up to you. I'm here only to teach you how. I want to empower you like I was empowered when I got the best advice I ever received from Kaya.

Kaya rarely gave me outright advice, but when she did, it was golden. When I was 19 years old, I was afraid that no one would love me for me and that I would die alone. I just accepted it as fact. She told me to imagine the man I wanted to be with in as great a detail as I could muster. Imagine what he looks like, what he wears. She told me to imagine how he walks and how he treats the waiter. She said to pin him down in as much detail as possible. And then she said, "when you have a clear picture in your head of the man you want to be with... *become him.*"

I was stunned. As the years marched on, I became more and more and *more* impressed with that bit of advice. Which piggybacks off something my father told me stemming from his relationship with his father. "You can only learn so much from what not to do." - which is ironic, considering our non-existent relationship now.

At 19 years old in a very small town, I had very few role models to pattern myself after. I knew plenty about what I didn't want. But I needed to figure out what I did want. I needed a goal.

You will need a goal too; you will need more direction than "not that." Not that enough to get started, but the sooner you start to carve out a goal for yourself for who you want to be, how you want to act, how you want people to think of you, the easier this process will become. You're bound to miss if you don't have a target. So, create yourself a role model. Piecemeal your future self from anything you want!

Pick cartoon characters or people from literature if need be. Personally, I have been obsessed with Sherlock Holmes since I saw him as a mouse detective. I loved his curiosity and wit. I loved his ability to notice tiny details to solve unsolvable things. That's probably why I wound up eventually obsessed with behavioral psychology. There is no bigger riddle than the human body, except the brain.

So, find the traits you resonate with and want to embody more of in your life. Look for inspiration in the attitudes, behaviors and outlooks you want to see more of in the world. Then, mimic them to the best of your ability. I think the "weird kids" from school do this well. At the cost of being constantly teased by the "normies" they live in their own worlds, playing a role. They wouldn't have been the weird kids if their homelives were "normal." I think they have really got it figured out, even if only on a biological level. They're just trying to NOT be like their family. So they chose to be Naruto instead...

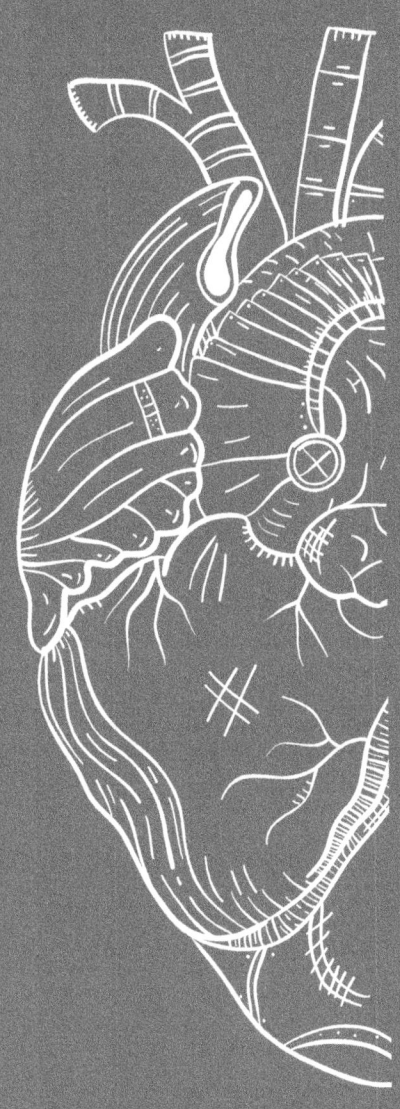

SECTION 3
STRENGTHNESSES
– YOUR HIDDEN
SUPERPOWERS

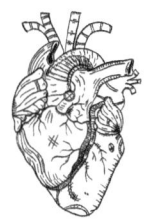

Congratulations! You made it through all the science stuff! See, I told you it wouldn't be that bad. Now you understand every piece of evidence in my airtight defense that **proves** you are NOT broken!! The case on your brokenness is officially closed, and you have been deemed NOT guilty.

As a recap in the last section, you learned:

- What your ACE scores and resiliency scores are.
- How to build more resiliency in your life today.
- What conditioning is and how it forms all of our habits and thoughts.
- What the Reticular Activating System is and how it can keep us in a negative mental cycle.
- How to reprogram the RAS through appropriate & proper "I am" mantras.
- Problems that occur when the brain & nervous system develop under chronic stress.
- How emotions are, in fact, logical, even the stupid ones.

It's an undeniable biological fact that you *responded appropriately to inappropriate circumstances*. So, right now, take a moment to check in with your body and reflect on what you've learned so far.

You may still have some resistance despite all the evidence we've covered. I get it. It's not because you don't believe me. It's not because you don't trust science but because that's how biology works. So, check in with your body. Do you still feel resistance? Do you feel any resting tension somewhere in your body?

If you do, take 60 seconds to let the truth of all this sink in. Set a timer on your phone right now for one minute. Close your eyes and be present with whatever your body feels like right now.

Mental resistance always has a physiological parallel. Mental tension is always accompanied by tension in our bodies. Any physical tension in your hands, shoulders, face or legs might signal that you have some residual mental resistance.

This is the power of conditioning. The resistance you feel is the RAS doing its job. It's just biology resisting updating its programming.

I told you _people don't change according to what they know. They change according to how they feel._ So how do you feel? How does it feel in your body to know that you are not broken? Can you describe it? Is it warm or cold? A swelling? A contracting? A relaxing?

Now that it's all settled that you are not broken, the only _real_ problem you have left is the lifelong struggle of trauma all survivors, **the struggle to maintain a well-regulated nervous system.**

Like in a court case, the verdict is the end of the trial. But it is also the beginning of the rest of your life. The verdict is merely the moment that the conclusion becomes mentally accepted. It takes time for the impact of a verdict to settle in.

This section is dedicated to helping you move the verdict from your mind squarely into your body. To do that, we need to do some convincing of your biology. You already know it's unsatisfied with even the most air-tight defense. What your biology needs to change are experiences.

This section is about providing your body and brain experiences that will allow your programming to calm down, stop seeing every little thing as a threat, and short-circuit your plans!

Strengthnesses for CSA people are not usually a conscious thing. They're not even a purposeful thing. These skills result from innate biological reactions to maintain safety in an unsafe environment. They're our best friends' worst enemies and superpowers all in one.

In this section, we will:

- Find your unique strengthness(es)
- Identify an environment or two in which your strengthnesses can thrive
- Learn to leverage those strengthnesses mindfully
- Learn to reprogram faulty defaults

It's time to find your unique skillsets and put you where you thrive!

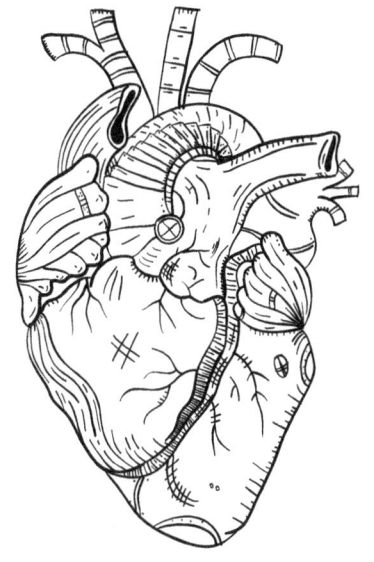

CHAPTER 13

WHAT IS A STRENGTHNESS?

The first thing to understand about strengthnesses is not everyone has them, but being CSA means you most likely do. Strengthnesses are basically *attributes* with an attitude. According to the Oxford English Dictionary, an attribute is *a quality or feature regarded as a characteristic or inherent part of someone or something.*

The difference between a strengthness and an attribute is an *attribute you can use or hold back as necessary.* An attribute is a facet of you that is under your control. That attribute becomes a *strengthness* when it is no longer within your control. Since we can't control the facet, we have to control the only other option: ***our context.***

Because a strengthness, when not adequately exercised, *commands its wielder instead of the right way round.* It is a facet of yourself, your personality, or your worldview that became so overdeveloped that we automatically lean on it, even when it's not the best choice.

A strengthness is created by repeatedly launching innate biological protection mechanisms in response to threatening or stressful situations. They were developed and strengthened by consistent successful short-term reliance on a single strategy to produce a single overly developed protection-focused aspect of our character.

Which if not recognized by us for what they are, protectors, and are not honored, meaning not utilized, our strengthnesses predispose us trauma survivors to launch self-protection responses in situations in which it is unnecessary and sometimes problematic.

If distress is experienced consistently enough, those protector pieces overdevelop to shield us from that constant stress. These overdeveloped facets of us are the demons we wrestle with from the introduction. These pillars of protection and personality are what I call Strengthnesses.

Before we dive straight into finding your strengthnesses, a story is in order. At this point, helping a person identify their strengthness(es) in person is second nature. It's nearly reflexive for me. But helping someone I don't know through words on a page has proven more challenging. So next are a few stories that will make finding your strengthnesses easier.

THE REFUGEE PHYSICIST

One of my favorite stories to tell is the story of being in Tijuana while working with Acupuncturists without Borders. We were there providing relief work for would-be immigrants and refugees. Most people don't know this, but the majority of refugees in Tijuana attempting to enter the US *legally*, are actually from Central and South America and Africa. Less than 30% of those seeking legal entry there are Mexicans. They have gone through unspeakable horrors to get to the relative safety of Mexico.

The problem for many of them is that the law in Mexico says they will take you as a refugee, providing you with legal asylum, but only if Mexico is your first country of entry after fleeing your war-torn home country. Most of these people have taken busses and trains, vans, tiny row boats, motorcycle rides and lots and lots of walking, sometimes thousands of miles, and sometimes through dozens of countries just to find safety.

For these people, even if they make it to Mexico, they still have to hide. If the local police see them and run their ID or name, they are very likely to be shipped out on the next boat back to whatever horrors they spent years risking their lives to flee.

Knowing this, Acupuncturists Without Borders held clinics for those who could come to us and went to those who could not. One of those places was a squat house for Cameroonian refugees. There, I met a man I will never forget for as long as I live. I had an incredible conversation that shocked me, healed him and was only an option due to one of my strengthnesses: *insatiability.*

Like all strengthnesses, my insatiability ripples out to many facets of my life, making me insatiable in many ways. I long for many things. But the thing I crave the most is belonging. One of the places I've always wanted to belong is with the smart people, like the elite IVY league schools. Since I didn't have that kind of money, brains or background, attending those schools was not an option for me. So, I did the next best thing. I spent a year and a half going through all of the Great Course's lectures on physics multiple times. I fell madly in love.

The great courses are a series of college and graduate-level lectures on any subject you could imagine. They hand-pick the best lecturers and experts the world has to offer so that average people like you and me are more engaged and actually learn the material. They come with downloadable lecture notes and PDFs for nerds like me.

My insatiability drove me to go through those lectures over and over and over again, printing PDFs and filling notebooks with notes, thoughts and ideas, which prepared me beautifully for one of the coolest, if not the coolest, conversations I've ever had.

When we showed up to offer care to the folks at this squat, everyone was a little trepidatious at first and for good reason. I'm sure they were thinking who are these white people walking up to us in the middle of the day? In their situation, it was sketchy – it was a risk just to talk to us. Depending on our intentions, they could have been shipped back to their villages the next day.

But one guy came over, and as we offered care, he reluctantly accepted. As soon as he did, he started asking for medical forms to fill out. We explained we understood the legalities of their situation, so we don't keep paper copies for their safety, which made him more nervous. We explained that we have protocols to keep patients and us safe and legal. He accepted this trepidatiously.

When the treatment began, which was just five tiny needles, not much bigger than a hair inserted in each ear, he asked how acupuncture worked. I knew by this point that *this guy was not like the rest.*

He was asking *very* specific questions that take a peculiarly high level of knowledge to even ask. He specifically asked how we calculate dosage. He pointed out that pharmaceutical interventions come in doses to ensure the patient gets exactly as much as they need. While our treatment was the same for everyone. So, he wanted to know how acupuncture as a whole, deals with the concept of dosage.

So you are aware, in this type of care, we treat everyone with five needles in each person's ear. So, asking about dosage is a reasonable question. But it's not a question that many acupuncturists can answer with any scientific rigor. Acupuncturists aren't exactly known for their deep understanding of physics or microbiology.

Since I'd become an insatiable learner as a way to deal with my baseline stress of feeling like an unwanted child, I had recently just finished all those physics courses and was able to explain to him about neuronal resting thresholds being stimulated by needle insertion. I explained that when the needle enters the body, an electrical charge is stimulated to the tune of .7 millivolts, which happens to be the resting threshold of a neuron in the human body. That's the electrical aspect.

I went on to say measurable changes also occur in the tension of the body's fascia from manipulating an inserted needle. That's the mechanical aspect. I explained further how electrons jumping orbits from the needle insertion cause electromagnetic waves to erupt with each jump. So, I explained that the patient's mass helps control dosage along with needling methods and retention time.

He was impressed with my answers and then explained that he has a doctorate in physics from the United States!! That's why he knew to ask about patient records and dosages and the fundamental physics behind why and how acupuncture works!

I was obviously completely blown away! Here was this man exceptionally highly educated, more educated than myself for sure, living his life, hiding in a squat house in Tijuana. To top it all off, he told me that the reason he came outside to us and agreed to treatment at all was because he had just found out just before we arrived the village that he calls home was burned to the ground by a rebel group. I told you there are a lot more types of traumatic experiences than those 10 ACE questions. This is a perfect example.

This man was disconnected from everything. He had to assume, at the time, that everyone he knew from back home was dead or permanently displaced. He no longer had a home. He had no one and nowhere to go back to. He was waiting and waiting to try to gain entry to the US, where he might hopefully be able to build a life for himself from the ground up, yet again.

If it weren't for my insatiability, which is most certainly both a strength and a weakness, *I would have never* dived into learning everything I could about the fundamentals of physics. At least enough to convince this guy that the people offering him care were competent and safe. I spent hours talking with this man. We connected at a time when he desperately needed connection.

The treatment that he received that day was not five needles in the ear, although that happened. His actual *treatment* was a conversation with another human about an area of competency in a crisis. Remember this in a few chapters. Competency plays a significant role for us as CSA people.

He had no control over his life at that time. He had nothing except his education. In that hellish situation, he reached out for stability through his established competency. He relied on what he knew, specialized in, and was already good at. What to me sounds like a strengthness for him.

He gravitated to a world that was comfortable and familiar- physics. Luckily for us both, my insatiability strengthness had also led me to that realm. I'm not a physicist by any stretch of the imagination, but thanks to my strengthness, I was prepared when the time came to have one conversation with one man that will stick with me forever.

The key to this working out as beautifully as it did was the context in which I found myself. I've already talked about how I do well in high-stress situations like emergency medicine due to the skills I developed to survive the stresses of my childhood.

This was undoubtedly a high-stress situation. More so for him than for me, obviously, but that's true in emergency medicine as well. What I want to draw your attention to most to help you find your strengthnesses is the *context* of my insatiability.

In this case, it brought me to a high-pressure situation, which I thrive in. But most importantly, that situation gave me a chance to use my insatiability strengthness in a way that helped someone.

I love understanding the how and why of things. Physics is a great topic to pursue with those kinds of interests. By spending dozens to hundreds of hours listening to lectures, looking at diagrams, and taking careful notes, my mindful use of my insatiability created a whole realm of knowledge that allowed me to have this incredible experience. These are the kinds of experiences that, to me, make a life worth living.

I was able to exercise my strengthness in a way that prepared me to have this opportunity to help a man in more anguish than I can imagine, with only a conversation. Having the ability to help that man on such a day... now that's power.

THE WEAKNESS SIDE OF MY INSATIABILITY

Let me tell you another story in which my insatiability was a problem. I have an ex, Eddie, whom I lived with for a little over a year. I was 21-22 then and had never even heard the term codependence yet. But boy, was I codependent. I would wake up for work hours before him and come home just minutes before him, and in that time, I would vacuum the floor, pull up the playlist he liked during his bath, start dinner and brace myself for whatever he was going to nitpick when he arrived. - I told you I tended to be with people who think nothing is ever good enough.

There was one day when he came home, I had just vacuumed, and when he walked in, I told him I vacuumed because he liked that, and asked what he wanted for dinner. He took just a few steps in the door, bent over, picked up the *only* piece of lint on the floor, and said, "you missed a spot." I just about lost my mind. I wanted to scream!

Yet, we did everything besides work together. So much so that when we would go grocery shopping, I couldn't even bring myself to walk down a different aisle than him.

You have to understand that I pride myself on being a pretty rational and frankly pathologically independent person. Rationally, it would have taken less time in the store if we split up, and he went to go grab the tilapia, and I grabbed the greens, but that never once occurred to me. Not till he pointed it out.

My need for connection and belonging was so insatiable at the time that I couldn't bring myself to take space from someone that was driving me absolutely mad!

This remained true up to the point that my need for connection and my need for expression were stifled at the same time. Two strengthness protectors popped up at once and ended up throwing a TV onto the floor. Eddie really liked Swiffer commercials.

One day, a new Swiffer commercial he had never seen came on. I was in mid-sentence when he noticed the commercial and shushed me. I don't do well with being shushed. So naturally walked over to the TV I bought and pushed it, face first, off the entertainment center and said in a terrifyingly calm voice, "You will never shush me again. Are we clear?" Needless to say, the relationship didn't last much longer after that.

Those are just two of the many instances, especially in my love life, in which my strengthnesses knee-jerk reaction was less than ideal. The key difference is context.

At the time I was with Eddie, I drank a lot. My job was burying people in the most high-profile job in the Air Force during Don't Ask, Don't Tell. Even my relationship was something I had to hide. I had almost no connection to myself. Yet, I felt chronic discomfort. That's what the drinking was for. It was too cut off from myself from knowing why I felt bad. But not so cut off that I didn't feel bad. To cut my connection to my discomfort, I drank more so I could continue to function while ignoring and denying my pain.

This is why maintaining connection with one's self is paramount for CSA people.

Most, if not all of us, have attachment issues, and those issues make us crave connection, sometimes, like in my case, insatiably. The worst part is, for many of us CSA personalities, our whole schtick is often predicated on acting and believing that we **don't** want connection, while we search it out subconsciously. Then we wonder why we wind up with toxic people.

Part of the context I had to consider at the time was that I had no connection. I had no connection to my mother or, father or sister. My brother was dead. The Air Force had just launched an investigation into my sexuality. So, I had no one; I didn't talk to my mother, my father, my sister, my brother was dead. I just had me and best friends Jack (Daniels) Jim (Beam) and Eddie.

As you evaluate the situations you wrote out in the exercises earlier, I want you to zoom way out. I want you to consider the broadest context you can. Think about the multitude of factors that were at play in exercises 3 and 4. To understand what was happening at the time, I couldn't just look at that day or that week. That was a rough year for me for lots of reasons. Each of those reasons played a role, and each is a part of the context I was in.

> *When I zoom out, it becomes apparent that everything about my life felt insecure at the time. Including the fact that the Air Force was making me switch jobs. All of which played into my strengthness showing its weakness side.*

What about you? What's your story? I know you have a bunch of them. I wish I could sit with you right now and listen to them. I'm sure you've got some doozies.

If I could sit with you and listen to your story after you emptied your heart, I would eventually ask you to think about all the factors at play. Compare your lists of strengths, weaknesses, core beliefs, and stories, good and bad, from your life and see if you can jigsaw them together. As I said before, this is not a clean one-to-one association. Take your time with this; spend days on it if necessary. Sleep on it, for sure. Come back to this section as many times as you need to.

This is the crux of the book. **This is the place you must meet yourself fully to unlock your superpowers.** You have to have an honest accounting of your strengths and weaknesses. Once you have a clear idea of what your strengthnesses are, you can finally start taking steps to put yourself in environments in which your strengthnesses are a blessing instead of a demon.

You adapted appropriately to inappropriate circumstances. Those adaptations are now well-developed skill sets that you can leverage at any moment in time – once you are aware of them.

You don't need to learn anything new. You don't need to change who you are. The entire point is to show you that you're already a badass. The skills that make you a badass are already fully developed. You just need to use them in the right place at the right time.

Using only a hammer to build an entire house wouldn't work very well. But a hammer will work when you need to nail something. We CSA folks have really big hammers. So, find a nail that needs pounding and pound away. You are ready right now today. No extra work or webinar is necessary for you to use your skillsets. You just need to recognize them and then use them in useful contexts. *It's literally that simple.*

ORIGINS OF MY "I'M TOO MUCH" STRENGTHNESS

I mentioned this earlier, but one of my most glaring core beliefs was "I'm too much." This one ran deep. It wasn't just a feeling I had. There was legitimate evidence of it from the moment I was born. I was 12lbs 1oz when I was born, about twice the size of the average baby. So, I was cut out of my mother's womb two weeks early to save both our lives. A regular vaginal delivery could have killed us both.

Compounding this, I learned I had to be a lot to get any attention, which is the plight of many a middle child. It also seems my mother also had a touch of postpartum depression. She has always avoided the doctor like a rabies patient avoids water, so she never got a formal diagnosis. At any rate, depression is more common among C-section mothers.

It seems to be related to many things. One theory is that the mother, due to the surgery part, does not receive the giant hormonal and neurochemical cascade that happens as a result of pushing a baby through the vaginal canal. That flood of hormones, including oxytocin, facilitates mothers bonding with their children. Without it, sometimes they struggle to bond. Which inevitably leads to an insecurely attached child. At no fault of the mother or child.

During depressive states, no matter the cause, mothers are not able to be as attentive as they would typically be to their child's needs. So, the child's needs and desires were met less than the child's biology expected. So, the child begins to expect less. *I began to expect less.* Because of it, I've grown to expect very little from everyone. It was a point of pride and a hallmark of my personality. I call it **surviving on crumbs**.

Love, attention, time, food, birthday presents, care, consideration; you name it, I don't need it. Because disappointment sucks, to become disappointed less the Child learns to expect less. We learn to have as few needs as possible, hopefully zero needs. All because my belief of "I'm too much" subconsciously extended to my needs. "I am too much" and "I have too many needs" became the same thing.

OTHER STRENGTHNESS EXAMPLES

I mentioned earlier that it's quite natural and seemingly inevitable that at some point on this path, you will reach a place in which you try to separate what is the "real you" and what's your trauma. The answer was and will always be: *it's all you, Booboo.*

There are many common trauma responses. And you're probably like me, and like the rest of us, in that you live out some of these common responses. I mentioned I fell into this trap in which I put a lot of time and effort into changing some of my trauma responses for the simple fact that they were common.

I thought that was how I was supposed to undo the damage of my trauma. Begin with the typical manifestations of trauma and work my way backward, retraining each of the habits I have that are a result of trauma. Unfortunately, that meant changing nearly everything about me.

I lost myself more than a bit during this process, and wow, it was uncomfortable and confusing. I had no sense of identity except *changing my identity*. Who I was during this too-long phase of my life was stressful because I created this state of limbo that was very uncomfortable and unhealthy for me.

So, I want to display just how silly that chapter of my life was for me in hopes that you do not fall into the same trap. I'm going to show you how one extremely common trauma response turned strengthness has changed my life for the better.

OVER-EXPLAINING

One of the more common trauma responses is known as "over explaining." Over-explaining is a typical trauma response launched by millions of people around the world. *It's a strategy designed to avoid conflict.*

The idea is, if I explain everything about what I'm doing, what I want, and why I want it from as many angles as possible, I can prevent all conflict. This, of course, is madness. It rarely works. It's also a natural extension of the fawning aspect of the fight, flight, freeze, and fawn strategies.

I hate confrontation, but I'm damn good at it. I've never been good at following the rules or doing what I'm told. Yet, displaying respect for those around me is also important to me. If I can articulate all the reasons that I do what I do or don't do what I should, then somewhere inside, I believe I stand a much better chance of being left alone or less punished for breaking the rules.

This has allowed me to practice articulating my thoughts, feelings, and logic, which has worked out wonderfully. It's also worked out less than ideal in other situations.

THE WEAKNESS SIDE: OVEREXPLAINING AS A TRAUMA RESPONSE

I had a situation with a CSA friend while writing this book. I had hired her to write some health articles for my health education website. She had written a few for me, and I was happy to upload them after a bit of editing. But the last article she sent me wasn't the kind of article I wanted to publish. So, I asked her to write one on the health benefits of dancing. She did, and it was a great article. It wasn't exactly what I wanted, but it was a well-written article.

But a problem occurred. Because the previous article was different from what I wanted, I got a message from her asking if it was publish-worthy. I had just opened it when she sent the message. So, my response to her was not filtered <u>at all</u>.

Now, I know myself. I know how harsh I can sound. It doesn't bother *me* much; I'm used to it because it's *my* inner voice. It's *my inner critic* that I have spent my entire life dealing with. So, I have learned to use that voice to my benefit. My friend Sandra has her inner voice and, therefore, doesn't hear mine. So when she asked me what I thought of the article, she got the totally unfiltered *inner Owl critique.*

She, of course, flipped out. She took everything I said personally, and being me, I tried to explain- or rather *over-explain* everything. Mind you, at this point, I had pissed off a really good friend. So, I was dysregulated as well.

In my dysregulated state, *I overexplained myself into a deeper and deeper hole.* I did my best and apologized for my harshness, but the damage had been done. She didn't speak to me for weeks when we were talking every few days at the time.

THE STRENGTH SIDE OF OVER-EXPLAINING.

The counterpoint to this, *you are reading right now.* If it hadn't been for having a lifetime of practicing over-explaining, I would not have been able to write this book. My deep, trauma-conditioned desire for peace and *conflict* resolution drove me to write it. Not just reducing conflict *for me* but reducing conflict for *people like me.*

The hundreds upon hundreds of times I inappropriately and obnoxiously over-explained myself allowed me to write this book. That includes times when overexplaining myself went well, and times it went not so well. Even when we have used our strengthnesses in ways that turned out not so great it was still practice! Practice doesn't make perfect. Practice makes improvement. Again, improvement is the goal, not perfection.

So, when I got it wrong in my life and hurt people with my strengthnesses, I still got better at that particular skill. So much better than with all my imposter syndrome crap, I still heard from enough people that I was good enough at explaining things I ought to write a book.

So here we are. The words you are reading right now are a direct descendent of one of the most common and seemingly boring of the common trauma responses. What separates these two events into being adaptive or maladaptive, a strength or a weakness is the crux of the whole rethinking strategy - **Context.**

COMPARING CONTEXTS

In the Sandy story, I told a close friend about her creativity and work via text. We all know how many misunderstandings happen over text. Texting during a situation like this in which a close friend and I are both wearing multiple hats, her as a friend and freelance writer and me as a friend and employer, was not an appropriate context in which to have this kind of conversation.

When you add the fact that I became dysregulated as soon as I knew I had pissed her off, and she rage quit, it became that much more evident that this was not the right place or the right time. Yet I persisted because that's *my* habit.

Right place and right time is what life as a CSA person is all about when it comes to leveraging our skill sets. We have to put ourselves in situations where our strengthnesses will be adaptive to our lives.

I racked my brain for weeks about how I could have done better in that situation with Sandra. But I couldn't. No matter how hard I tried, I couldn't come up with a way I could have changed the outcome of that particular situation. I believed everything I said in the text was valid and appropriate feedback, even while it was too harsh for her. Especially if I wanted her to continue to write for me.

In my life, if I can't find a way that I could have prevented an unnecessary conflict, I try to find a way to learn from it to avoid future similar conflicts. So now I have a paragraph rule in texting. If I notice that I have written three paragraphs in a single text message, I know I need to sleep on it before I send it.

This prevents me from overexplaining myself to someone likely going to read a very different message than the one I meticulously but dysregulatedly wrote out. It's not uncommon for me to want to spend 15 -30 minutes composing a single text. But I've noticed I don't do that if there isn't a problem. I mostly feel the need to get granular when there is a perceived problem or threat. Why would I bother otherwise? That's an insane amount of time to spend on a text message.

But I still do it occasionally. And thanks to my conditioning, in my mind, if I can explain everything that happened, like who said what, how it was interpreted, the influence the state of biology had on such an interpretation, I can eliminate any conflict through clarity. But clarity doesn't typically come during dysregulated states.

The conflict with Sandy was a perfect example of that. I wrote out so many things and felt I was solving the issue by noting where and how she misunderstood me. You can guess how well that went over.

Had I had access to the clarity I thought I had at that time, I would have seen sooner that the damage had been done, and what was needed was space and time to let things cool off. You'll be happy to hear later; that is precisely what happened. I waited a few weeks for things to cool off, reached out, and we patched things right up. In my experience, this kind of conditional conflict is often unavoidable between CSA people. The willingness for reparation is the key. I'm not going to beat myself up that my conditioning and her conditioning butt heads. What matters is we both chose to rise above and repair.

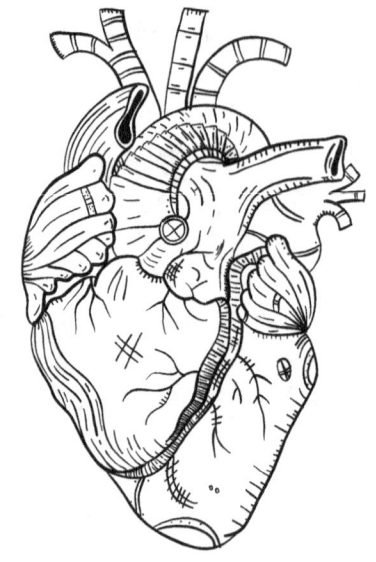

CHAPTER 14

FINDING YOUR STRENGTHNESS

O K, let's get to it! Now that you've heard about some of my strengthnesses, You have a better idea of how this might work. So let's find your superpower right now! Once you know what your strengthness or strengthnesses are, you will be on your way to the life you've always deserved.

Some strengthnesses are identified quickly, and some are harder to see. Some are best found in simple statements, and some through comparing and contrasting your strengths and weaknesses and the context each occurs in. Then I will walk you through a few ways I have helped others identify their strengthnesses.

Don't worry if you need help figuring it out. We are going to use multiple exercises to try and identify these slippery little skills.

FINDING YOUR STRENGTHNESS EXERCISES

EXERCISE #1 STRENGTHS AND WEAKNESSES

The first way to ID your strengthness is as simple as it gets. Create a list of your known strengths and weaknesses. The ones you already know about you. Write out as many as you can come up with.

It was hard for me, and it might be for you too. I could list a few, literally two, and then I had to ask friends. I'm not the only person I know who struggled with this.

One of my best friends, Emily, who works in sales, did the same. After she and I talked about the concept, she asked her closest friends and family members to be honest with her and tell her her greatest strengths and weaknesses. The feedback she got was insightful and went a long way in helping her conceptualize her strengthness skills.

Our close friends are often a fantastic resource for getting to know oneself. She was bold enough to ask her children, who gave marvelous and insightful feedback! One child she has notices cause and effect in most things. His feedback listed very specific strengths, which he instinctively tied to their weak counterparts for her!

If you need help writing out your strengths and weaknesses, please reach out to the people you're closest to and ask them. They might have some valuable feedback you aren't aware of!

Once your list is complete, look at which ones seem most related to each other. If you can see some way that a strength and a weakness could be two sides of the same coin, congratulations, you have found yourself a strengthness!

For example:

Strengths: I'm a fighter, I work hard, I'm creative, I treat others well, I'm tough, I'm kind.

Weaknesses: I'm a fighter (when I probably shouldn't) I'm erratic, I take things too seriously, I'm chaotic.

Note: I'm a fighter I listed as both a strength and a weakness. In some circumstances, it's a gift. In others, it's more of a curse. Which means being a fighter is a strengthness of mine.

One last thing: self-help books, more than any other type of book, get shared from hand to hand. That said, the following workbook sections are meant for you to fill out. However, if you like this book enough you might loaning it to a friend? Writing your personal stuff out in these pages might understandably stop you from doing that.

So, in the back of the book, after the acknowledgments, are additional copies of the blank lines of these exercises for you to use. There are three additional sets of each of the exercises. This way, if you want to give the book away after you find your strength-nesses, you don't have to share all your secrets to do so. Simply write your answers in the back, rather than within the lines below. Then, when you're done, if you want, rip those pages right out! Then, share to your heart's content!

Some folks might cringe at that, but it makes the irreverent part of me very happy. I encourage you to write in the very very back and rip your details out when you're done! Then, you'll be free to share the book with a friend and keep all your stuff to yourself. I apologize in advance for those pages not being perforated. It would have raised the cost of printing the book.

Finding your strengthness: Exercise 1, Strengths and Weaknesses

(Strengths list)   (Weakness list)

_____   _____

_____   _____

_____   _____

_____   _____

_____   _____

_____   _____

_____   _____

_____   _____

Now that your list is complete, look at which ones seem most related to each other. If you can see some way that a strength and a weakness could be two sides of the same coin, congratulations, you have found yourself a strengthness!

This usually takes a little time to see. It's a bit abstract for some, so set a 3-minute timer and look at the lists you wrote. By the end of just 3 minutes, you'll be able to see the connections more intuitively.

Exercise #1 is done! Not too bad, right? Did you find any pairs that are obviously or could be tied together in some way? What strength do you have on that list that might have a downside in a different or opposite context?

What strength at work do you find is a weakness at home? What weakness at work is a gift to those you love at home?

That is the first and most straightforward way to find a strengthness. If you are still waiting to see something obvious, don't worry. I've got a few more exercises for you. They'll come.

EXERCISE #2, CORE BELIEFS

You probably already know what core beliefs are: a set of ideas about ourselves and our world that we believe so deeply those beliefs color every interpretation, interaction and thought we have. They are the ideas, beliefs and associations running in the background of our minds all the time. It's only possible to do the work that is the heart of this book by dealing with core beliefs.

Another way to find strengthnesses is to write out some of your core beliefs. Core beliefs can be strengthnesses too if they play a prominent role in our lives. Core beliefs are deeply held beliefs about yourself and the world. They are often quick, off-the-cuff phrases and always profoundly impact a person's perception and decision-making. Unsurprisingly, many are inherited from our families and childhood.

Core beliefs typically fall into one of 4 categories: They are beliefs about

Likeability: like "I am unlovable." or "I am unlikable."

Goodness: I'm a good or bad person or other people are good or bad

The world itself: "The world is fundamentally unfair." "the world is my oyster."

Competence: "No matter what I do I fail", or "If I try hard enough, I will succeed."

As I said, core beliefs are short and broad enough to be applied to nearly any situation. They are blanket statements. So, list the blanket statements you believe to be true about each of those categories.

Most categories will have more than one core belief. Often, core beliefs contradict one another in some way. Don't worry if those core beliefs are already listed in your strengths or weaknesses in the previous exercise. There is *always* going to be overlap. If anything on that list has both served you and hurt you, that's a clue to help you find your strengthness.

Even quirky family mottos have a way of becoming core beliefs. My favorite of my mother's mother was "Suck it up, buttercup." That wasn't just for the boys. There were no boys. She raised three tough and adoring daughters with that as a core belief. It's become one of mine as a result. I just try to temper it a bit when appropriate.

If you get confused, don't worry; this is just to get some more juices flowing.

Here are a few of mine:

- I'm always in the way
- I'm kind
- I'm a bull in a China shop
- I'm generous
- I'm honest
- I'm insatiable
- I'm like a dog with a bone
- I'm a klutz
- life's a bitch and then you die
- people are stupid
- individuals are smart

Some others you may have learned from religion or a religion-founded culture like I did:

- I was born a flawed sinner in need of saving/healing

Pro tip: If you can't think of anything and the blank page is freaking you out on the first line, write "I have no effing clue" or something similar. Sometimes, a blank page can be a mental barrier. That'll get the page dirty, and the rest might come easier.

Write out some core beliefs you have here:

_____

_____

_____

_____

_____

_____

_____

_____

_____

_____

_____

_____

_____

_____

_____

_____

_____

As you look at your list of core beliefs, do you see any that could be useful in certain situations while being less so in others?

For example: *Life's a bitch then you die* is a core belief that, depending on other beliefs, could be horrible. It could easily keep a person in perpetual depression. If accompanied by certain other beliefs and perspectives, that same philosophy acts as carte blanche to do whatever you want!

If life's a bitch to everyone, we all have it hard. So rather than groan about it, you can accept the challenge and do whatever you want! Got something hard you want to do? Why not do it? If life's a bitch, then you die? Then life will be a bitch whether you're doing something hard or not!

It may take time to see how these core beliefs subconsciously influence our decision-making in stressful situations. Take all the time you need to feel your way through these. Keep looking back at what you wrote. Come back to it in an hour or tomorrow if you need to.

The power of pausing and reflecting cannot be overstated. It took time to develop these patterns, and we are only now beginning to uncover them. Observing and understanding your patterns of behavior is a skill that takes time to develop. Be patient with yourself. Over time you'll be a pro, and your life will be much better for it.

EXERCISE #3 SKILLFULNESS

I want you to think about a situation where you did something well. Think of a time when something happened, you stepped in, and *others* told you you were *skillful*. Or you were just the right person for the job. *These situations can point you to times when you used your strengthnesses well.*

This is the *streng*th side of the strengthness coin. Maybe you're *good in a crisis*. Or maybe you're a peacekeeper. You may be able to see an interpersonal problem arising, and you have a magical ability to respond in a way that prevents the future disaster you saw coming. Write a few examples of when you felt you were really on fire.

Be sure to be as specific as you can. The demons are in the details. Include some dynamics of the situation, the people or the types of people involved. Was it with family or strangers? It could be with co-workers. What was the environment you were in at the time? What were the specific actions you took that led to the positive outcome? What exactly was the positive feedback from others? Try to remember their exact words.

Was it indoors or outdoors? Was it peaceful or chaotic? Were there lots of people, or were you with just a few folks? These generic context clues may seem irrelevant at first, but it's the stuff that helps us most. Write them all out below.

Finding your strengthness: Exercise 3, The Good Stuff

If you skipped that section, I understand. You probably skipped it, telling yourself that you'll do it later… Good try, but go back right now and do the exercise! I know it's uncomfortable, but you can do it.

There is simply no way that you have made it this far in life without doing a single thing right. Even if sometimes it feels that way. Any resistance you felt during this exercise is your biological conditioning raging against new conditioning from your newfound perspectives. It doesn't make sense to the biology of a broken person to look for positive reinforcement. It's incongruous that a "broken person" would have entirely positive actions. No matter the context.

<u>So, if you skipped this exercise, un-skip it - now</u>

Thank you, and you're welcome.

If you're anything like me, you want accuracy and balance in your life - and now you know about the negative bias in the brain. In the *pursuit of balance and equanimity, you must cheer yourself at least as much as you critique yourself! It's the only fair way!*

It's easier to critique ourselves. We do it naturally. And sometimes it's a good thing. Still, if we want to suffer less and feel balanced, we absolutely have to learn to cheer for ourselves as much as we criticize ourselves. It's only fair, not to mention the effect it will have on your RAS. Wink wink, nudge, nudge.

Now that you have completed this exercise. I want you to notice the feelings, thoughts, and sensations in your body right now. Become familiar with that feeling. The resistance and uncomfortable yet exciting awkwardness that you feel writing exclusively good things about yourself is the exact feeling of overcoming your biological programming in real time!!

If you set out to memorize this feeling, you will know from today forward. Throughout your life if you are successfully rewriting your trauma programming! I told you this is an uphill battle. It never stops being uphill, but it does get easier.

One of the ways it gets easier is that the uncertainty we feel while reprogramming becomes less painful or at least less terrifying once we know what it *feels* like to reprogram ourselves! The unusual sensations get interpreted as purposeful reprogramming instead of something strange and, therefore, potentially dangerous that needs stopped.

Yes, it feels weird. Yes, it feels uncomfortable. But does it *feel bad*? So far, when I ask, folks unanimously decide it's uncomfortable, but it doesn't feel *bad*. It's scary for some, and peaceful for others. But so far, no one has found the sensations or reprogramming unilaterally unpleasant or painful. So to me, it's a sensation worth getting very familiar with.

EXERCISE #4 THE NOT-SO-GREAT STUFF

Now it's time to dig into some less proud moments. As sure as I am that you haven't made it this far in life without doing something right, I'm equally confident that there have been times in your life when your reactions were less-than-ideal.

Maybe you spoke up when you shouldn't have or said nothing when you ought to. There have undoubtedly been times when you were in the wrong place at the wrong time. I want you to start digging through your recent memories to find and write down instances in which you wish you had handled things differently.

So, think of those times when, at the end of it all, you may have thought to yourself, "My God, I must be broken." Or, OK, well, that may have been a bit extreme."

The good news is that thanks to that negative bias in all of our human brains, you'll probably have a much easier time remembering the situations you screwed up than the ones you were great in. It also feels less uncomfortable because your RAS is currently programmed to find things wrong with you.

The same rules apply here as in the previous exercises. Think long and deeply. Be as specific as possible. Be sure to include as many of the dynamics of the event as possible, like what the environment was like, how you responded, and how you wish you had responded.

Finding your strengthness: Exercise 4, The Not-so-great Stuff

_____

_____

_____

_____

_____

_____

_____

_____

_____

_____

_____

_____

_____

How was that? Take some time to breathe and feel your body again. I know it can be dysregulating to go through all that. Check in with your body see if there is something kind you can do for yourself. Make a cup of tea or go for a walk. Bring this book with you.

PUTTING IT ALL TOGETHER TO FIND YOUR STRENGTHNESS

Well done! Firstly, I apologize for making you dig into the less fun details. Those experiences are not usually fun to relive. But you made it and for many people, it beats the hell out of reliving the worst shit from childhood. So well done! You're done! You've written them out. If you feel extra inspired by any of these exercises, please don't limit yourself to the tiny lines in this book. Use the spare pages in the back, a notebook, or your phone to write out more examples.

Now, you have evaluated yourself in 4 ways.

- You've looked at your strengths and weaknesses.
- You wrote out your core values into four categories.

- You've taken a closer look than you've probably ever taken at the times when you've performed well and should be proud.
- Lastly, you've looked into a few examples from your life that you probably interpreted as evidence of brokenness before all this. So, let's put these pieces together.

Exercising your strengthness: the puppy analogy

You now know what your strengthnesses are. You've done the work to figure out which strategies little you's biology employed to keep yourself safe. You understand how those strategies become habituated through conditioning. You also know that those automated habits get you into trouble at times.

The things that, prior to reading this book, you would have considered evidence of your brokenness. Now you know are actually evidence of an incredible and frankly annoyingly efficient survival mechanism. But surviving wasn't good enough for me, and it seems it isn't good enough for you either.

How can we honor our protectors, our strengthnesses, while not allowing them to shoot us in the foot? Like I said before, when those protective attributes grow strong enough to be a strengthness, they develop their own personality and goals. But they're simple. Each has one goal, and that's to protect you. The way to conceptualize how to deal with a strengthness is to think of it like a puppy.

Imagine your strengthness is a 6-month-old golden lab. What is the most critical thing for that dog to have other than food and water if you want it to be healthy? It's *exercise*.

What happens when you have a 6-month-old puppy at home that doesn't get enough attention and exercise? It acts out. Dogs have an innate instinct to protect. They were bred from wild dogs to live in tandem with humans. They warn of and protect us from danger, and we, in turn, give them food. That was the original contract or at least a part of it. Now the contract has changed because we don't need their protection. A pug couldn't protect me from a lion anyway.

That's very similar to the relationship we have with our strengthnesses. The protection it was bred for is no longer necessary for us. But your strengthness is too big now. He got too big to be able to ignore. Now he is that puppy. If you don't allow a dog to feel like he's doing his job, you'll wind up with a dog who barks at leaves blowing across the yard.

A puppy who never gets an opportunity to serve its purpose will create a purpose. Depending on how much he had to protect himself and you, he might snap at strangers or bark himself hoarse whenever the doorbell rings. He'll chew up all your furniture and eat your shoes. This is what our strengthnesses do too.

If we don't honor what these protectors were created for, what they were designed for and recognize the value they offer us, they always make our lives more difficult. Not out of maliciousness but out of a protective compulsion. Because of nature. It is their nature. All strengthnesses were, at one point, just grunt-level protectors. So, no matter how big one gets, he is still a protector

at heart, even when he's gotten too big for his britches. That ought to be honored.

I've said that you aren't in the same environment that you were as a kid, and if you think about it, you'd be glad. This is why. You chose to leave that environment because it was unhealthy. But you learned how to survive quite well in that unhealthy environment thanks to your strengthness puppies.

By changing and adapting your environment to suit you and your strengthnesses, you can unlock your hidden power. I'm not suggesting you become an MMA fighter just because your dad was a violent alcoholic. But I _am_ saying that if you were to, you'd probably have an edge.

Exercising your strengthness is honoring your hard-won skills. I know it fucked up in more ways than one. Surviving a violent childhood or being sexually molested is unequivocally awful. Until we have honored how horrible it was for us, we inevitably experience a lot of resistance to the thought that something positive could come out of such a unanimously terrible situation, which brings me to my next point.

There is a phrase floating around in the self-help world that says.

"The wound is the gift."

Although I understand where the sentiment comes from, I feel I need to take this opportunity to say loud and clear, "Fuck you!" to that sentiment. My wound is NOT my gift. My wounds, your wounds, our trauma is exactly what I've described it as; an effing wound. Trauma is in no way a gift. I know that surviving wounds inflicted by the circumstances of my life has granted me some skills. Those skills can be a gift and a curse. But the wound is just that, a wound.

You're learning how to identify and use the skills you developed as a result of your surviving trauma to your advantage. Not from the trauma itself. The skills are rudimentary reactions at first. They are rough, unrefined, and without the right mindset and knowledge, they often harm us as much as they help us. That is, until we make them conscious.

Your wounds, my wounds are wounds. I'm not going to pretend they're anything else. Doing so may help people with less traumatic events in their past. Some small t trauma folks may be able to immediately see the truth in this from their experiences without getting deeply offended. But for those of us with big T trauma, this kind of framing is frankly insulting. You don't deserve that. Your wound is a wound. But you can heal it because you can integrate it. Make it a part of you, make it whole, and make it beautiful.

Claim your Strengthness!

Now you've completed all four exercises! I know this still probably feels incomplete. You may not know exactly how to describe your strengthnesses even though you feel you have a sense of what It may be.

Next, please write out some of your strengthnesses. Just like in the exercises, they may be most easily described as a phrase or maybe as a single word. It may be an - I am - statement like "I'm a fighter." Give yourself a moment to reflect on what you're naturally good at in the light of the exercises you just did.

Fill the lines below with phrases and statements that describe the positive aspects of who you are. Your strengthnesses will show up as you write. You will begin to understand what I mean as you write. This is all still new to some of you, so don't be surprised if it feels a little awkward for you. The more time you spend writing, the clearer it will become. Even if what you write makes little to no sense.

Here is where you solidify for yourself the strengths of your adaptation strategies. Using what you write below, we will find a place for you. A place you belong, as you are, right now today.

My Strengthness(es)

_____

_____

_____

_____

_____

_____

_____

_____

_____

_____

_____

_____

You did it!! You know what your strengthnesses are! I hope you feel proud of yourself. I'm proud of you. Climbing our way out of the trappings of trauma isn't easy, but it is rewarding. Now that you've got your personal superpower pinned down. It's time to figure out when and where to use it!

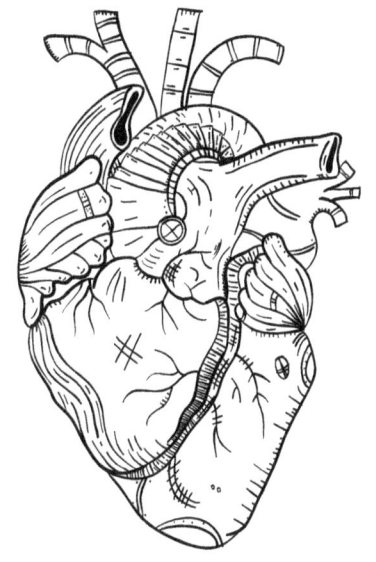

CHAPTER 15
LEVERAGE YOUR ENVIRONMENT

Change up your environment in ways that leverage your strengthnesses! That's the next step. In biology, experiencing is believing. So, I learned to switch up my environment to prove to my overly dramatic physiology that I am useful exactly as I am! Flaws and all. Being *"too much"* in a situation that is also, *"too much"* means I'm *"just enough."*

There are a lot of ways to describe a thing and trauma, big T or little, can be also be described as an unfinished or incomplete stress response. With it being unfinished, it desires resolution for itself. Our body desires, as much as a body can, that we complete the stress response. We have to move our nervous system into that post-stress-response, resting, refractory period – that ever-elusive *rest and digest* mode.

What we are doing by putting you in an environment in which your strengthness can thrive is completing the stress response, over and over, creating a positive outcome, rather than the one we had when the trauma happened. This is what updates the biology. It changes our narrative on a biological level.

Putting ourselves in an environment where we naturally shine is purposefully conditioning ourselves for the better. It's doing the same thing as in our romantic relationships we talked about before. A relationship has to start toxic for us to change the ending and complete the stress response. To complete a stress response, we must first be in a situation or environment that is... you guessed it! Stressful.

In this chapter I'm going to give you some examples of how you can leverage your skills, immediately. I'll share some examples of folks who have managed to leverage their strengthnesses themselves.

MATCHING STRENGTHNESSES TO ENVIRONMENTS.

As I mentioned before, occasionally using your strengthness happens naturally. It did for me. If you were physically hit as a kid, you might shine in emergency medicine as an EMT or paramedic. Emergency medicine allows you to intervene in someone else's crisis, taking a person under threat and bringing them to safety.

The chaotic environment I had as a child fostered an ability to focus on subliminal details, threat evaluation, ignore my emotions, repress my reactions, and hopefully change the outcome of a terrible situation, providing a sense of power over time. Not to mention, it kept me as safe as I could be.

As an EMT in the Air Force, my mind had to be focused on observation of facts, staying aware of but not getting lost in the emotions of the situation. That's how people die. My job was to evaluate every observable detail of the patient to assess the situation to determine which life-saving interventions should be applied and in what order. That's why I was good at it and loved it so much. Emergency Medicine played to my strengthnesses, before I knew what a strengthness was. That sense of power, when repeated, becomes a felt experience of *competency.*

Competency is the point. It tells me that I'm not broken. It's just that big parts of me were built for an unsafe environment. Emergency medicine provided me with proof that I had innate skills that were useful. I was no longer just screwing myself over. If I'm genuinely competent, I can't be *that* broken. Right? Especially since the thing that originally created my competency, *was* surviving my trauma!

Let's make some simple correlations so you get a sense of how every strengthness has a context in which it's useful. I gave examples of I am statements in the last section. Let's use some of those to find a valuable context for each.

- I'm always in the way – standing up for people bullied or oppressed.
- I'm kind – working with children with behavioral issues.
- I'm a bull in a China shop – build a Start-up! There's nothing to break!
- I'm generous – disaster relief work, where your generosity can be most impactful.
- I'm honest – Become a therapist, coaching.
- I'm insatiable – work in higher education and get paid to learn forever!
- I'm like a dog with a bone – Long-term projects, write a book or play, be tenacious
- I'm a klutz – physical forms of expression like circus, where fumbling is mandatory.

These are just a few examples and obviously in no way complete. This list is to get you to see the trend. I don't know what your strengthnesses are. I don't know what you wrote down, so I can't give you the perfect suggestion for your unique skill set.

So instead, you have to do it. Take a look at the strengthnesses you wrote out. Are any of them similar to the examples? Is there a context that parallels the suggested ways to use your strengthness? Is there an environment that comes to mind in which you could use it? I bet you forgot a very old desire somewhere in there.

When I was a child, the only person I wanted to be, other than Sherlock Holmes - mouse detective, was Dr. Quinn, Medicine Woman. Reflecting on my life now, it's hilarious that I do a nearly identical, modern-day version of exactly what she did in the show. And it took leveraging all of my strengthnesses to do it.

You may have a similar childhood dream. If you can, try to adapt an environment from that. Maybe you are too old to become an astronaut but you might still thrive working in a highly regulated, detail focused government job you find inspiring. Maybe you wanted to become a firefighter, but now you're close to retirement. Being a 911 dispatcher could fill a similar void.

USING STRENGTHNESSES ACCIDENTALLY

You're almost guaranteed to have already used your strengthnesses accidentally. That's basically what Finding Your Strengthness Exercise 3 was. But when you exercise a strengthness consciously for the first time, which again means to purposefully put yourself into situations where your strengthnesses are being used to help another person, it's life-changing.

When you do this for the first time, please pay close attention to your body and what's happening inside it. Focus on the physical sensation that you have in those moments of reflection. The deeper you dive into the sensation, the deeper the experience of competency is driven into your biology. *Pause & reflect.*

All your body has is sensation. That's the only thing it has to interact with the world with.

The mind arises as a function of the brain and body. However the brain is a physical organ that is also affected by sensation. *So, make sure you really sit with why you changed your environment.* Whether you did that by finding a new job or hobby, volunteering once a week, or choosing to live in a van. Sit with the sensations that arise when you are experiencing and reflect on how applying your strengthnesses is making someone's life better.

This provides a necessary sense of global good. It makes us feel like we are worth something because we are helping someone. For 3 million years, humans have depended on each other. We fundamentally needed each other to survive. The things that helped us survive were acts of kindness, generosity and reciprocity in our community. It's tough to beat oneself up while helping someone else. *That's the point.* But we talk more about that in the Service chapter in section 4.

The point is to change your opinion of yourself and the skills that you developed. The point is to see your strengthnesses a useful tools instead of evidence of your brokenness. To see yourself as someone who, no matter what's happening in your life, understands you are still fundamentally good or, at the very least, fundamentally useful.

For me, I shot for useful first. Believing I was fundamentally good after a fundamentalist Christian upbringing was hard. Actually, it was impossible when I started, and now, I see how fucked up that is. The whole religion is predicated on us being flawed lost sheep in need of saving.

Your strengthnesses have spent your entire life protecting you. They've worked hard to become big and strong so they *can* protect you. And if they don't get proper exercise, this amazing protective friend you have had becomes your worst enemy. Like any other part of us that is repressed or ignored, strengthnesses will show up in the most inopportune places and times.

Say your mother was a perfectionist, and because of that, you learned to predict her desires, needs, and particularities before they ever came up. If you aren't using that talent, you can likely already think of times when you judged so much, you concluded you hated everyone in the room, before they ever had a chance.

Or maybe, rather than nitpick others, you do it to yourself. You might be one of those people who could be a gold medalist Olympian at finding each thing you did that was less than perfect then evicerate yourself over it. I'm not talking about looking at your screw-ups to learn from them, either. I'm talking about looking at the things that went fairly well and *still* coming up with all the ways you ***should*** have done it better.

This is not new. In fact, many CSA people I call friends have, throughout their lives, found ways to maximize their childhood trauma skills.

I briefly mentioned my friend Emily, a top seller in her organization. Sales is all about relationships. People don't buy things. People buy people. So, when you're selling anything, what you are really selling is yourself. This can be a sketchy path for CSA folks whose worth gets tied up in their work.

For Emily, her ability to quickly evaluate a person to understand who they see themselves as, how they think and what their goals are, is one of her strengthnesses. She has another strengthness she calls "I cut off." She can separate herself from anything and anyone at the drop of a hat.

That strengthness was a painful lesson stemming from experiences with her mother. But because she found her way into a job in which she can use not one but two of her strengthnesses, she makes six figures a year and doesn't often have to stress about money, which was very important to her when she had kids.

For me, my first accidental foray into a strengthness was in the military. My narcissistic, perfectionist, homophobic, Bible-thumping father trained me well for a career in which we were literally told every day our job was to be perfect. Once, I even got written up for having dry skin on my face after shaving for a televised ceremony in the Honor Guard. That's how <u>perfect</u> we had to be.

I had to hide all my flaws, including my thoughts, from my family, and I continued to hide them from Uncle Sam. The experience was incredible, but it took a toll on my soul. Not just the job in which my primary duty was burying military members in Arlington National Cemetery, but also the pretending to be something I'm not, still hiding the fact I was gay from my family and my government too.

Still, the skill of appearing perfect provided a very meaningful moment for the people I was serving. When the families of a deceased military member are at their loved one's funeral, they remember that day forever. In the Honor Guard, a full day was six funerals. Over my four years there, I did well over a thousand funerals. The most we did in a day was 22 from a bomber that crashed.

My perfectionism, which is both a strengthness and a massive enemy to mental health and self-worth when unchecked, was also the thing that made those families experience something special. We may have performed six funerals that day, but each family *only got one*. They only get one chance to bury their loved ones. This is a perfect example of how a strengthness can be leveraged. Even subconsciously.

The next place I found myself leaning into my strengthnesses was medicine. I was terrified of my mother growing up - terrified. She worked very hard, and I was always quaking with fear that she would come home volatile because of it.

To prevent one of her lousy moods from turning volatile, I got good at noticing what she noticed so I could see the writing on the wall and hopefully prevent what felt like a nuclear meltdown.

So, in medicine in the military, I got to work with some fantastic people who were happy to teach an eager, bright young student, even with all my harsh edges. They showed me what details to look for and what they might mean for the patient.

So, every day I went to work, I got to use a strengthness from childhood in a way that was beneficial for *me and those around me*. That was a massive step in the right direction, even if I hadn't figured out *why*. I just knew medicine made me feel good.

So, you see, this is a natural process. It's a biological process. It happens spontaneously in many of us, like in my and Emily's lives. By recognizing and leveraging this, we can skip some of the trial and error of finding a different way and go straight to the most effective way to use our skills. By moving this process from sometimes happening unconsciously to happening consciously, we are fast-tracking the healing process, which is to say, fast-tracking the integration process.

The last big story of me finding ways to cope with my stuff using environmental factors was the years I spent in van life. It's not quite as obvious of a shift, so sharing it with you is important. There are many ways to add a variety of environments to your life.

Not everyone's strengthnesses are so overdeveloped that they need to find a whole new career or life path. That's what I needed to do. But that honestly also wasn't enough either. I needed more. This next section is the more. Many folks may not need to make extreme changes to their lives. Either because their trauma didn't make as massive of a strengthness, or because one way or another their strengthnesses have gotten a little less unwieldy as they do, over time. For these folk, a less dramatic approach may do the trick.

Van-Life Part Two: Environmental Prosthetics.

I love van life. I spent most of 2013-2020 living in a vehicle of some sort and I'm back at it yet again! The reason I love it so much was unknown to me at the beginning but eventually clicked. It does back yet again to that phrase "I'm *too much*." I've already described how I slowly changed this core belief over time.

Because "too much" is so common among CSA people, I want to talk about it from yet another angle here. It wasn't enough for me to adjust the way I thought about myself to change that narrative. It wasn't enough for me to change my mantras alone.

To successfully change the "too much" narrative I had, it took experience. To facilitate the experiences, I set up what I now call environmental prosthetics. Which are ways to manipulate my environment that set me up to feel the way I want to feel about myself to upgrade my self-concept.

Believing I was "too much" meant I felt extremely uncomfortable in any social setting. Alcohol was a way that I dealt with the feeling. Because I needed to present like a badass or not appear "weak," a straight-jacket for midwestern men, I did a lot of drinking at all social events.

We all know it doesn't take long for a person <u>who isn't too much to *become* too much under the influence of alcohol.</u> So that not only was alcohol a bad short-term plan, it was a worse long-term plan. I needed something else.

A more long-term fix eventually fell into my lap. It helped me so much. My first major *environmental prosthetic* was the ability to have my house everywhere! If I ever felt *off* or *"too much"* I could hide. I could retreat to my converted van, where I can't embarrass myself or get so dysregulated I say something I'll regret.

My van is a perfect example of an *environmental prosthetic*. It's honestly the *best* example because it hits so many of my *soft* spots. Having a van to retreat to allows me to remove myself from any situation I no longer want to be in. That helps me not feel trapped, which is triggering for me. Additionally, no one worries about me because they know I have my van. I worry about people worrying about me because part of my trauma is feeling like a burden. I don't want to be a burden. That might be my biggest fear in life.

An *environmental prosthetic* is something physical or tangible - like a van - that allows a CSA person to have the tools we need to facilitate us to live our best and most peaceful lives. *They allow us to maintain regulation of our nervous system* and keep an eye on our environment and our reactions. They help us feel like we have our trauma bases covered.

I have C-PTSD – So my trauma responses vary greatly depending on what was happening seconds to minutes to hours before. It feels like I have every classic trauma response conditioned into me, and I'm not always sure which one will pop out. Remember when I said runners never stop looking for exits, fighters never stop looking for a fight, and fawners never stop looking for friends? A good environmental prosthetic helps you have the things you need.

In my van, I have so many things that are helpful to me and my trauma. I have all of my favorite pastimes, which help soothe and regulate me. In there, I have my fantastic sound system to dance to, one of the best ways to move and resolve my anxious energy. I have my guitar to help me emote when I'm having big feelings but can't tell what the feeling is. I have a whole library of medical and acupuncture references. That not only helps me be and feel competent, but also makes me feel I belong with the "smart people" like I always wanted.

Whenever I get dysregulated, I can walk away, return to my van, and lay down for a bit of decompression and re-regulation. I'm free to do whatever I need to to regroup, and then, if I choose, I can return to re-engage later. All of my re-regulation strategies can be done with no resistance from the safety of my van.

Social engagement can be incredibly taxing on CSA people because of that whole hypervigilance thing. After social engagements, I need to have time alone to recoup. But funnily enough, I didn't even know that about myself until I had lived in my van for multiple years. I hadn't had an opportunity until then to find this out. It finally became clear as I became less permanently energetic due to aging. The price of not resting became more pronounced.

There are many ways to *adjust your environment* including a time and place in which you engage specifically to let your strengthnesses run free, as well as *environmental prosthetics* to help you have the support you need.

At first, I didn't know how much I needed the support of my van, a safe place to withdraw so that others leave me alone. A place I know is mine and respect as my space, but I could stay close and not feel rejected by the group, which is incredibly impactful.

You may already be doing this to some degree. You probably are. You may have a job in which you help people out of sticky situations. If so, but you still occasionally feel broken, you may not need to add an entirely new environment to your life.

It may suffice for your situation to become consciously aware of which skills you are using, where they came from, and reflect on those skills' impact on other people's lives. The simple recognition of that can make a profound shift in your self-concept.

If not, consider finding a soup kitchen or a tree planting group or some way to volunteer your time to people. You can find a job or shoot for a promotion that would allow you to use the skills you attained in chronic stress to be helpful to you instead of accidentally sabotaging yourself.

Changing your environment not just to use your skills but to provide yourself with the shameless support you need is also essential. My van did both for me! It allowed me to *travel and retreat* whenever possible. It let me get to the people who needed my skills in my pop-up clinics, as well as hide when I needed to.

My language there gives away a piece of info about myself. The fact that I still call it hiding instead of recuperating or relaxing or me time shows how much self-judgment still exists in me, even after ten years of this process. I hope you understand by now that I'm far from perfect. Like I said, I learned most of this through reflection. I only recently systemized it to use as I desire.

So don't beat yourself up. You've survived enough of that. Be shameless about your own needs. You've been shamed your whole life for having them. First, by those around you, but then your RAS took over and continued their work for them. Now, only you can undo that. The only way to do it is by putting yourself in real-world situations with focused, purposeful effort.

If you need to "hide" in your van, do it. If you need to go to the bathroom six times daily to cry it out, then do that. As a CSA person, the single most important thing is maintaining a well-regulated nervous system. Leveraging strengthnesses in appropriate environments as well as establishing *environmental prosthetics* for ourselves is how we facilitate that regulation. Be shameless about meeting your needs. It's the only way to truly be helpful to others.

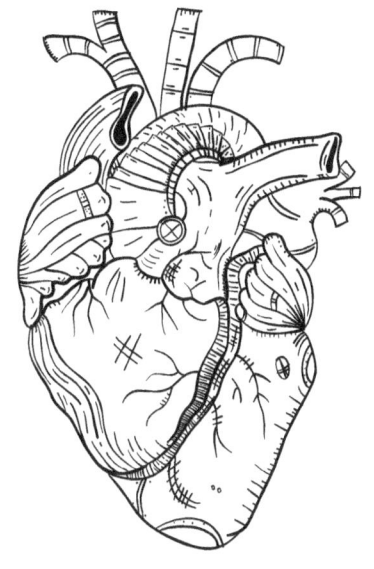

CHAPTER 16
REPROGRAMMING

Once we reach adulthood, we gain access to our higher brain functions. We gain access to more complicated neurological concepts like self-control, empathy and complex understanding. That's when we finally train our bodies to react differently in stressful situations.

But boy, is it hard. As adults, all those developmental windows we had access to in childhood are closed. In theory, their job is complete. To our brain, the programming is complete regardless if it's faulty. So, the innate ability of a young brain to adjust synapses through experience and learning isn't as readily available.

As far as your body is concerned, you know how to do everything you must to stay alive. And that's good enough for biology. Again our biology is focused on *survival*. It doesn't matter if you do those survival things well. You just need to do them well enough to survive. <u>If you want to thrive as a CSA person, you'll *have* to overcome some of your biological drives.</u>

Since the ability to reorganize our synaptic connections is not automatic as adults, there must be more than passive experiences to change our hardware. What is that process now? You know how your brain gets programmed - conditioning. Even passive experiences throughout those developmental windows automatically form and organize synapses and synaptic networks. Does that change once the plasticity isn't readily available?

Actually, no. Changing our hardware is basically the same process as building our hardware. But this time, we have our work cut out for us. Without those developmental windows granting us automatic access to neuroplasticity, making changes is more challenging. But it's not impossible.

Each of us has different habits and automations. We experience differing levels of dysregulation. There are people reading this whose hardware is a little buggy or *lags* a tad on occasion. For those folks, the reprogramming process, while more challenging than childhood, will struggle to change their programming less than others. As they have less, that demands change. Meanwhile, others' hardware seems to be constantly freezing, glitching, or crashing, and they always feel like they need to reboot.

If your hardware functions ok most of the time, you might just need a software update to fix bugs. If that's the case, all you need to do is download the software update, which is the equivalent of finding someone who embodies the changes you want to make.

Then, you - *download and install* - the update by simply spending time with them. That's the easiest way. After all, we are all the average of the five people we spend the most time with.

If you're less lucky like I was and can't find a role model for your behaviors, you'll have to do it the harder way. You are going to have to troubleshoot. Doing it this way takes much more time, attention, and effort, but it can be done. It is what I had to do.

TROUBLESHOOTING OUR WET COMPUTERS

Most of us have little to no knowledge of the hardware in our computers at home. We don't usually need to. We only learn what we need to, to make our computers functional enough to be used for whatever we use them for. Some people might know there is a motherboard, processor, graphics card, and cooling system. We might even know that the components are wired together in some kind of sequence, but that's probably about it. We usually know more about our software though.

If you work with computers, you probably know a few tricks about what to do when your computer freezes up or crashes. Most people know to close out open tabs, check their connection, and, if need be, restart the computer.

Yet, many of us need to learn how to take care of the incredible wet computer we live inside. When a CSA person gets overwhelmed, we often give up. When things we want lag too much, we disengage out of frustration. When we feel disconnected, we self-medicate.

But luckily, there are *analogs* for each of these in CSA people. When our brains lag, we can close tabs. The analog to this is reducing our expectations and cutting out less critical tasks. When we feel disconnected or alone, we can check our connection. The analog here is emotional connection. We can reach out to a friend. And when all else fails, we can force a restart. We can take a nap.

In early life, the brain is designed so that our most emotional experiences become hardware extremely quickly because neuronal plasticity is naturally available to us.

But that also means if you experienced lots of chronic stress during your development, which for an infant being around consistent unpleasant emotions absolutely counts, especially under the age of three, that emotional software creates hardware designed by and for an environment of chronic, stressful and unpleasant experiences.

Since we are meant to play out the algorithms of our early life for the rest of our lives, our hardware will have errors in its operations in *any environment* that's *not unpleasant and stressful!* I don't know about you, but I try not to spend too much time in unpleasant or stressful environments—except when I do it on purpose, to exercise my strengthness puppies.

The best way to handle our hardware errors when we have a lot of them is to surround ourselves with people we want to be more like. Just by being themselves, they're modeling the behavior we want to see more of in ourselves.

Say you want to be less reactive in general. Getting yourself a therapist is a great way to observe how non-reactive humans can be! Therapists spend a lot of time practicing non-reactivity in school.

Second, if we only have a few things we want to change in our hardware, we can troubleshoot them individually. Which means dealing with our issues as they come up. If we feel disconnected, we can call a friend to feel more connected instead of letting our minds tell us everyone hates us. That tape is played out.

We can minimize overstimulation by simplifying our lives by focusing only on the top two most important things on our list. And on the really bad days, we can take a nap! Those things all help keep us well-regulated.

Keeping with the theme of this book – context. The best advice is always contextual. Since, again, I don't know you nearly as well as I would like, I can't give you personal advice. But I do know most people tend to lean one way or another as a baseline. If you know your baseline, you can have at least a general idea of what direction you might want to adjust toward.

BASELINES

Everyone has a baseline. Your baseline is the state you are in when you are at rest. For our purposes were less interested in the resting state but the direction our stress responses take us when we leave our resting state. Your hardware determines this. Specifically, your mid- and low-brain hardware determine the most considerable portion of your baseline. Since our brain's hardware is 90% developed by the time we are three, we've only about a 10% margin for change over the next 30 or so years.

Since the middle brain is in charge of processing our emotions, it's our middle brain that we need to change. It's our lower and middle brain together that establish our baselines. Since our plasticity windows are closed as adults, how do we change the midbrain? The answer is from the top down. Unfortunately, that takes time, and maintaining *consistent effort while feeling stressed.*

You have probably heard the term "top-down regulation" floating around. What is meant by that is that those later developed higher brain functions must learn to regulate the mid and lower brain - emotional reaction - functions.

The trouble here happens when the midbrain is fired up. When we are highly emotional, access to the top part of that *top-down regulation* can be all but impossible. When we are in highly emotional states, we can't always choose what we do with those emotions.

Depending on what your strategy for surviving your particular cocktail of chronic stress was, most bodies choose one of two fundamental strategies as a baseline stress response.

Hypo and Hyper Reactivity

Everyone with trauma falls into one of two basic categories. They are either hypo (under) reactive or hyper (over) reactive. Hyperreactive people blow up on others, while hypoactive people implode on themselves or just shut down. It could even be viewed as anxious people (hyperreactive) versus depressed (hyporeactive.) Each strategy is biological and has their own costs and benefits.

We all know people who launch themselves into frantic action as soon as something unexpected happens. We also know someone who shuts down at the first sign of bad news. They could be described as anxious or depressive people, respectively. Maybe not clinically, but many of us are certainly on that spectrum to one degree or another.

This hyper and hypo reactivity concept relates to the F's we covered earlier. Those Fs are broken up into two basic strategies for dealing with stress—activated coping, i.e., fight/flight – or passive coping strategies Freeze/Fawn.

Whichever strategy we lean on most will fit into one of the two piles: the activated stress pile or the passive stress response pile—making each of us hyper-reactive if our responses are activated (fight/flight) or hypo-reactive (freeze/fawn) if their passive responses.

Most of the stories that whisper in our ears, "You're broken," have something to do with sins of omission or commission. People with hypo-reactive baselines are usually guilty of what my very Christian upbringing would call sins of omission. They didn't do or say something when they felt they ought to have. While, hyperreactive, anxious types tend to open their mouths when they might have preferred to keep them closed. That's the commission part. *Committing* an act, we didn't want to.

For these folks, whichever party you belong to, team over function or team under function, both have to adjust their baselines. Team hyper needs to learn how to ramp down, and team hypo needs to learn how to ramp up!

Personally, I'm a hyperreactive person in general. I probably would have been even without my trauma, but I'll never know. I've said for years that I don't have fight, flight, freeze. I have *fight, fight and fuck you*! Which is still hilarious to me, but it also doesn't work out all that well in some situations. When your response to everything is to fight, you tend to create enemies quickly. So, I had to learn how to ramp down my reactivity to make fewer enemies.

My goal was to take my generally hyper-reactive system and down-regulate it. It could be the other way around for you. Since our hardware is designed to be pretty damn permanent after those developmental windows close, any permanent positive change is going to come from conscious, consistent effort from our PFC.

When I was in the Honor Guard, I was forced to develop a more hypoactive baseline in one realm and had limited success. There were things I could relatively easily pay no heed to (suppression). Things that didn't bother me that deeply bothered most people. *Death* was at the top of that list because of my burying people for a living. A hypoactive baseline is usually hypoactive in a particular set of circumstances but not in all. In other circumstances, we may be the opposite.

We have to identify our baseline reactivity for as many aspects of life as we can and try to average them out to get a good read on and then adjust the entire system as a whole.

Each time we make the harder decision, repeating that decision gets easier. Each time you think a thought, it is easier to think it again. That's the way brain networks function and exactly why consistency is key.

Anytime you executive-function (PFC) yourself into making a good decision when a less effective or more destructive decision is what your hardware really wants, it becomes easier to do the same thing again the next time!

This is how the "top-down process" happens on a neurological level. This software (decisions) influences and becomes hardware (default neural programming) over time.

Lastly, it's essential to understand that activating neural plasticity once those windows are closed, takes *stress*.

It's all because of this other neurotransmitter called acetylcholine, but don't worry. You don't need to remember this one. It's just the compound that marks a synapse for up-dating! And acetylcholine is released when we are focused. Focus happens automatically when we feel threatened for obvious reasons. Without a threat it's harder.

Without a real threat we have to manufacture a similar level of stressed focus to mark a synapse for changes. This means that each change you want to make will require you to *feel stressed*, and you must push through it.

This is easier for hyperreactive people and harder for hyporeactive ones. Please hear me when I say both types *will* want to give up. Please don't. Hyporeactive folks might feel it's not worth the stress and reach toward something comforting. While hyperreactive folks might search for a different, more dopaminergic type of adventure.

If the strengthness you have predisposes you toward shutting down when you feel stressed, even if it's for good reasons, you will have to learn to differentiate between the feeling of danger that often accompanies stress and the stress itself.

Feeling stressed and not giving up is required to mark something in the brain as important enough to change. I told you it was going to be extra work. Marking a synapse for plasticity so it can update is a *stressful experience by default.* It's how our bodies are designed. It's so worth it though, and with practice, you will be able to recognize the mental resistance that you feel as a necessary step to making the changes you want to make.

A FELT SENSE OF SAFETY

The counterpoint to this is yet another catch-22. *C'est la Vie! Feeling stressed and not giving up* is mandatory to mark a synapse for change. But it's also equally important to understand that a "felt sense of safety" is required for learning.

I'm all about pushing through the hard stuff. It's harder for me, as a hyperreactive person, to remember that I can push all I want, but if I don't also feel safe while doing it, I will learn nothing. Again, this is just the way biology works. And it makes evolutionary sense.

We don't need to conscious learn fear conditioning. That's an innate survival strategy build into our biology as a default. Conscious learning things, especially pleasant things, or things that challenge our preconceived notions, is not a biological default.

If your great, great, great, great, grandma was running from a cougar and ran past a berry bush? Do you think her brain would track precisely where the bush was? Of course not. She was focused, she was present, but she was not safe.

Suppose she was wandering with the other Gatherers and found the same patch. Does she have a better chance of remembering it? Of course she does.

This is why I loved Emergency medicine so much. The first step to any situation as a first responder is *BSI, body safety index.* The first thing you are trained to do when you arrive on scene as an EMT or first responder is to say out loud, "BSI, is my scene safe?" A dead medic can't help anyone.

Evaluating and understanding my level of safety before entering any scenario is fundamental. I don't care whether it's a house fire, a gunshot victim, or Thanksgiving. To this day, I still do what's called pre-coping in DBT, Dialectical Behavioral Therapy. I look ahead at the situation and try to guess the likely things to go wrong. Family gatherings are a perfect place for that strategy. But it doesn't end there.

Evaluating what my actual levels of safety will be, in upcoming scenarios is one way I make sure I can be present while in it and learn during the interactions that would otherwise just be stressful.

So, if you're going to visit your family for the holidays, evaluate beforehand if there is any chance that the interaction you are dreading will cause you actual physical harm. If the answer is no, then walk into it knowing that whatever dysregulation you feel at your racist uncle or your nitpicking father is only uncomfortable and not actually dangerous. That will help your mid and low brain stay regulated.

You must stick to it, through the hard stuff. But it's equally important that you prioritize your own safety. We're simply built in that if we want to learn we must have a felt sense of safety. Whatever you must do to make yourself feel safe, is good enough. Just make sure you actually *feel* safe and you're not just *telling* yourself to feel it.

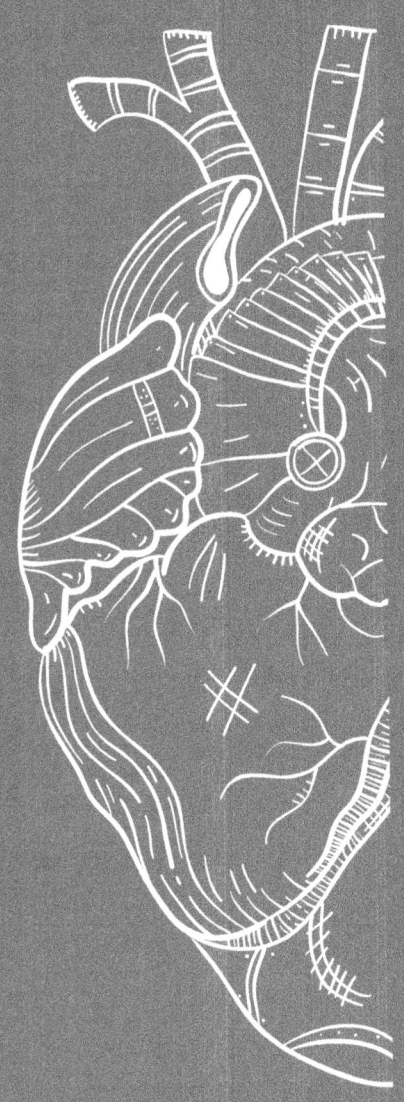

SECTION 4

PRACTICES FOR THE PATH

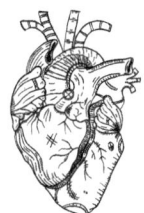

Congratulations! You made it to the final section of the book! Now you know:

- You aren't broken. You're chronic stress adapted
- the biology behind why you once thought you were broken
- the changes that happened in your body as a result of chronic stress in early life
- how those changes affect you now
- what environmental prosthetics are & how to use them
- which strengthnesses you developed from adapting to your chronic stress
- a place or two where you can utilize those skills to your advantage!

The conceptual heavy lifting is done! You've got everything you need to know to make any change you want to make in your life! But we all know that making a change is easy. Sticking to it is what is hard. So, the rest of this book is about the - sticking to it - part.

No matter how good our intentions are or even how excited we feel about the new changes we want to make in our lives, sticking to those changes can be challenging. Honestly, it's usually the hardest part. Humans love novelty. Making changes, especially seemingly massive changes, ticks that novelty box. At first, it can feel easy-breezy. Once the novelty wears off, I don't want you slipping back into old habits.

It's inevitable that you will eventually and probably repeatedly. It's a part of the process. When the novelty wears off, that's when the *consistency battle begins*. The real battle is maintenance. Maintaining a well-regulated nervous system, as we've discussed, is essential, but maintaining some habits of behavior that help us maintain the adjustments we want to make to our baseline.

When we start the maintenance part of this work, we start the long slog. After reviewing the specific brain changes CSA people have in section 2, you know the importance of consistent inputs.

Maintaining consistent interventions and interruptions to our old patterns ensures the things we want to stick around do. Thus begins the uphill battle against our biological programming.

So, for good measure and to start you off right, I want to sprinkle a few more things on top. In this section, you're going to learn about how to take care of your future with:

- Creating compassionate narratives
- Asking for help
- Setting healthy boundaries
- Identifying and setting non-negotiable boundaries
- Practicing mindfulness
- Moving your body
- Take good notes
- The power of service

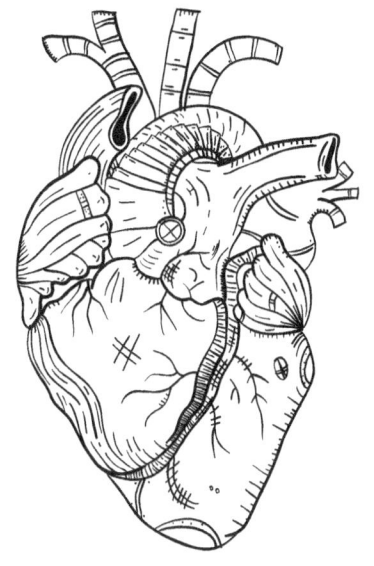

CHAPTER 17
COMPASSIONATE NARRATIVES

The single most difficult and important thing I struggled to learn in my journey is finding compassionate narratives—especially for me. Everything that humans understand, we understand as part of a story. The story itself, as well as how that story is told, is a narrative.

Trauma is not what happened to you; it's the story you tell yourself about the event.

> "Trauma happens in the absence of an empathetic witness."
> Gabor Mate' MD, Trauma expert

To start integrating all of us, we must make it a regular practice to find compassionate narratives. Everyone is different; for some people, *it may be easiest* to start with finding *compassionate narratives for others*. It was easier for me that way. I didn't find much self-compassion until I found compassion for others.

Try this the next time you are upset with someone at work; try to find a narrative that is compassionate to them. Please stick with me. This may seem like a silly example, but it's a good one. This whole book is a bit heavy. It is about childhood trauma, after all. But practicing these skills in seemingly silly places allows us to practice so we can use them when it matters.

Say someone ate your lunch. It would be easy to assume that whoever ate your lunch is a total jerk. It is easy to assume it was on purpose. Unfortunately, being mad at the phantom sandwich thief isn't going to get your sandwich back. But now you are hungry, and you have no sandwich.

To practice finding a compassionate narrative, try coming up with a story that could explain why your sandwich is gone that is compassionate toward the thief. Maybe someone was not paying attention, and maybe if you ask, you can figure out who it was, and they will give you their lunch in exchange.

Just out of curiosity, at any point, did you think, "Well, I guess I shouldn't have left my sandwich at the work fridge?" Or "Well, did I have it labeled?" These are ways to discharge the pain of losing the sandwich that discharges it at *yourself.* If this is what your mind came up with, I want you to create a compassionate narrative for yourself.

If you can't remember whether you labeled your lunch, a person with less trauma might go, "Oh shoot, I forgot to label it!! And then they're off for a quick grab-and-go bite without a second thought.

A hyporeactive CSA person might very well say something like, "Well, I'm the dumbass who didn't label my sandwich, I guess I'm not eating today." Does this story sound familiar? I couldn't count all the times I've done this type of thing to myself if I tried. Another hyperactive CSA person might have the opposite reaction and think that someone is out to get them and make a massive scene about their missing sandwich and put up missing sandwich posters.

One time, I went hiking with some friends. It was a last-minute but strenuous hike. I had little time to pack, so I threw a few things together. I left behind my headphones, water and all my food. Rather than ask to share with one of my hiking buddies, I kept it to myself, to the point that I was so weak from a lack of food and water that I slowed us all down.

That's when one of them said something, to which I explained, "No, it's fine, I don't need your food. I'm the one who forgot my stuff. It's my failure and my problem to deal with." Never mind the fact that I was slowing us all down. So, it was, in fact, their problem too.

Do you see how blind I was to the reality of the situation because of my fixation on what I messed up? What I was missing here was self-compassion. A more compassionate narrative for myself could have made the entire situation more enjoyable for us all.

These reactions are not usually a conscious thing. They were programmed into us too. At some point, we learned to survive by taking responsibility for things we shouldn't. If that protector of "taking responsibility" gets too big for his britches, it can put us in situations like this, where we take so much responsibility for not labeling our Tupperware that we excuse the loss of the sandwich as the price we must pay for our stupidity. That is ridiculous! Even as it's painful and true.

So, try coming up with a different compassionate narrative for yourself. Narratives provide us with perspectives to try on, like sunglasses.

HOW TO FIND COMPASSIONATE NARRATIVES

1. Make up a story that puts the subject in a positive light
2. Try the narrative on like sunglasses and see how it feels. Is it reasonable?
3. If it's not reasonable, change it! Try a new story!
4. Rinse and repeat!

Try on as many narratives as you need. Maybe you were in a hurry and didn't notice it wasn't labeled. Maybe it's "Even if I didn't label my lunch, I didn't deserve for it to be eaten." The more narratives you try on, the better. The best part is you only need **one** compassionate narrative for it to matter. So keep at it.

Trying on many narratives is a good practice and a protective factor for CSA folks because our default programming is quite strong. Trying on new narratives and perspectives alters our neural networks.

For me, a go-to narrative that often pops up is something like "I don't need nobody." I know that when I start thinking that way, I am dysregulated, not just because of the use of the double negative either. But because I'm hearing the narrative of one of my already identified strengthnesses: the autonomous lone wolf, aka hyper-independence.

He, like all strengthnesses, has a singular narrative. And when that part of us gets going, it's very hard, if not damned impossible, to stop it. Which means we get stuck in one narrative - our strengthnesses narratives. Each strengthness has its narrative.

By practicing trying on other narratives like sunglasses, we get to discharge a lot of the frustration of a situation when we find one that fits. The practice of finding compassionate narratives also helps us not get locked into one narrative, one way of thinking or being. Being stuck in one narrative while the rest of the world thinks there's room for multiple is part of what makes us feel broken.

Try this at home, at work, with your kids. You already do it with people you love, if mostly subconsciously. We tend not to get as mad at our good-hearted friends because we know them well enough to know that whatever they did, we assume their motivation wasn't vindictive or malicious. By giving our friends the benefit of the doubt, we have a much more peaceful experience.

You'll probably get upset if you get hit in the side of the head with a basketball. It hurts. If you look in the direction the ball came from and see someone falling, you probably assume that they did it by accident, and you feel less unpleasant than you would if you looked and saw someone glaring at you, and you believe they did it on purpose.

Though the pain in your face would be more or less the same either way, the rest of you could be upset the whole day because they *purposefully* hit you in the face.

Finding a compassionate narrative is not just for the person you're narrating for either. It's a tool to help you regulate yourself. I mean it. Just like the basketball. How do you feel when you believe someone purposefully slighted you versus if it was an accident?

It's usually much easier to deal with an accidental pain, and it doesn't cause the same magnitude of reaction. Compassionate narratives are at the heart of healing for CSA people. Boy, do we need them for ourselves?

Another place where it really matters is when we look into our pasts. Every person who identifies enough with its title to read this book probably has memories in the deep, dark recesses of their minds. Ones that are purposefully rarely brought to light.

You believed pieces of you were unlovable because there was no empathetic presence there to provide you with a compassionate narrative to tell you otherwise.

The dark recesses of our minds are still dark because we believe there isn't room or reason for compassion for those pieces.
Compassion and understanding are the light.

By practicing compassionate narratives in our lives, for ourselves and others, we are practicing the exact thing that we need to clean out those recesses. By trying on narratives like sunglasses, you actively build the skills and perspectives you desire to upgrade.

Whenever you are ready, face those dark recesses and shine some compassion on yourself in those cobweb-filled corners. When you do this, you will know beyond a shadow of a doubt that you are not now, nor have you ever been broken. You made it through hard things, and no one at the time was able to make you feel like they gave a shit. At least not the ones who mattered most.

COMPASSIONATE NARRATIVE EXERCISE:

It's time to put the pieces together again. This process is more straightforward for my clients in my coaching practice than in this format. But we'll do our best here. The in-person practice would go something like this.

The client shares an experience with me just like the one you wrote out in finding your strengthness Exercise 4. They describe a situation that feels like evidence of their brokenness. Then, I reflect on their statement to ensure I understand their version correctly. Then, I reword their narrative for them in a compassionate way.

This process has to include two aspects:

The new narrative must be #1 True & #2 Compassionate.

I reflect to the client another narrative for their story that they can try on based on the science we covered in section 2. By focusing on the truths we have learned so far and using those truths as the foundations for our narratives, rather than how we feel or think of ourselves, we can objectively see what happened.

Now you know many reasons you are wired the way you are. You understand why it is you do the things you do. So, all that's left is to use that information to justify dropping the judgment. CSA people are excellent at justifications of all sorts, as I'm sure you know.

We can justify almost anything. We have had to find justifiable excuses for our whole lives, beginning with excusing the chronic stress that formed us. The one area that we suck at justifying is justifying any opinion that says we don't suck!

That's why having someone there with you when you do this the first couple of times can be very helpful. It can be an insightful, compassionate friend, a coach, or a therapist. But it can be done successfully by one's self as well.

In person, I put words in my clients' mouths. I will speak for them, narrating their story using those new truths as critical perspectives. Then, I have them repeat the narrative in their own words, keeping anything that feels right and changing anything that doesn't.

In this way, we reshape their perspective of what happened in a way that is both accurate and fair to them. If this kind of reframing had happened at the time of our exposure to our traumatic situations and chronic stress, we would carry less trauma inside us. These are doing for us now what the variables in the resiliency questionnaire did or would have done had we had them back when we needed them most.

Resiliency comes from, in part, our ability to second-guess our own automated story. The unfortunate reality for CSA people is that our narrative defaults to being something about us being at fault.

MY FRIEND REN

For example, a friend of mine, Ren, came to visit me recently, and she had just gone through a rough conversation with her boyfriend. Like most of my favorite people, Ren has a hell of a story. She is an incredible person with profound insight and a capability to hold a depth and weight uncommon for people with fewer traumas in their lives. She shared a story that she was kind enough to let me share with you.

She and her boyfriend had known each other for a few years but had only been dating for about six months. She hadn't been transparent with him about her traumatic past yet, but she had reasons. On this night, she came clean about it all. All the crap from her past. She told him everything all at once, which is admittedly a rough way to do it and was part of why she felt twisted about it.

He responded wonderfully. Understandably, he was taken aback some because Ren has quite the story. He was in shock a little and felt confused. But he said he would take some time to integrate or come to terms with the news. He even said he would find a therapist to talk to about it.

To me, that was a tremendous response. But Ren was still struggling with it due to her past. She felt she had screwed everything up because things were "too good" or "too quiet." That *is* what a broken person does, after all.

Every CSA person knows this feeling and situation intimately. We often have had moments when things were good, we stirred the pot.

There is a belief that permeates CSA people. It says when things are good, we always screw it up. I have a few things to say about this perspective. Although that is most certainly something that can and does happen. It usually happens early in our integration journey, but we eventually grow out of it.

Ren is no longer in the early stages of recognizing and integrating her trauma. Not even close. She's pretty insightful in her processes. But, she was in a significantly dysregulated state because of the emotional weight of the situation. As a CSA person, we know now that makes accurate perception and recall of events difficult.

So, I did what I usually do: I asked for more details. The demons are always in the details. So, I had her walk me through her experience of the whole day.

She told me she had a craniosacral treatment earlier that day, which brought up a lot of stuff for her that she was sorting through. It stirred up lots of feelings and concepts that she felt needed to be shared.

When she walked me through the details of the story, which was only a few days old, so it was still pretty fresh in her mind, I reflected a few things back to her that I picked up on that she did not see at the time.

She revealed the treatment was a stimulus to open up to her boyfriend about her past. She also initially told me that the conversation was a dinner conversation. But it turned out it wasn't. She actually waited until *after* they had a nice dinner out to open up. She told him everything on the ride home, not at dinner.

So what I did with her was present a different narrative than the easy, go-to self-blaming; things were good, so I had to screw them up, a narrative that nearly all CSA people use all too often. I just pointed out a few details that opened up another option. The fact that she waited until after dinner to share her story with him, I thought, was thoughtful and mature. In contrast, she had forgotten that important bit.

The revealing of our traumatic pasts as CSA people can be terrifying. We have no control over how another person will react to our story. The more interested and attached we are to that person, the scarier it is. So, she made a wise, albeit seemingly subconscious, decision to wait until things were good to have the conversation.

All I did for her was point out that if we don't have these types of conversations when things are good, the alternative is to do it during a fight. And we all know how well that works out.

Upon prodding into other similar situations in her past, she said she had an experience with her last partner in which she opened up to him very quickly - too quickly. It was the cause of a major point of contention early in their relationship. One she thought put a permanent chip on the shoulder of that relationship.

When someone tells you on day two of dating all the details of their past, the abuses they suffered and continue to deal with in their own life and as a result of their family it can undoubtedly be a put-off.

Because of this event, she had decided that she wouldn't just dump all that on a person on the second date in future relationships. Which is a smart move if you want the relationship to stand much of a chance. So, here she is a few years later with a new love interest, and she smartly kept those cards a little closer to her chest this time to prevent the same thing from happening again.

She waited to share the weighty stuff with him. Maybe six months was too long to wait, but there's no way to know that for sure. So, speculation is useless. Regardless, the decision to wait was reasonable and logical based on recent, legitimate personal experience.

As we covered before, in her dysregulated state, she couldn't even see this poignant detail. Once she did, along with the recognition that waiting until after dinner was, in fact a wise decision, she was able to put all the pieces together for herself and rewrite her narrative accurately and compassionately.

This was a situation that, before the reframing, to Ren felt like proof of her brokenness. Once she took the time to calmly reflect on the details of the situation, which, as we learned, is harder for CSA people due to the changes to our memory and threat systems, especially when dysregulated. She saw that what she did was almost perfect!

Of course, it's possible to argue she should have told him sooner. It's also equally possible that telling him sooner wouldn't have changed the result. As I said, his response was beautiful.

He was a little shocked, but he immediately went to "what can I do to make this situation as good as it can be?" Including saying he wanted to find a therapist to understand her better. So, it's equally as valid to argue that his response was as good as it could have been, regardless of *when* she told him.

As far as I'm concerned, wishing we would have done things better ought to be reserved for situations when the outcome was an undesirable one. In this case, it wasn't. Ren, in her dysregulated state, was beating herself up, plain and simple.

She learned that two days is too short and six months arguably may have been longer than necessary. But for her, the takeaway was to make this entire process more conscious. Because if she has to go through this process again, she wants to be more purposeful about sharing this information with potential partners or love interests.

The key to this is that this story, before reevaluation, was proof of her brokenness. Once seen through the lens of a compassionate narrative for her as a CSA person, that is to say, the accounting for common CSA factors like the effects of dysregulation, self-blame, fawning, the changes in the memory and threat systems, she proved she is more than just not broken. She handled the situation *exceptionally well! She didn't do anything wrong at all but initially felt that she had screwed up massively.*

This is the process CSA people must focus on for ourselves. This kind of situation happens to CSA people every day. This probably happens to you many times a week, but you don't realize you are blaming yourself for doing nothing wrong. Many times, it's just a situation that, like in Ren's case, was out of her control, and the situation itself has an inherent friction to it.

CSA people automatically find ways to blame themselves when they feel that friction, even when it's not their fault or responsibility. Finding compassionate narratives for ourselves is how we retrain our brains to see ourselves as CSA instead of broken. It's how we take back our power.

We only need to repeat this process for these types of situations over and over until we do it automatically. We too quickly blame ourselves when we are dysregulated. Just like in this story, the outcome was positive, yet she carried so much pain, shame, and fear about it that she thought she ruined everything.

Finding a *compassionate narrative for herself* was all she needed, to let go of the pain, fear, and shame that came part and parcel with her dysregulation over the situation with her boyfriend.

This is what I want you to do for yourselves, too. Go back to exercise 4 and find another perspective you can take that is true and compassionate. Start with the factors that we have covered so far. If you were dysregulated in the situation, think about how dysregulation affects you and where it came from in that particular instance.

Look into the hours preceding the event. Remember the effects on your memory system. Is there something you forgot at that moment that would have been helpful? If so, that's trauma in action. That's not your fault. But again, it is your responsibility. Next time, maybe try to be just a little more mindful.

Was there a substantial reward somewhere in your story? What was the reward? Think in terms of biological and logical rewards. Most of the time, thanks to our trauma, our biological rewards are not always harmonious with the rewards we logically desire. So look closely.

In your story, were you unable to put on the brakes? Remember that you have a more challenging time braking because of the effects of chronic stress on the vagus nerve. In this case, being more in touch with your body can illuminate the earliest signs of dysregulation, preventing you from needing your E-brake because you were able to let off the gas.

Try writing out your new accurate and compassionate narrative in the lines below.

_____

_____

_____

_____

_____

_____

_____

_____

_____

_____

_____

_____

_____

_____

If you need more room, grab a sheet of paper or go to the back of the book to write out the details surrounding the event again. Be as detailed as possible. Then, when you're done, flip that page over, and write out your new story on the back. Write out your compassionate narrative. Make sure it's compassionate and accurate. When you come up with a story, make it simple. It helps to have a balance between the old and new story.

The broken narratives that we fall into are quippy. They're generic and easy to toss out. So, we need something just as easy and quippy to replace it.

Ren's was something like, "I stirred the pot because things were too good and calm." After all, that's what I always do." Which can be counterbalanced by something like, "I was burned by sharing too soon, so I purposefully waited to share the heaviest stuff this time." That is a compassionate narrative. It was a rough conversation, yes, because talking about trauma is always uncomfortable, but he deserved to know. Maybe it wasn't perfect, but it was good enough.

If you're like me, this might be hard for you. I have always hated "good enough." Good enough, in my experience, was the excuse given to justify the laziness and incompetence of people I was forced to depend on that consistently failed me. Yet, good enough is exactly the goal we must strive for in our compassionate narratives.

Ren's boyfriend's reaction may not have been the fantasy reaction she wanted, which might sound something like, "Oh my god! I can't believe all that happened to you! I'm so sorry! You're so strong! I had no idea! I never would have guessed! I'm so glad you told me. You're amazing! Let's have incredible sex!"

The reality was that he said, and I'm paraphrasing here, "This is a lot. I need time to process what all this means. I want to talk to a professional about how to navigate all this." To me, that response is just incredible. It's not the fantasy answer, but the reality never is - That's why it's a fantasy!

Her goal in sharing this information with him was not just to be totally honest and transparent but also to have him respond in a way that wouldn't make him run away screaming. That goal was certainly achieved.

Which then feeds right into remembering the importance of our goals. Not just big goals about the direction of our lives but our more minor, everyday goals too. Like becoming aware of what we want out of a conversation. By becoming aware of the goal for an interaction, the feeling of brokenness immediately dissipates when we recognize the goal was achieved in some way – in this case- he didn't run away from Ren screaming.

Isn't it funny how we do this to ourselves? This is just one example of a CSA person handling their trauma very well. And yet, she still left the situation feeling like she screwed things up massively - *a classic CSA move.*

In exercise 4 of finding your strengthnesses, what was your goal? What was the thing you were trying to accomplish? Did you accomplish it? Not perfectly, of course. But did you accomplish it at all? Is there any way you could compassionately reframe it now, that makes whatever you did poorly, good enough? Knowing what you know now about your nervous system, what narratives might you come up with for yourself that are true and compassionate?

It's all CSA folks' default programming to obsessively look at what we did wrong and what we can improve or should have done better. It's easy for us to see our screwups. That's built-in. The skill we have to train is to *put the same amount of time and effort into looking at what we did right.* We have to spend as much time cheering ourselves as we do criticizing.

But sometimes that's not so easy. Doing this exercise can be challenging by one's self. Some people can reconfigure their experiences in ways that are compassionate for themselves, but they're rare. The rest of us will probably need help. If you need help, *ask for it.*

ASKING FOR HELP

You can stop making that face now. I know you don't want to. I know you don't like to. I know a relatively large portion of most CSA personalities are predicated on *never* having to ask for help. Too bad. That's a basic bitch, biological response. It's time to upgrade that biological response and make it logical. It's time to grow up and learn *when* to ask for help.

Infants of nearly every species are born with their most basic biological survival instincts more or less intact. Baby turtles are born able to flap their flippers, waddle and skooch their way from their nests to the ocean. Baby giraffes can run within 10 hours of being born, which is a useful skill for the uncoordinated, lanky prey of lions. Human babies, too, display our most important instincts almost immediately after birth. As soon as we are born, we cry for help.

This implies that asking for help *may* be the most important human survival instinct. As infants, we can't even regulate our own body temperature. Without mom or some caretaker there to warm us, we would die in minutes to hours.

I know *asking for help* is at the top of the list of least favorite things for many CSA folks. It was for me. Until I truly began integrating the information shared with you in this book, asking for help was basically my least favorite thing in the world.

It's still high on my list, but at least it's not at the top anymore. I'm working on it. That's because I assumed problems were my fault and responsibility alone to respond to. I was sure that asking for help would make whoever I asked think I was too weak to do it, too stupid to figure it out, too lazy to try, or was just looking to pass off my responsibility to someone else.

You've heard some of my story. Can you imagine my closeted lesbian, midwestern factory worker mother's reaction when I asked her for help? She flat-out told me she couldn't help me with my homework in school. Even if she could have, she had too many struggles of her own to deal with. She didn't have the time or bandwidth. I saw her tough it out and suck it up every day. You know what I never saw her do— not even once? I never saw her ask for help.

But asking for help is paramount for us all. We might need to ask for help for a few reasons, and we will cover some of them in this section.

The *first reason* is that *trauma is isolating*. We have talked about biological v logical decisions. Turning biological decisions into logical ones lies at the heart of recovery for the CSA person.

Traumas' tendency to isolate us is a biological decision. It's a primary imperative to seek pleasure and avoid pain. Trauma is painful, so it's only natural that we want to avoid that pain as well as the people who brought it. But avoidance as a general strategy will never allow us to thrive.

The *second reason* we need to learn to ask for help is because we sometimes need help *reality-checking*. Due to our negative self-focus imprinted on our nervous system, we have an unfair, unbalanced view of ourselves. So, when something in our life goes sideways, that negative self-view is magnified even more, and we are often unable to see an interpretation of the events that's accurate or fair to us.

In these instances, we must reach out to a friend or someone we trust to help us *reality check* to provide a more balanced and honest narrative, as I did for Ren in the last section.

The *final reason* we need to ask for help is because it forces us to *interact* with the world around us. This goes back to the isolating nature of trauma. We don't like asking for help because it displays our vulnerability. Our biology doesn't like that. Sure, it would be nice to be at the top of whatever proverbial pile we are part of. But knowing where we lie in the grand scheme of things is a comfort. At least compared to not knowing it is. For primates like us, even being at the absolute bottom of a hierarchy is less stressful than not knowing where we are.

UNCERTAIN SOCIAL STATUS IS STRESSFUL.

There is fascinating data on when baboons are most stressed and it's all about losing context. Dr Robert Sapolsky performed the study as a young scientist. One of his summer jobs was to watch a group of African baboons and note when they exhibited the most signs of stress, then tranquilize them and take some labs to confirm stress levels.

The most stressed a baboon can be is when he gets knocked down the hierarchy - a social demotion - when he isn't sure where his place is at all, according to blood panels. Even the baboons on the very bottom of the social hierarchy were more relaxed than those recently demoted and, therefore, uncertain of their social status, according to blood levels.

What a cool way to show how extremely stressful uncertainty is for us large primates. Isolation removes us from our social hierarchies, and if it happens long enough, we don't know where we fit in. That uncertainty is dysregulating, especially when we try to reenter the hierarchy.

I have so many times been in a dark place and wanted nothing more than just to be welcomed into a group of people. I desperately wanted to be with the group, but I wouldn't even attempt because joining the group would place me somewhere in that social hierarchy.

I had been so far removed from it for so long that wondering where I might land, what role I would play, and how people would like me or not like me was so scary to me that I, more often than not, opted out of the very thing – interaction- that would have helped me. Of course, at first, it was just a feeling that I was only later able to recognize for what it was.

You and I have every reason to isolate and mistrust the people around you. That's a biological reaction. But to thrive, you still need to ask for help. There's a valid reason for all the horrible things in the world. You know where this fear, and yes, it is a fear, is coming from.

It's up to you to do something better than react. That's what responsibility is - _the ability to respond_. When you were young, you needed help because you couldn't help yourself. If you asked and help was refused, in a very real way, infant you faced threat of death.

To this day, when I have to ask for help for something big, I still have that same fear. It may not be very conscious for you, but often, that feeling is still there. That vague fear that's a little too strong to be reasonable still lingers.

But you're tough and resilient and don't have to ask for help. You can figure it out like you always do. And indeed, you can do that. The skills and resiliency you have earned in this life grant you that.

If you can accomplish a thing by yourself, you will. And honestly, that's just fine! Because, like everything else in this book and life, it's all about context. If you CAN do it alone, you don't *need* to ask for help.

But how many truly wonderful things were formed in isolation? Most, if not all, meaningful advancements humans have made for thousands of years were group efforts. Civilizations, bridges, railroads, and the internet were all group efforts.

Even having babies is a group effort. Unless you live somewhere where you can own slaves or have the financial independence to pay wages for everyone you would need to accomplish your worthwhile undertaking, you are going to have to ask for help in one way or another at some point or another.

One way or another, every single major break and advancement that has helped humankind was a group effort. Either all at once, like the Amish raising a barn in a day. Or over time, through the written word, adding to our scientific understanding. Stuff like math and physics have been compiled generation after generation, leading to more and more exciting breakthroughs by standing on the shoulders of giants like Isaac Newton.

I'm not saying you need to ask for help all the time. I'm saying you need to be able to ask for help *when you could use it*. So you don't slow down your friends on what could have been a fun day hike because you're unprepared, hyper-independent, self-punishing and stubborn. Don't let your desire to be independent prevent you from doing all you want. And definitely don't let it stop you from, say, phoning a friend when you're upset.

REALITY CHECKING

Reality-checking is a crucial intersection of maintaining a regulated nervous system and asking for help. Essentially, as CSA people, when something unusual happens in our life, if we have a **big** reaction to it, it often serves us well to *phone a friend* for a "reality check," as I mentioned in the last section. We expect our friends to be honest with us and help us figure out what's actually happening and what's a dramatized trauma perspective.

A reality check consists of comparing your inner reality and assumptions to what's objectively happening in the outer world around you. If what you feel inside and what you are noticing outside yourself matches up, you're good.

Although, as CSA people, much of our work centers around learning to trust ourselves again, for many of us, more damaged folks, our sensors were programmed wonky, and we occasionally need help. If this is the case for you, asking a friend you know and trust, who also knows and trusts you, to tell you what they think about the situation can be a godsend.

We should, of course, be mindful not to become overly dependent on asking others' opinions, even our friends. But asking a trusted friend to help us evaluate a situation we are unsure of can be paramount to learning to trust ourselves again, especially at first but also throughout our lives.

All humans in dysregulated states - like when feeling threatened or afraid - interpret neutral data as more threatening. (Sapolsky) As explained earlier, CSA people's dysregulated states are more intense and last longer than others.

So for us, it's much more critical to "reality check" regularly - to prevent me from thinking that my boyfriend's tired face is actually an "I'm mad at you, and no, I'm not going to tell you why!" face.

Frankly, just *not* having a fight or being riddled with fear near my significant other after a long day is very much worth the awkwardness and discomfort of doing a reality check.

Note: Don't reality check with the person you feel weird about. Unless you trust them completely, to be honest with you, consider calling a different friend who is not the cause or target of your dysregulation at the moment. It can get messy being dysregulated and trying to find out if your dysregulated perceptions are accurate from the person whose face happens to be the face making you feel crazy. Call somebody else.

INTERACT!

Since trauma has this tendency to pull us out of our current time and place back to a past one, interacting with people is crucial. Yes, even the ones you don't like, eventually. But you're safe for now. Regularly interacting with people forces us to practice being present.

I mentioned early in this book that there are things unique about each of us, and there are things that many of us share. Hyper-independence is one of those things. Some people may become severely dependent or codependent due to their experiences. Still, typically, in cases of abuse or neglect, hyper-independence is a common choice our young bodies make for us to help keep us from fracturing under the pressure. That is why asking for help is so hard for so many CSA.

Unfortunately, If you expect to be abused or neglected, then you are less likely to engage with anything or anyone who could abuse you. You assume the outcome will be the same as it was for some particular event or series of events in the past. And you could be right. If you are right, you get the pleasure of telling yourself, "I told you so." Which feels pretty good but still leaves a person isolated. Doing this in a way that will be functional and beneficial in the long-term means doing it purposefully with focus.

When you talk to the lovely lady behind you in the cashier's line, remember that the simple act of engaging with them primes you for harder conversations with a long-lost friend or a lover later. Opening up about even meaningless things with strangers primes the brain's circuits for opening up about more impactful stuff with someone you trust later. So, every interaction helps.

Practicing interacting on any level is beneficial to this process. Much of this work is time-consuming, takes focus, and can feel heavy.

Think of interact as a simple rule for engaging in the world in a risk-free way.

Interact doesn't mean impress. Interact doesn't mean make a new best friend. Interact doesn't even mean have a good time.

Interact means to engage with the people, places, and things around you. You don't need to have any expectations of how the interaction will turn out. You just need a willingness to engage in the world, uncertain of how it will go, which builds bravery and resiliency.

Notice I haven't included any prescription as to how one should interact. This is purposeful. The most beneficial ways for people to interact vary significantly, as do the amount and type of interactions we each need. So, play around with it.

Try something like:

- Say hi to your neighbors

- Make small talk about the weather
- Make conversation with the barista at your coffee shop
- Ask the bus driver how their kids are
- Tell someone their dog is cute

The only rule to interact is to do so regularly! Even in seemingly meaningless way, being with others still assures our ancient biology that we are with others and belong – at least a little. The goal is to interact enough that social settings feel uncomfortable but are no longer paralyzing. Keep your social interactions regular enough that they're not excruciating.

A little bit of bad does a whole lot of good.

The mother of invention is necessity.
3rd Century Proverb

Only when the pressure is on in the moment do we really put our all into something. Nothing makes that more evident than the massive worldwide response to COVID-19.

Our bodies weren't designed for the psychological stress of navigating the existential dread of a post-capitalist world actively crumbling around us. Our biology is still that of our hunter-gatherer ancestors when we were designed to run away from bears. So, when we feel off, and we can't find any motivation to do what we ought to, or we find ourselves overwhelmed by stress, worry, anxiety, or fear. All we need to do is shift *the kind of stress* we experience.

Replace *psychological stress* with *physical stress for* profound results!

When you feel mentally overwhelmed, you *take a cold shower*, and suddenly your body remembers what stress and overwhelm really feel like. Suddenly, problems are smaller and the world is a better, calmer place. Maybe not during those short seconds to minutes in the cold, but certainly after.

If you do this repeatedly, building a routine of willingly exposing yourself to unpleasant events, it builds your resiliency to all stress!! You will be able to take on the challenges that seem overwhelming. You can face your most significant challenges and accomplish any goal. The ones you have been putting on the back burner your whole life because they're too scary.

If you have massive goals you have always been afraid of pursuing, this might be huge for you. If you have big dreams but often find yourself overwhelmed and under-motivated, aka a hyporeactive baseline, this is your golden ticket. Willingly exposing ourselves to discomfort regularly is the most sure-fire way to motivate yourself and stay that way when things get not so fun.

What exactly am I talking about? This principle can be applied to just about any area of life. My favorite example is also one of the best studied, thanks to a guy named Wim Hof.

Wim Hof is known as *the Iceman*, and he has popularized an ancient type of breathing combined with mindfulness that he uses during cold exposure that has shown mind-boggling results. He has shown miraculous changes to his immune system and neurology due to his protocols.

I'm going to focus on just the neurological effects that take place in the brain as a result of cold exposure because that's what matters the most for CSA people. But so that you know, these breathing and cold protocols stopped E.coli dead in its tracks after he and a group of his followers volunteered to be injected with the virus for the sake of science. It's worth looking into if that sort of thing interests you.

Regardless of the very cool immune responses, something magical happens when we purposefully put ourselves into stressful situations. Every time a person takes a cold shower, does a polar bear plunge or an ice bath, they powerfully rewire their nervous system and brain.

When we willingly expose ourselves to uncomfortable situations, we activate our prefrontal cortex to direct our actions. That's the definition of top-down regulation! When we stay in the cold beyond the moment our body tells us to "get out," we change the conversation between the amygdala and the PFC. While exposed to the cold, the amygdala screams at us, "Get out, get out, get out NOW!! Threat! threat! threat!" When we stay in anyway, it's our PFC saying "Naw dude you got this! it's just cold water, not battery acid." The more times and the longer we willingly expose our physical bodies to this stress, the more we change the conversation.

When dysregulated or in a highly emotional state, including feeling threated by cold, the conversation between the amygdala and the PFC becomes one-sided. The amygdala becomes the one doing all the talking or screaming, as it were. Communication becomes one way - bottom-up – rather than top-down - which is exactly what we CSA are trying to prevent. That's when our programming chooses our responses. Which means we are not able to direct our choices. We can't access any of our executive functioning while under that level of stress.

Being CSA means that our amygdalas are more reactive than they are for other people. By remaining in the cold, we exercise our executive function in a dysregulated state. Staying in an uncomfortable situation for the long-term benefits it will provide is an executive decision.

By putting ourselves in the cold, we get experiential practice in facing the hard things we need to face psychologically. By remaining in the cold when our whole body is screaming get out, we are engaging in executive function while in a stressful state!

It's always going to be uncomfortable. The water in an ice bath will *always* be cold. The unpleasantness is always present. Like fear is, just like pain is always there. Using cold exposure, whatever fear stops you from achieving your goals can be overcome without identifying it! If you willingly put yourself through physical distress to show your body who is boss (PFC and not amygdala), you win.

It also wires the PFC and amygdala together in a way that predisposes that 2-way communication between them to be more strongly PFC down instead of amygdala up, even when dysregulated. You're neurologically training yourself to have more self-control and increase your executive functions even in the most challenging situations.

Quite literally, you're putting mind over matter. But instead of parlor tricks and bending spoons, you become the master of your destiny by taking charge and rewiring the conversation dynamics between your threat response with your highest cognitive abilities, just with a bit of regular exposure to noxious, cold, stimuli.

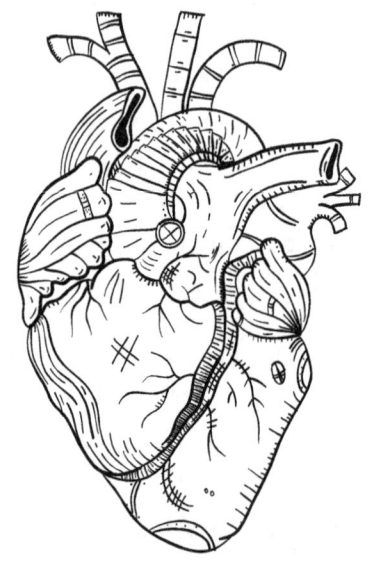

CHAPTER 18

BOUNDARIES

What are boundaries?

Y ou've probably heard the term. The concept has made its way into pop culture, especially pop psychology. There are many ways to describe them, but the best description I've heard about boundaries is

"Good boundaries maintain the distance at which you can love someone else and yourself at the same time." Prentis Hemphill

Why do we need boundaries? Essentially, a boundary is a psychological fence that allows us to say no. Saying no is a necessary skill for all people to protect themselves. There are only so many hours in a day and so much energy available each day. Boundaries allow us to use our finite energy efficiently.

If you or anyone you know has difficulty saying no, it could be said that you or they have "bad boundaries." However, the term is misleading because bad boundaries are most often a *lack* of boundaries. The primary way to be bad at boundaries or to have bad boundaries is not to have or not enforce your boundaries.

How do you know if you need to work on your boundaries? Things to look for

- You have a hard time making decisions
- You're a people-pleasing person
- You take care of everyone but yourself
- You tend to overshare
- You get mad at someone else's boundaries or lack thereof
- You take on other people's problems.
- Passive-aggressiveness
- You stonewall or stop communicating quickly
- You have a fear of rejection and abandonment - sexual

Interestingly, *all* clinical personality disorders have trouble with boundaries.

Almost everyone is bad at boundaries. We are trained as children to do what our parents and teachers say. (Considering they're usually better at keeping themselves alive than a small child, that's not necessarily bad.) In adulthood, still, no one sits us down and tells us what boundaries are, what they're for, or how and when to set them. This runs us into problems later in life.

Let's say you have a friend who talks a lot. You are tired from a long day at work after a long week of work. All you want to do is go home and be vegetative. But your good-hearted, perpetually cheerful, and talkative friend wants to come over. They text you, "Hey, I'm 5 min away. Can I swing by? I miss you! Let's hang!"

What do boundaries look like in this situation? The truth is boundaries are incredibly personal and context-dependent. It will be different for every person in this position each time. So, let's look at a few options.

Working from our definition of (good) boundaries, keep others at a distance where we can love them and ourselves. At the same time, we will eventually need to say no to protect ourselves, even from our favorite people.

If person A is tired after a long week, is sure that if talkative friend B were to come over, friend A wouldn't be able to muster up the energy to enjoy the company, which means things might go south. Friend A might take a joke wrong.

Maybe Friend A gets low-key mad at Friend B for texting when 5 minutes away, making them feel pressured into socialization.

Maybe Friend A feels pressured into socialization but decides that socialization is what they're constantly told they need, so they say, "Yes, of course, come on over," knowing that it will exhaust them more, but, in their head, it's the *right thing to do.*

A good boundary embraces discomfort over resentment, so in this situation, a good boundary might sound something like, "Hey thanks for thinking of me! I've had a long week and a very long day today. I need some time to recoup before I people again. I hope you have a great night, and I look forward to the next time we get to hang out."

I included a few things in addition to the boundary here because they are valuable tools to make boundary setting easier for those of us just learning. As well as for those who tend not to set boundaries because they feel bad, which is most people. But we'll get to those a little later. The boundary in this example was stating, "I'm exhausted and need to recoup before I people again." That's what I call a soft "no."

SETTING BOUNDARIES: SOFT NOS AND HARD NOS

If you have difficulty setting boundaries with people, this section is especially for you.

A "soft no" in boundary setting means saying no without saying the actual word no. There are specific upper socioeconomic status stratifications in which the avoidance of an outright no is a primary communication style. It's kinder sounding not to say no, and for many people, it's easier to receive a soft no because a soft no isn't definitive. Instead of outright saying no, a soft no shares a reason that implies no. In this case, "I'm exhausted and need to recoup before I can people again" implies the no.

On the other hand, a hard no is a statement that includes the word no in clear reference to the question or subject at hand. In this case, a hard no could look similar to a soft one but must include the word no.

One option might sound like this. "Unfortunately, not today, I'm exhausted and need to recoup… etc. Hard no's are helpful because they make it clear that no is the answer, leaving no confusion about your boundary.

A hard no can be as hard as you want it to be. Another perfectly acceptable boundary statement in this situation might be, "Hey! sorry, that's a no today." Or even just "no." After all, no is a complete sentence.

We all need help with boundaries, CSA and non-CSA alike. In my future ideal world, where we are all rethinking what it means to be broken and carving out beautiful, unique paths for ourselves, we will all be on the giving and receiving end of boundaries. So, let's look at boundaries from the receiving end to be prepared for the inevitable.

Imagine hearing "I'm sorry but that's a no today" from a close friend. Now imagine just receiving the word "no" in response to a "let's hang out" text request. It hurts a little, right? "I'm sorry, but that's a no today" is a little disappointing. No by itself can hurt. There's no reason given, no explanation. None is needed. No is a complete sentence, after all.

This is the trouble most people have with hard nos though. The harder the no, the greater the chance it injures the relationship. This is why we have soft noes. In addition to soft noes, we have another handy concept the Air Force called a shit sandwich.

Sometimes soft no's are too soft, and a hard no seems overkill, so we create a combination of the two with an explanation, including the word no, and if we are concerned with the feelings of the other person, we give them our boundary in a shit sandwich.

SAYING NO MAKES ME FEEL BAD: USE A SHIT SANDWICH

Join the club Love. Pretty much everyone except sociopaths feels bad when setting boundaries. It's inevitable. Boundaries separate things. They separate the requests, wants, and needs of another person from your own and prioritize one thing over another. That's uncomfortable, especially for the people we are close to.

It's inevitably uncomfortable to have one's needs stratified, especially when you're just learning how to set boundaries. So, to make it easier, you can do a few things to make yourself feel less bad during boundary setting besides just hard and soft nos.

The original boundary statement we used was what I call a "high-quality" boundary statement. "Hey, thanks for thinking of me! I've had a long week ending in a very long day today. I need some time to recoup before I people again. So that's going to be a no for me. Thanks anyway, though!

Looking forward to the next time we get to hang out." Most of that statement, about 2/3rds, isn't a boundary.

Firstly, it's employing the soft no strategy, but there's more than that. None of the rest of the statement was necessary as part of the boundary, but it can be very helpful for those who feel bad during the process. This is a high-quality boundary statement, but it is also an example of that "shit sandwich" I mentioned earlier.

Every military branch is big on this one. And it's been a super helpful skill for me. In the military, you get lots of practice receiving and eventually giving criticism. When you make a high enough rank, it becomes your job to give criticism or correction, like when you're in charge of other people. In the Air Force, at least, we are trained to do so with what's called a shit sandwich. Think of it like this.

Whatever the thing that needs to be corrected, in the case of boundary setting, saying no is the correction. The correction or "no," whether soft or hard, is essentially the "turd." The turd is the "meat" of the sandwich, the substance, the important bit, in this case, the boundary.

But turds are assumed to taste pretty awful, or at least I assume so. So, the bread on either side that makes it a turd sandwich and not just a turd should be something genuine and positive. It helps the turd go down easier.

The formula is if you have to say something hard to hear, start with a compliment, then the hard thing, then another compliment. There you have the making of a "shit sandwich."

In the military, they teach anyone who makes the rank of sergeant this tactic. It's meant to make it easier to set expectations and hear criticism. But as a CSA, people-pleasing person, it also makes it easier for me to say no because I'm actively taking steps to avoid hurting the feelings of the person with whom I need the boundary while also getting the space that I need.

Most CSA folks are like me in this matter. *Saying no can be and often is much harder than hearing no.* The shit sandwich not only makes hearing no easier. More importantly, for our purposes, it also makes *saying* no more accessible.

I view myself as a bit of a rebel. I always have been getting myself into trouble by finding out what the rules are so that I can break them. But somehow, it's still my instinct to say yes to nearly everything asked of me. I also hate that, especially when it comes to socialization and connection and especially as a person working on their anxious attachment tendencies.

No matter how much of a rebel I feel, it is still difficult to say no to people I'm close with. That becomes even more true if they're close friends or already close by.

For me, boundaries get sticky on a whole other level if our relationship is sexual or romantic. It is still very easy and natural for me to say, "Yeah, totally, it's fine, come on over!" If I do that when I'm not feeling it, I betray myself and my needs.

Self-betrayal is one of the prices we pay for having bad boundaries. Self-betrayal leads to self-loathing. It reinforces that my needs are not important, leading to a whole stack of issues. If we don't respect our boundaries, why would anyone else?

Bad boundaries lead to exhaustion and burnout.

Bad boundaries mean we don't know how to say no. Which means we are doing something for someone else all the time. That is its own reward, which makes setting boundaries that much harder. It's a complicated task to balance our needs with the needs of our community.

Most of us enjoy doing stuff for other people. It's rewarding for our species. We want and need to do stuff for other people and vice-versa. We (in theory) want them to help us, too, when we need it. Even if we don't want to ask, that's what community is.

But if we can't say no to the people in our community, we will resent them for how much they ask of us, and they'll know it. For folks without boundaries, it eventually begins to feel like the entire world constantly demands something from us. So, we begin to resent our whole world and become reclusive. Isolating ourselves and making everything we struggle with harder.

Boundaries help us to choose <u>discomfort now over resentment later</u>.

Is everyone bad at boundaries?

Basically Yes. Everyone has to learn boundaries. Yet, in our culture, they just aren't taught. No one sits down and teaches us what boundaries are, why we need them, or how to set them, which is why nearly everyone across the board struggles with boundaries. Struggling with boundary setting is understandable for two reasons.

Reason one is an evolutionary perspective. It is a fundamental, functional aspect of our nature as a social species to be liked. And I don't mean that in a hippy way. Humans have almost always done things in groups, from hunting to sleeping, shelter building, and foraging for food.

Because of this, belonging to a group of humans, such as your village, clan, friend group or clique, provides safety, food and shelter. Being liked is a big part of the reason setting boundaries is hard for everyone. Good boundaries go against our biological desire to be liked and belong.

Reason two is cultural. In many parts of America, the response to "why?" from a small child will often be met with an answer like "Because I'm your mother/father and I say so."

Though this sentiment may be more intense or repeated more often in CSA homes, this statement seems to be a ubiquitous response to the ever-present "Why" of tiny American children with exhausted parents across the country.

The heart of that response informs the child when someone in authority says "do this," they must do it. No questions asked, regardless of the reasoning. This is part of why, as a culture, we make excellent and obedient workers for the hierarchies that employ us. It's a wholly congruous and natural biological process, even if it's also gross or problematic in ways.

Even those who grew up with minimal chronic stress push themselves beyond their physical limits for their employer. Many wind up sacrificing their minds, bodies, and happiness for their job. Which has created the most anxious, depressed, addicted and medicated culture the world has ever known.

For CSA folks, it's even more complicated. Saying no as a child is all but forbidden if not *actually* forbidden in many chronic stress filled American households. And I say households for a reason.

If you're CSA, your parents were almost certainly CSA as well. You probably figured out a long time ago that your parents weren't Zen masters in disguise who lived their own internal lives in perfect peace while stressing you just for the hell of it.

If your parents were stressed out of their minds your entire childhood, guess what behavior you will model? What do you think your default programming will be?

Most adults are pretty terrible at setting boundaries, mainly because they were never taught either; even non-CSA, as we established, could be better at them. In reference to boundaries, what makes a non-CSA person is that they got instilled in them a fundamental form of self-worth at a young age.

Saying no happens more naturally and automatically if you have genuine, secure self-worth. Self-worth is the tiny voice that supposed to live in your head that tells you you deserve to have your needs met.

The sense of deservedness instilled in non-CSA folks may be a thin layer, but it's a critical layer of protection that makes it easier for them to have boundaries. Even they will still need a lot of practice to get good at them though. We CSA, on the other hand, have to learn self-worth consciously later in life. Self The only way to learn boundaries is to do them.

The reason it's most challenging for CSA folks is as simple as this. For a human to learn anything, meaning to engage the learning network in our brain, we must first experience a sense of safety.

To get good at something, any human must also practice said thing. Boundaries are extra challenging for CSA folks because, as we established in section 2, we didn't experience enough psychological safety to develop brain structures the way we were engineered to fully.

It makes sense that we would have almost no chance to say or practice saying no. Let alone learn the self-evaluation skills necessary to make good boundary decisions.

A boundary is all about being able to say no without it costing us a bunch of time and energy. We need to be able to say no so we don't overextend ourselves and get ourselves hurt or sick physically or mentally. Our boundaries change; they move, and we need to be able to adjust them when appropriate.

If you want to have friends and peace, you will need to be able to move your fences to make room for the people you want in your life. It's a tricky tightrope to walk, balancing the needs of the many with the needs of the self, but it's paramount to our survival and health that we do.

Struggling to find and maintain that balance is a fundamental challenge of the human condition.

Good boundaries maintain a distance at which I can love myself and someone else simultaneously. I know it's hard to do, but I promise your life will be much better when you start choosing discomfort now over resentment later.

Choose boundaries!

THIS IS NOT A BLAME-THE-PARENT GAME.

This may come as a surprise to you, or it may not. Either way, there is little room for playing the blame game. There are two reasons and one partial, but only partial, exception for this. Let me explain....

I know first-hand that it's easy, with all of this talk of childhood trauma, to want to throw all the blame on our parents. We've spent the entire book so far talking about the impacts that parents have on their children. I spent 10 years not speaking to either of my parents because of the crap I went through while under their care.

But like I said in the introduction, each person who has ever walked this earth has a story that will break your heart, including your parents and mine. No matter how f*cked up they are or were.

MOST PARENTS DO THEIR BEST

Most of us had parents who did their best. They screwed up, but damn did they try. Any parents reading this already understand this implicitly. Those efforts ought to be recognized at least. Probably even commended. Raising a child is the hardest, most thankless job on the planet. The older we get, the more we realize that this is true.

It is nearly impossible to raise a mentally and emotionally healthy child in our modern world. Things we've talked about that are out of any parent's control have a massive effect on a Child. Things like the nuclear family replacing multigenerational living, increased dependence on old folks' and assisted living homes which isolating the generations that need each other - to every household in the country having to be a two-and-a-half-income household to pay the bills, makes rearing an emotionally and mentally intact child nearly impossible today.

Depending on the experiences you had as a child, you may automatically understand that your parents, and indeed most parents, tried their best. In today's world, that's worth a lot in my book. Most parents fall into this category.

It is absolutely possible and even probable that you as a child were injured in real and lasting ways by a parent who was doing everything they could. Just because someone tries their best does not mean they win first place. It's true for parents as well. Some of our parents, like my mother, were doing the best with what they had at the time.

She was screwed from the beginning. First off, she didn't even have a fully formed brain when she started developing mine! Not to mention being married to my father must have been an absolute nightmare.

The psychological damage I live with from all my crap with her, from her anger and physical violence as a kid to the abandonment trauma to the sense of neglect I still deal with, sucks. It was absolutely real and did affect me. But that doesn't make her a bad mother.

My mother called me one time while writing this book. She did so for one reason. She called and said she wanted to apologize if she "had ever been a bad mother." I can't tell you how weird, and surreal this moment was for me.

I'm a painfully honest person. I always have been. So I've never been the type to say tell a white lie to make a person feel better. That's problematic to me. Instead I took the opportunity to tell her a few things that were important for me to say and for her to hear. I want all CSA people who are struggling with their dynamics with their parents. I told her.

> I think she's a good mom, but not perfect.
> No parent is perfect
> I *was* deeply injured by many things that happened in childhood, things she did.
> Although it could have been better, I don't think it's possible for that to not have happened. No one rides for free.
> And that if a child makes it to 40 and still talks to you, that's good enough.

That last one might benefit from an explanation. I told you I didn't speak to my mother or father for almost ten years and I still don't speak to my father, and that gap's been going strong for 16 years.

So, let me tell you about the last straw I had with my father. Because although the seeing demons things was crazy, that wasn't even the last straw. What happened after I joined the military was. Then I'll tell you about how my mother worked her way back into my life, even after the childhood I had.

My father would send me care packages when I first joined the military. A care package is just a mailed parcel of goodies. They more common for deployments, but you can send one anytime. Well, after my brother died, Bruce sent me the very last one I would ever receive.

That's because his care packages I took to calling BOBs or Boxes of Bigotry. There would be one nice thing in the box and then a bunch of… bigotry. When I opened this last box, the nice thing was right on top.

On the very top of the BOB was a small square blue-grey pillow with a deer in the center of it. I immediately recognized it as Caleb, my dead brothers' pillow. Underneath the pillow was, as usual, a stack of literature, and the reason I called them BOBs.

Among that relatively large stack were pamphlets entitled "AIDS the Wrath of God" and "Islam the Heart of Terrorism" as well as literature for Straight Away Camps, some of which even came complete with electroshock therapy! Straight-away camps, for those who don't know, were places that homosexuals or usually their homophobic families, could pay money to send their gays to for a few weeks or months to try to pray and shock the gay away.

In Bruce's head, I'm sure he was doing *his best* to save my eternal soul from damnation. From my perspective, it was more proof that I was wrong and an embarrassment to him. That kind of behavior is precisely why I have no relationship with my father. In my life, you either accept me fully or I dont accept you at all. Failing to do something as simple as accept your child means your best simply is not good enough. There is no reason to let people who don't accept and love you fully remain in your life, at all…

My mother on the other hand, when Caleb died, he had only recently spoken to her. They hadn't spoken since he moved in with our father when he was about 13. I don't know exactly what was going on in her head when he died. But during that conversation, I got to tell her exactly why I choose to have a relationship with her now.

I can't imagine losing a child. Losing my brother was bad enough. Losing a son who all but hated you must be an unbearable burden. When Caleb died the two of them had no relationship and it was her fault. I know it was her fault because frankly, after all the info presented in this book, fuck you, if you try to blame children for their behavior. Children without exception, are products of their environment. So yes, them not having a relationship was her fault. He died basically hating her guts, only having just barely began to forgive her for his childhood crap.

I think that she realized that too. Because she set out to do the work to weasel her way back onto my life. She found a way to find my number from my sister or cousin or someone repeatedly. She used it to text me nearly every workday for years and years. It was always something innane about the weather and a have a good day equivalent. She kept up texting a black hole for ages because I refused to reply. Eventually, I would reply a few times a year. But she kept at it, regardless of whether I texted back. Eventually, I would reply a few times a month, until now, when I respond almost da

ily. Which is the best response rate anyone ought to expect from me anyway.

I told her, her consistent effort over the years is what "fixed it" for me. There was a lot that went wrong in my childhood. Only in some of it did she have much influence or control.

One of the things she did have *some* control over was making me feel unwanted, unimportant and inconsequential. So, *when she did the work* to prioritize me for no other reason than she felt she ought to, the chasm between us could finally be bridged.

I know that parents, especially CSA parents, have very little chance of changing. If it weren't for the death of my brother, I don't think my mom would have changed. I don't think we would have any relationship. But occasionally, miracles or nightmares occur that cause people to change.

Some will change, and some will not. That's ok. The ones who want to change and show you through action that you are important and they want to repair things. Let them. For those unwilling to change, those who have labeled you as the problem, fuck 'em.

My father believes to this day that I'm just a drug addict. That's fine. I've taken a long and hard enough look at my crap that it doesn't bother me much when I'm misunderstood, misrepresented, or even demonized, even by him.

It's hard when those who are supposed to love us, hurt us, and maintain their hurtful positions. If you're dealing with that in your family, *when they maintain their position, maintain your distance.* Because…

WHEN ONE'S BEST SIMPLY ISN'T GOOD ENOUGH.

1 in 6 boys and 1 in 4 girls are estimated to be sexually abused by the age of 180F. 30-40% of those cases are estimated to have been perpetrated by an immediate family member. In my world, "Trying ones best" is not a justifiable rationalization for these statistics.

It's well documented that experiencing sexual abuse makes a person much more likely to become an abuser. So, it's also likely that many, if not most, abusers were abused themselves. And if *trying one's best* to prevent all sexual assault and violence from one generation to the next, then "they tried their best" would be all that needs to be said. But it doesn't. So, it's not...

So, I want to make this crystal clear. While I do think all parents do try their best, *sometimes a parent's best is simply not fucking good enough*! I don't know what you went through. Hell, I'm not even sure of the entirety of what *I* went through, thanks to my own stress-induced memory gaps.

I'm not saying that your parents deserve your forgiveness. Maybe they do, and maybe they don't. Most probably do. But I want every single person who reads this to understand that some of the atrocities that some parents inflict on their children are far beyond what I can gloss over as "trying their best." Sexual and physical abuse are obvious examples of this. But that's not the only kind.

DON'T LET BLAME TURN TO HATE

No matter how hard your parents tried or how awful they may have treated you, blaming them has limited utility. *Blame is a way to discharge pain.* When we blame our parents, we are attempting to discharge the pain we feel by shifting it onto someone or something external, something other than us.

Pain genuinely blocks us from thinking clearly, so blame can serve a temporary purpose. It can allow us to evaluate some specific things more accurately. But our vision will always be blurred when we look at the place that we have pointed that blame.

We naturally get angry when we feel we have been wronged or hurt as a way to protect ourselves. As CSA people, we carry that hurt with us in our nervous system every moment of every day. Most of the time, it is just there, not activated, but always waiting to be.

That's what makes us triggerable. When we focus on the blame, we focus on the anger and the pain. When so much anger gets focused in one place, that anger can quickly turn into hate. Hate is the easiest place to become blind and lost.

For those of us who did suffer in ways that stirred hatred in our hearts, I'm no longer a religious person, but I pray that you don't get lost in your hate of *a person*. Get mad, get angry, scream, and punch a pillow if you need to, and I *highly* suggest you get a therapist you vibe with.

Anger is a powerful protector and friend. He wants to keep you safe. The residual anger you carry over the injustices you experienced might be mild, or it might be a raging housefire. Either way, that anger is telling you to protect yourself. Listen to it. Protect yourself. And when you have made yourself safe again, have a conversation with that anger.

Say thank you. That's how you let it go.

Use it, then thank it. But try not to let it turn into hate. If you can't help but hate, use it as a fuel to propel yourself to the safety (boundary) you should have had all along and once it's gotten you to safety, I hope you will honor it, thank it and let it go, so the hate can't fester.

Some anger certainly remains in me, and I don't think it will ever go away completely. Nor do I think it should. Now, that anger is utilized. It's focused on balancing the injustices I faced personally on a larger scale and not on the perpetrators who injured me. ***Not because my perpetrators deserve forgiveness but because I deserve peace.***

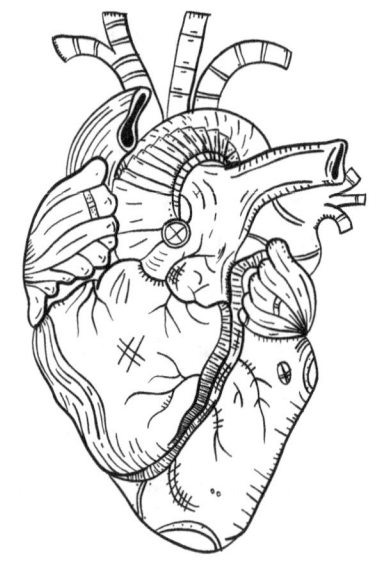

CHAPTER 19

NON-NEGOTIABLES

B eing CSA often means having lived our lives in situations in which we were not allowed to express our opinions. If we were, they probably would have been complaints about our treatment, and that just was not allowed. So many of us learned to negotiate our realities. What do I mean by negotiating our reality?

This goes back to the Stockholm aspect of being raised in an abusive home. If people, especially children, cannot express themselves - their thoughts, feelings and opinions, they will stop having them.

It sounds unbelievable, I know, but again, it's a biological process. Any aspect of our neurology that is not beneficial doesn't get used, and over time, it gets pruned.

Have you ever been put on the spot and asked what you want? Did you feel like a deer caught in the headlights? It's dysregulating for many CSA people because many of us learned to shut those pieces of ourselves down. The piece of us that knows what we want in life or this moment is just not easily accessible any longer.

We are usually very good at knowing what everyone else wants. We can often feel who they are, what they want and what will happen if they don't get it. We are uniquely adapted to this because of our trauma.

Since childhood, we were trained by our environments to help other people, starting with our parents and then our siblings. Since each person is unique, we all have different goals. Certainly, at some point in the life of a CSA child, there comes a moment in which our goal is to not feel neglected or abused.

Sharing that desire can be a huge issue. It's every parent's goal to see themselves as a *good parent*. If your child tells you they feel they are being abused or neglected, that would, of course, make you feel like you are failing at being a good parent.

So, what happens then? What happens in that child's experience? One thing that happens often in CSA homes is our CSA moms and dads deny the reality of the child because it doesn't match with theirs. "I don't abuse you; you're being a baby," "You're not neglected, you're just needy," and "You think this is worth crying about? I'll give you something to cry about" are all common responses many grew up with - myself included. Just writing and reading these phrases still brings up some echoes of unpleasant emotions and memories for me.

This is a fundamental aspect of why it's so important to reach out to other people to help us reality check; our realities were denied, and we had to learn how to negotiate and even sometimes dismiss our experiences as figments of our imagination—adopting a narrative counter to our reality.

These are the realities that CSA kids face. We learn to ignore our reality to have peace and safety in our homes of origin. When you ignore something long enough, you suppress it. When something is *suppressed* long enough, it gets automatically suppressed. It becomes *repressed*.

So, we often become *incredibly* defensive when someone finally asks us what we want. It's almost like we're mad no one asked sooner. But all we feel in that moment is attacked.

What's happening is we are trying to access a part of us that hasn't been activated since we learned to suppress it. Access to that part of our brain was pruned from lack of use.

Back then, we were in incredible distress. And touching it again triggers that distress, like a biological flashback, even if we are not consciously aware of it.

We have learned to deny our reality automatically, especially when it comes to situations in which our reality conflicts with someone else's. Especially someone close to us, with more power than us or with people we love. This can be a serious problem for us as adults.

When CSA folks' reality bumps up against anything that causes friction, we abandon our reality automatically and are totally unaware. This is true in our relationships, our work life, and basically everywhere else too.

Everyone you know knows you as the person you were before you read this book. By the time you finish this book, you will be different. You already are in this moment. But everyone you know will expect you to be the same you that *they* know.

The expectations other people have of the *old* you will bump up against your new goals and identity as a *CSA* rather than *a broken* person. When that happens, *it is paramount that you have non-negotiables.*

There have to be things in the life of a recovering CSA person that were utterly non-negotiable. Like the fact, we couldn't fight our parents or run away from abusive situations. We are so good at negotiating away our reality to display congruous, Stockholm-y feelings of comfort, belonging, and peace that without them, we will continue doing it forever and, therefore, never heal.

This is never truer than in our romantic relationships. When we fall in love, CSA folks tend to fawn almost automatically anytime there is friction. Doing that keeps us locked into this small and broken version of ourselves; for those of us from enmeshed families or who had an abusive or narcissistic parent, it's vital we set boundaries ahead of time around our most sensitive areas. That's where our non-negotiables go.

In relationships, what is critical for you? Is it quality time? What about work? With your friends? What gives you a sense of peace and places you firmly in your body in a way that makes you feel grounded, centered, and calm? That ought to be your non-negotiables.

I have trauma around my music. I always wanted to be a singer. It's the only thing I wanted to be—until the day that changed. I'll never forget it. My mother asked me what I wanted to do in college. I said I wanted to major in music. She responded, and

I'll never forget -word for word, "You're not good enough, you won't get anywhere, don't waste your time."

This little story might be the biggest reason I'm writing this book instead of releasing an album. So, a non-negotiable thing in my relationships is that I can sing and play music.

I need to be able to do it any time, any place, without rude or snarky comments. If I hear those types of things from someone I'm romantically involved with, the knife gets twisted, and the pain is incredible.

It makes me want to fight everything in sight. I can become enraged in a millisecond. I get so angry so fast that there's almost no way for the rest of the interaction to end well. That's the clue for you. If there is something you know for sure sets you off in a nearly unrecoverable way. Slap a non-negotiable there.

For me, hushing me, telling me to keep it down, or even someone saying, "Take it into the other room." constitutes a resounding goodbye. I'm immediately filled with a burning desire to scream, "Get the fuck out of here! Get the hell out of my life forever."

My mother said those words to me at such a vulnerable, formative time. It cut me so deep that I'm still working on repairing the damage.

I'm so sensitive to it that the slightest resemblance will make me want to explode or shut down immediately. Yet it remains a goal Im desperate to pursue. So, I view my need to practice singing right next to food, water, shelter, and connection. If you have a problem with me practicing and singing quite literally during almost all waking hours, then we are just not going to be a fit.

Now, you might ask, is it "fair" that I have this demand? It seems dramatic. It seems unfair to my prospective partners. And you're right.

Still, from my perspective, and in my experience, you bet your ass it is fair! From a prospective partner's perspective, it could definitely seem a little suspect or unfair. After all, why can't he ask me to go into the other room or "keep it down"? Those are, after all, reasonable requests.

Yes, they are reasonable requests if the context didn't include **me**. But it does include me. It includes all of me. **What is fair for me must include all of me**, including my past experiences, my present reality, and my future desires. Because of the damage from that story with my Mom and the wound I *still* carry as a result, those kinds of seemingly innocuous responses hurt me worse than being punched in the face. So yes, it's absolutely fair that I set up that as a non-negotiable.

There is no right or wrong place to put your non-negotiables. They're unique to you and your story. Non-negotiable boundaries exist to protect you from reinjury of your most sensitive experiences and nothing else. Non-negotiables exist to help change the ending of a traumatic story that played out in your childhood.

By establishing your non-negotiables up front, you are saying this thing, this expression, this freedom, this control, is essential to me. It's important I don't experience whatever that non-negotiable boundary is in place to protect me from. Non-negotiable boundaries make our realities as CSA humans who are carrying painful experiences in our neurology more pleasant.

They teach the biological you that you are worth protecting, even in ways that may seem slightly unfair initially. They also teach others how you expect to be treated. Since birth, our sense of self was determined by how we felt about how others responded to us. Non-negotiables force other people to respond to our presence in a self-affirming way.

Non-negotiables are non negotiable, for many, if not all, CSA folks. Meaning we all need them. It's where we make our first and most fundamental stand for ourselves. It's where we say for the first time, "I will not allow myself to be treated this way." To say that and have it respected is a powerful type of healing.

Every CSA person ought to create at least one for themselves to heal, and grow – free of having our deepest wounds picked at, at least till we are ready for the picking.

Your first non-negotiable will likely be overzealous if you choose it in a heated moment. If that's the case, move it. You have that right. You reserve that right – for the rest of your life, you reserve it. You're the only one who can move it or choose where to put it next. They are, again, your *response-ability*.

Start by making your first non-negotiable in a place that protects your deepest wounds. Whatever sets you off or hurt you most, put a non-negotiable around it. If you need to move it later, fine, you're learning where they belong. And ***don't you dare feel bad*** about it either. <u>Non-negotiables are built into our non-CSA counterparts</u>.

It arrives in them from a feeling they have instilled from a childhood in which they felt safe, loved, wanted and respected. They walk away from situations where their boundaries are crossed rather than spending all their energy convincing someone why they should have been respected. That's part of how their wiring works better for them than us CSA people.

They have an innate sense of deservedness. During their development, they felt they received the things they needed when they needed them. So that sets them up to expect it where CSA people expect to have them crossed or altogether ignored.

Non-negotiables are how we close the gap between CSA and non-CSA folks. Especially big T-CSA people, but it applies to all. This is the first step to feeling different about ourselves. We demand different treatment of ourselves in the areas that matter most.

Again, your non-negotiable will be personal to you, like my music is personal to me. To help you find one for yourself. Think back to the moments in life whose echoes have held you back most. What do you remember? What was that about? How might you set up your life and future intimate relationships in a way that supports healing for that wound?

NON-NEGOTIABLES SOUND A LOT LIKE BOUNDARIES; ARE THEY THE SAME THING?

They are similar! Non-negotiables are just more hard-core. It's kind of like the square and rectangle thing. All rectangles are squares, but not all squares are rectangles. All non-negotiables are boundaries, but not all boundaries should be non-negotiable.

I think of boundaries as fence-like. I imagine one of those pretty crisscrossed old-world wooden fences in places in the rural west like Montana and Utah. I think of them like this because although it's work to move one of those boundaries, it can be done. And there's pretty much no reason ever to adjust a non-negotiable. Thus, the name.

Boundaries are something CSA people need for breakfast, lunch, and dinner. They help us navigate all our relationships in life. Outside of self-worth, it might be the thing we lack most. They protect us and our energy at home, work, school, and on the street while passing a stranger.

Boundaries ought to be plentiful, while non-negotiables should be much fewer and further between. And the only people who usually run up against our non-negotiables are those closest to us. It's most often only our most intimate inner circle.

If boundaries are fences, non-negotiables are stone walls. I placed a stone wall where I needed to feel safe to pursue music without shame. The only people I need to know about this non-negotiable are those I choose to live with.

The people we live with are the closest to us. Therefore, if they hurt us even accidentally, the hurt is much worse, which is why knowing and explaining your non-negotiables up front in a relationship is also non-negotiable.

Boundaries and non-negotiables limit our energy output, so we can reserve the energy we would spend on re-regulating and relationship repairing – and use it for ourselves to heal and orchestrate our lives so that we can make beautiful music.

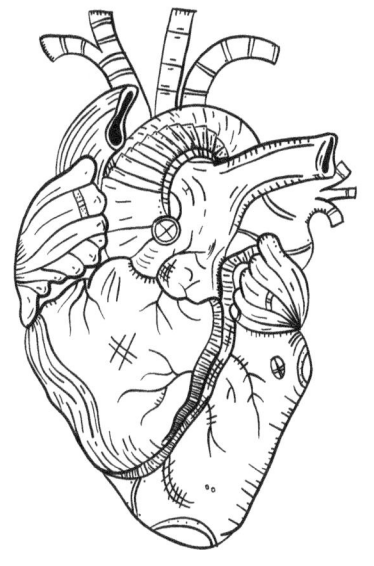

CHAPTER 20

MINDFULNESS

Mindfulness is *the single most powerful tool* available for CSA people. Pound for pound, nothing else I've found has the power to better our experience of life as quickly or easily as mindfulness.

WHAT EXACTLY IS MINDFULNESS?

The best way to think of mindfulness for someone who doesn't have much personal experience is to think of it like reading. Both are skills. We teach our children reading as soon as their little brains can grasp it. Mindfulness? Not so much.

Is reading good for you? Most people would say yes. Reading is a skill that has been one of the single most important in the history of humankind.

Reading allows a person to access a lifetime of someone else's knowledge and understanding without that person needing to be there or even be alive. It allows us to access ancient wisdom that, without reading, would be lost forever. Reading has fundamentally changed what it means to be a human being in this world.

Reading allows us to access an entire universe of knowledge that would, in its absence, be impossible to attain. It is how science "stands on the shoulders of giants." Without language and reading, we wouldn't have many shoulders to stand on. The same is true for mindfulness.

There are many health benefits of mindfulness:

- It reduces damage to the brain from age.
- It improves concentration and memory.
- It improves immune function.

These things are great, but they're still not the main reason you should meditate.

Both reading and meditation open up an entire universe of knowledge previously inaccessible. Reading gives access to incredible knowledge based on someone else's experiences. Meditation gives you access to incredible knowledge based on *your own* experience.

Okay, I was using the term mindfulness, and now I'm using meditation. Why the switch? What's the difference?

Mindfulness is a skill that's developed through the practice of meditation.

A practice is something a person does repeatedly to achieve a goal. In meditation, that goal is mindfulness. What is my definition of mindfulness?

Mindfulness is when my attention is focused on my experience.

So, when my mind wanders, as soon as I become aware of the fact that it has wandered off of wherever I have told it to stay, usually *my breath*, I am meditating. Whenever I become aware that my attention has shifted away from or back toward a thing, my attention is focused on my experience, which means *I am meditating*.

Throughout our lives, our bodies move through various states, all while thousands of things around us fight for our attention. Only some of them grab our attention. Each thing that gets our attention affects our body, shifting it yet again. Mindfulness is the quality of being aware of your state as it shifts and, eventually, the things shifting it. Meditation is setting aside time to practice becoming aware of the things in your awareness.

The Buddha represents the pinnacle of that goal. You've probably heard of him. Long story short, The Buddha meditated for so long, in so many ways, that he was able to attain a state of enlightenment. Which, in our practical terms, means he reached a place where he was able to remain mindful in every moment for the rest of his life.

That's a pretty unrealistic goal for most of us. Instead, we CSA folk benefit most from regular short meditations to free ourselves from our sometimes-faulty algorithms.

You already know that the RAS's job is to filter out most of that stuff. But people in the modern world need additional help, especially CSA people. We are unwittingly caught in this cyclone created by the breakneck pace of the modern world, our traumatic early life training and the natural functioning of the RAS.

More than anyone else, CSA people need to be able to watch our experiences closely. It's how we learn to become less "*triggerable*." Due to our strengthnesses, when we aren't in the right environment, we default to reactions that may not be helpful.

Mindfulness allows us to access the entire universe of our experience. We give ourselves the best chance to slow down and pay attention to what happens in our bodies during our experiences. So we can detect changes earlier and redirect our reactions.

MEDITATION CREATES MINDFULNESS

Meditation is the practice that facilitates the development of mindfulness - which is a skill. Like reading, there are skill levels. Although they aren't defined in mindfulness, the way that reading is broken up into second, third, or tenth-grade level reading. There is a parallel. If we had grading scales in mindfulness, there might be less confusion. But since there isn't, we struggle. We don't have much to go on to tell us if we are meditating successfully or correctly.

This lack of teachers means there is no one to give us feedback about how we are doing, which causes the biggest problems for most Westerners beginning a meditation practice. We need to find a way to know if we are doing it right. We need a yardstick to measure how mindful we are in a given moment. In this chapter, I will provide you with all of that in a realistic way.

PRACTICING MINDFULNESS

Mindfulness is a skill, a difficult one at that. Cultivating mindfulness is no different than cultivating any other skill. Imagine learning algebra or trigonometry without a teacher. How frustrating would that be?

Learning the skill of mindfulness is at least as difficult as reading or arithmetic. Still, again, we have no teachers to help us, which means that for those without teachers - frustration, confusion, and an uncomfortable feeling of uncertainty and anxiety are part and parcel. It's guaranteed that you experience them. That doesn't mean you're doing it wrong.

Which again is why this little phrase is so damn useful. Anyone of any level can and should use this description as a mindfulness touchstone. Use it to know whether you are being mindful or not.

**Meditation is about *this*, not that,
here, not there, *now*, not then.**

If you want to know if you're meditating, just notice if what you are thinking about is: *this or that. Here or there? Then or now?* There's your yardstick. Using this yardstick is easy.

- When you sit down on your pillow or walk to practice mindfulness, your only job is to observe.
- When you are observing, and your mind wanders from this thing to that other thing, notice it.
- When your mind wanders from the present moment, to a past memory, notice that too.
- When your awareness moves from where you are now, to anywhere else, notice that.
- Notice the changes that happen in your body due to the mind's natural wandering. Was there a change in the tension or temperature of your body?

Each time you notice these things happening during meditation, the practice is, the entire point is, that we bring our minds *back* to the present moment. Each time we bring back our attention from wherever it wanders off to the present moment, that is a mindfulness rep.

Just like if you were in the gym, each extension then contraction is called a rep, short for repitition. With our arms, we do reps to make our biceps stronger. It's the same with mindfulness. Each time you call your attention back, you're working your mindfulness muscles and getting stronger.

Each time we bring our focus back, we get better at bringing our focus to whatever we intend to focus on. That trains our attention, which is the first step and the initial goal of any meditation practice.

There are many paths and styles of meditation. Each is unique and has its own style and purpose. But before we can do any of those more complicated ones, we must first train our attention. Other more advanced forms of meditation use that trained attention in specific ways to achieve specific goals.

We cannot focus on anything without the ability to *command our attention*. If you stop and think about it for a minute - *focus is the most valuable resource on the planet.*

Everything cool or impactful that has *ever* happened, good or bad, was because one or more people focused for days, weeks, years or generations to accomplish it. *If we can't control our attention, we will always be tossed around by the situations we find ourselves in.* That's the opposite of what I want.

MINDFULNESS FOR THE CHRONIC STRESS ADAPTED

Mindfulness is being used every day in some surprising places like the VA to help veterans with PTSD like me. It works incredibly well. Mindfulness is a skill that everyone benefits from, but no one benefits quite as much as CSA folks, partly because being CSA is a lot like having PTSD or C-PTSD.

PTSD from a first-person experience pulls the sufferer out of the context of the present moment mentally or emotionally, and their body responds as if they were actually in another place and time. Usually, one in which they were under threat.

Though details differ between PTSD and CSA, the first-person experience can be similar. When a CSA person gets pulled out of the present moment by a trigger, they don't necessarily have a specific memory they are entering, making the event difficult to describe and predict.

CSA folks may not have even noticed the trigger, as that, too, might not have made it into the consciousness recall part of our brain when it happened. CSA people experience many of the same feelings and sensations as folks with PTSD, but often without a conscious direct link to the traumatic event. Mindfulness gives us a buffer, warning bells for our triggerability.

It's one thing to say - I was pulled out of the present moment and found myself reacting like I was diving from gunshots in Afghanistan again. Awful, but at least that's describable. It's another, even *harder* thing to say. I was pulled out of the current moment, but I can't say where, *and* I don't know what triggered it.

This is a common experience among C-PTSD and CSA people. Our traumas were too numerous, and we were too young for our brains to remember the details of what led up to the trauma. When the brain remembers and catalogs the happenings leading up to a traumatic event later, those things can become what is called a trigger. But if you were a child or if everything seemed unsafe, the brain could not categorize the triggers in our conscious memory; our body and subconscious retain the biological memory.

You've had the experience of biological memory because you have had the experience of muscle memory. You stop doing something for a long time, and you come back to it, and somehow, your body remembers how to do it better than your brain, like riding a bike. The same thing occurs here. While your body remembers the trauma and the events leading up to it, for CSA folks, it's likely that no conscious part of you has access to that memory anymore at least not without some psychedelic intervention. But that's a topic for another book.

When CSA people get triggered, it feels very similar to the experience of a person with PTSD, but CSA people are more likely not to remember the traumatic event. You may not have even noticed the trigger, making the experience that much more confusing. Last but definitely not least. It also makes us feel crazy because we have difficulty describing what is happening to us.

In chronic stress-adapted people like you and me, our RAS, which we covered in Chapter 6, is still doing its thing in the background, constantly scanning the environment for threats because responding to threatening situations has been an essential part of our lives. Not to mention that from a survival perspective, the second we let our guard down is the second we become most vulnerable to being eaten by a bear. Or our mothers if our mothers were our bear.

Remember how I said that the emotional and rational minds have the same job but accomplish it with different data? That job is to protect the host, which to the brain is the entirely physical body. Their job is to keep you alive. So naturally, the mind, both minds drift whenever possible to wherever our nearest discomfort is to protect us.

The kicker is that most of us only face a few present problems directly. At least not problems our body is greatly concerned with. Most of our problems exist only in our heads. Our problems are often the social situations we butchered ten years ago or the list of crap we're going to have to do later today or tomorrow. Worrying about your recent uncle's diagnosis and what you're going to say to your boss to get that raise you know you deserve.

These things are important, but they are only rarely present as - *this, here, or now* - for a few seconds. Yet we spend so much time thinking about them. And every moment we think about them is another moment we get upset about them and probably do nothing to change it.

Most of our time and energy is spent thinking about and getting upset over past problems, future problems, and, more often than not, problems that never actually happen. And they probably never will. How many times have you worried yourself sick over something that never happened? Mindfulness is your way out.

Still, our hard-working, obedient RAS is doing its job, trying to keep us queued into our environment and letting in only the essential things. Since noticing threats to our bodies is vital to survival, our awareness is designed to drift to the nearest threat. In our modern world, **the nearest threat is usually the one that's in our head**s. So, we worry. We worry about that, instead of this, what's happening there instead of here, focused on then rather than now.

HOW MINDFULNESS ACTUALLY WORKS.

Now you understand why your mind wanders all the time. It's designed to. It's just doing its job. And it's doing it well, so don't be mad at it for doing its job. If your brain's job is to wander off to scout for safety, then your job is to bring it back. By repeatedly bringing your mind back to this present moment, what you're doing is practice—practicing for what? You are practicing controlling your mind.

Or you could say that you are training your mind. You're training yourself to become aware of what's happening in the present moment. Why is that important? Because most of the time in the 21st century, we are not in imminent physical danger. This means when we start to feel bothered by something, we can learn to let it go more quickly and easily, since we don't have a lot of lions left.

Regular mindfulness practice teaches your body that the present moment is the safest place a person can be. That's right. Observing your surroundings without judgment is the safest place on the planet.

I know the world is a bit of a shit show right now from a lot of perspectives. There's been a global pandemic that lasted years and tanked global economies. The ocean is full of piles of plastic the size of a small European country. The earth is getting hotter by the day, and there's supposedly only 60 years of farmable soil left on the planet!

All of these are real issues that are important. As a society, we must do something about them. But getting depressed and feeling lost about it is simply ineffective. That's what happens when we let our minds control what we think about.

I'll say it yet again because it's worth repeating. Your mind, both *emotional & rational*, is interested solely in your survival, not your pleasure or health. <u>Which means if you let either one of them dominate your mind, your life will be focused solely on what might kill you</u>. That is a miserable existence.

HOW MUCH MINDFULNESS IS ENOUGH?

Okay, so now you're on board. You understand mindfulness, why you need it, and how it works. You're ready. You finally get it and are excited to start your meditation practice, but you foresee a problem. You don't have 2 hours a day to stare at a wall.

You've got to do your job and take care of the kids and the rest of the family. You're exhausted every day, and frankly, you're desperate to veg-out, after keeping up with our fast-paced world. You don't have time to do what initially seems like "nothing." I've got good news for you. Not only is meditation not nothing. It doesn't take much time at all to change your life!

Just 5 minutes a day, every day, of meditation is all it takes to have profound effects on your life! Seriously, just 5 minutes a day! You have 5 minutes to spare. Just replace 5 minutes of doom scrolling, which I know you do. Don't try to lie about it. I don't even need to know you to know you better than that. Replace that with 5 minutes of meditation daily, and it will change your life. And when I say profound, I mean it.

I promised you wouldn't have to sit and meditate for hours. There are infinite ways to practice mindfulness, and meditation is only one. But meditation is the place to begin because the big secret that no one tells you is you can't do it wrong. Seriously!

As a beginner, the more uncomfortable it feels, the more it's probably working. Or said another way, the more wrong it feels, the more right you're doing it. Some days will be better than others, certainly. But meditation *can't* be done wrong. Meditation is always mindfulness remember? The human mind wanders by design. Meditation is the practice of bringing that mind back to the present moment.

___What people think of as lousy meditation is actually good meditation___!!

But without a teacher to tell us that, it feels so uncomfortable we quit. A session of what I used to think was failed meditation was sitting down on a pillow or lying on my back, softening my eyes, and letting my mind go blank.

My mind, having no anchor, would wander off to god knows where so many times in a single session I assumed I was doing it wrong. I wish someone would have told me when I first started meditating that that's not wrong. *It's the whole thing*!

Bringing your mind back from tomorrow's bills and last week's fight with your spouse *is* mindfulness. The more times you have to bring it back, the more mindful you are being. When it comes to mindfulness as a Westerner, the more you feel like a failure at it, the better you are probably doing.

I understand resisting meditation though. I fought meditation for a long time. Although I was in the medical field and knew about meditation, I didn't start practicing meditation until I got out of the military. I found myself feeling so lost after separating; it felt like I had to meditate to feel sane.

When I left the clinic in Texas and became a civilian again, I felt lost during the transition from my controlled military life to so much freedom. Meditation felt just as important as air and food during that time.

The most annoying part was that even though it felt important, I still didn't *want* to do it. I have always been an action-oriented person. Sitting still and trying to think about nothing - which is what I thought meditation was at the time - sounded not just way out of character but also *torturous*. But once I started a regular practice of meditation, all that changed, and it will for you too.

It is called a practice for a reason. *There isn't good meditation or bad meditation.* In order to meditate, just stop doing other things, and when your mind wanders off, bring it back to this, here, and now present moment. **That's it.**

Okay, but like… *what if I'm a big baby and I hate meditation?* Maybe you've tried it, and you just don't like it, or you think it's just not for you?

I understand and if you absolutely refuse to do meditation fine. Do you, booboo. Just understand you are utterly screwing yourself. Seriously you're fucking yourself over now and in your future by refusing to meditate.

But if you really won't for any reason and you are willing to accept that you're missing out on the single easiest way to learn to be in touch with and regulate yourself, have peace and feel put together, then go for it. Continue doing whatever you're doing. I still have a suggestion for you.

There is a fantastic book called *Zen and the Art of Motorcycle Maintenance* by Robert M Pirsig. It describes how the author struggled with meditation but realized that he had the experience of mindfulness every time he worked on his motorcycle. It's a marvelous bit of insight and a great intro to mindfulness for the resistant.

Now, I need to admit something that may sound a little hypocritical. My favorite form of mindfulness is not meditation. I have a regular, indispensable meditation practice, but my favorite mindfulness practice is one-on-one care.

One of my strengthnesses as an ADHD CSA person is the ability hyper-attune for long amounts of time to the biggest threat in the room. In a medical setting, that makes me a keen observer of my patients and their ailments. When I'm doing a treatment or a session with someone, there is no better feeling in the world. I love that I get to disappear completely. I forget I exist for a while and am entirely enveloped in the session.

It feels like I *become* my fingertips, and I can feel everything my clients and patients feel, large and small. That deep level of empathy and attention to detail gained from my chaotic childhood provides perceptive skills that help me feel and understand what's happening in a patient. Then, I can better know what the next best step is.

During my sessions, my goal is to all but disappear entirely. Every time my mind wanders, and it does, I bring my mind back to the present moment, to the patient or client and their experience.

Part of the reason I love it so much is because it helps me a lot. It Zen's me deeply to be so attuned to another person. It's exactly what I needed from my mother, but she was too depressed, stressed, or whatever she was to be able to attune to me appropriately.

Maybe you, too, can relate to some of your personality traits being the ones that you needed when you were young. But also, in this environment in which I am an expert facilitator, I must attune to my clients right here, right now. I'm not dealing the trauma they had last week or month. I'm not treating a disease either. I'm helping the person that is in front of me.

It's my favorite form of mindfulness because it forces me to unify all my observation skills at once. I come face to face with the reality that even when a problem does exist, even one big enough that help is needed to solve it, it is still usually not life threatening. At least since I left emergency medicine, that is.

This is extremely important for CSA folks. It's common for us to experience the feeling of being unsafe much more profoundly and often than non-CSA people. For us, experiencing being unsafe in a certain way can feel like life or death, even though it no longer is.

But we have a hard time convincing our bodies of that. For CSA folks, the physical sensations that go along with not being safe were set up early enough in childhood that being unloved, unwanted, or unsafe meant death. So, we still have a lingering feeling of that threat of death.

GETTING STARTED WITH MEDITATION

Just so we are all on the same page, I will assume that you have never meditated before and walk you through how easy it is. Here is how you can meditate.

- Find a spot in which you can sit comfortably.
- Find a position for your body that will keep you both relaxed and alert. You can cross your legs if you want and rest your hands palms up or down on the legs or in your lap.
- Once you're in position, set a 5-minute timer on your phone.
- Before you press start on your timer, soften your eyes and relax any tension in your body that isn't helping to hold you upright.
- Take one big breath, and as you let it out, I want you to make some noise. I don't care what kind. "F" sounds work well for this. I know it's weird. Try it anyway.

Vocalizing on the exhale squeezes the vocal cords together, pressurizing the lung cavity so you get better oxygen exchange, which calms the body.

- Breathe like that for the entirety of the 5 minutes or just in the first breath; it's up to you. Are you ready? Of course you are!
- Now press the start button!

Congratulations, you're meditating! When your mind wanders, bring it back to your present experience.

How was that? Was it weird? A little awkward? How does your body feel now? What did you notice? What might you do differently for tomorrow's round?

How was the place you chose for your meditation? Most meditation guides suggest you find a quiet place where you won't be interrupted. But that's nearly impossible to do for anyone with children. And parents are probably the people who need mindfulness most! It also needs to be more practical. Practice how you play! You're not going to be feeling dysregulated in a peaceful room alone.

Being alone in a quiet room is a serious disservice to a new meditator. Mindfulness is all about managing attention. Our minds have to keep up with the pace of the modern world all day, every day. The average person makes an estimated 30 thousand decisions daily because the world moves so fast. That sounds exhausting.

Meditation is asking you to be able to control your attention by putting the brakes on your attention to slow it from functioning at *the speed of the modern world* to functioning at the *speed of mother nature.* That's hard enough as it is.

If you add sitting alone in a quiet room as a prerequisite to meditating, especially as a beginner, that is like asking your mind to go from the speed of capitalism to a complete stop in seconds. If you try to force yourself to do it "the right way" - like I did initially, in a quiet room? I promise you. You're setting yourself up for a lot of frustration. Don't take it so seriously.

Try to meditate in a place that reflects nature's speed over a dead stop. Softly gazing out a window lost can be meditation too. Watch birds fly or light a candle and get lost in the dance of its flames. These things can all be done mindfully and to great benefit. They're definitely easier and, therefore, more effective than staring at a wall.

I really love the candle trick. That was one thing we did every Tai-Chi class in acupuncture school. Every class ended the same: the teacher lit a small candle in the center of the room, and the class sat in a circle and focused on it. Something about flame, no matter how small, holds our attention fairly easily. Having the candle as a focus made things much easier for me.

Your mind is the only thing stimulating in a quiet, empty room. So, of course, it's going to do the *most*. It's going to wander off, and it's going to do it even more than normal because it's used to a ton of stimulation, and in an empty room, there's nothing around to keep our attention interested.

So meditate outside, if you can, with other people too. If you have things like motorcycle maintenance or patient care where you feel you get to disappear and drop into the present moment, lean into that to develop mindfulness in your life too.

"I regret having a meditation practice," said no one **ever...**

MINDFULNESS AND MOVEMENT

A few thousand years ago, some very smart, now dead people realized that mindfully reflecting on stuff was beneficial. Some ways were better than others, and many types of mindfulness have been explored, as well as pairing mindfulness with doing other stuff. It's often paired with breathing, which makes some intuitive sense when you realize in a quiet room all by yourself that breathing is the only thing guaranteed to happen, so it's the only anchor you have.

But mindfulness has been paired with many other things besides breathing and meditation. One of its most profound pairings has been with *movement*. It is so profound in fact, that one country - India - ingrained it in the *culture itself*. Giving birth to another truly profound regulation tool. *Yoga.*

In India, mindfulness goes hand in hand with movement in the form of yoga, which is what the next chapter is about. This combination of presentness of mind during physical movements has incredible, inexplicable health benefits. There's new science coming out nearly every day with more evidence for how good yoga is for the body and mind. The difference between yoga and most other forms of movement is how they tie movement with attention and breath.

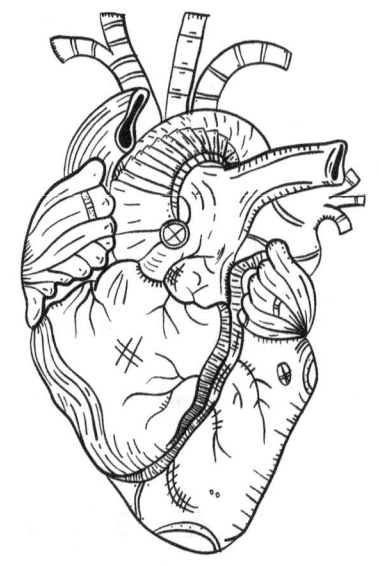

CHAPTER 21

MOVEMENT

I love the term movement. Movement makes me think of playing in the yard or wrestling with my dog. It makes me think of cartwheels, back bends, tree climbing, walks on the beach and hikes in the mountains. It makes me think of tai chi, yoga and dance. Movement has a connotation that feels free. You can do anything besides sit still, and it counts as movement. It also turns out that movement in how I use it is even better for our health than traditional "exercise."

But since the branch of science that studies this area calls basically all forms of movement, especially aerobic movement exercise, I will use the term exercise when referring to the research. I'll explain the difference between the two and why it matters in just a minute.

MOVEMENT AND THE BRAIN.

Some exciting stuff has come out in recent years about precisely what happens to specific parts of the brain when we exercise. Most interestingly, for CSA folks, the hippocampus and the prefrontal cortex (PFC), which we covered before, undergo some important and valuable changes due to exercise.

The first thing people usually want to know about movement or exercise is how much is enough. Time is short, so we want to know how much of our life we are going to have to commit to movement to reap its life-changing benefits. You'll be surprised at the answer. It's less than you think.

We all know exercising is good for us. But many of us need to prioritize it. There are a lot of reasons for this. Not the least of which is doing hard things today to make our future easier. But that has little draw as a strategy when you have spent much of your life in survival mode. Many CSA folks have spent much of our lives trying to make *today* tolerable. *Tomorrow* is all too often *a future me problem*. Today me has enough on their plate.

I also think for many CSA folks, we resist because doing what we're told hasn't been a strategy that's worked out well for us.

We are often a very evidence-based group. We want to know what the evidence is, not just that it exists. We want to know the why. Thanks to our general distrust of basically everything, "Why?" for CSA people has a powerful attraction. So let me explain the why...

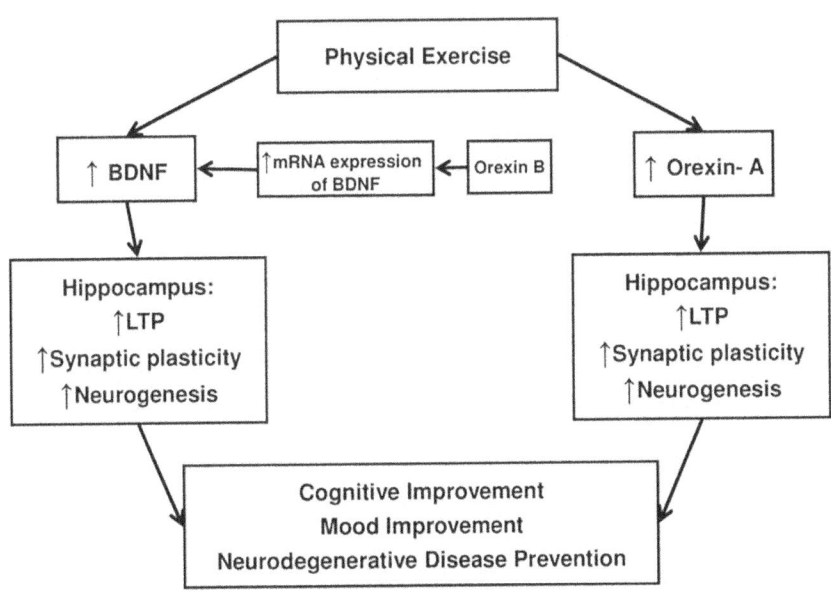

https://www.ncbi.nlm.nih.gov/pmc/articles/PMC5306252/

EXERCISE REPROGRAMS CSA BRAINS

I know this chart looks science, but fear not. It's pretty simple once you know a few pieces of terminology. This chart looks at what happens downstream in the brain when we exercise. That's why exercise is at the top.

This chart says when we exercise, two things happen (following the arrows down): There is an increase in BDNF, which is a brain-derived neurotropic factor. We simultaneously get an increase (see the little arrow to the left of the words) in orexin -A, both of which share a function (following the arrows again) of talking to the hippocampus.

As a result of the conversations had by Orexin B and BDNF Inside the Hippocampus (everything after the colon), we see some important things.

We see an increase in Long-term potentiation (LTP), defined as "a process involving persistent strengthening of synapses that leads to a long-lasting increase in signal transmission." Which is the brain science way of saying "practice makes permanent," or "fire-together wire-together."

LTP is the physical analog of the principle that says - whatever you do the most, you'll become most efficient at, just like our strengthnesses. This is how new habits become concretized, context-independent habits. It sounds a lot like *conditioning*. That's because it is.

Remember when I said consistent effort over the long haul makes permanent changes? Well, now you know the brain science word for it, LTP. Synaptic plasticity means that whatever your synapses are used to doing can change; that's the plastic part. It's the ability to adapt to new information. This is the mechanism that rewires the RAS. Synaptic plasticity is the ability of neurons to change their mind about which neighbors they talk to and why.

Lastly, neurogenesis is the mother effing game changer that put our understanding of neurology on its head in 1998. It's the secret weapon we were told was impossible for our whole lives. I and most folks growing up were told that it's impossible to grow new brain cells. But science is continually updating itself. It turns out that it's not true!

The term for growing new (genesis) brain cells (neuro) is neurogenesis. What was once thought impossible is not only possible but happens regularly *and is stimulated by exercise.*

It is essential for CSA folks wanting to change their default programming. Neurogenesis happens in two places significant to CSA people: the hippocampus and the prefrontal cortex.

The last bubble in our little flow chart here is self-explanatory. We experience improvements in our ability to think clearly and in our mood, as well as prevention of some of the most terrible diseases known to man, like dementia and Alzheimer's.

I'm sure you know why I hammered the why of movement before telling you how much. The PFC and Hippocampal changes resulting from exercise are the perfect storm for us CSA folks.

It's nearly everything we need to rewire our nervous systems! These changes are fundamental to overcoming those Chronic Stress adaptations that can sometimes get in our way and make us feel broken. Ok, now on to the how much part. How much exercise is enough to change our programming?

Just 30 min of movement that increases your heart rate & causes sweating is enough!

Yep, that's it. 30 min of exercise 3 times a week is enough to change the brain regions most heavily affected by childhood adversity. If you're not a gym or even a yoga person, you can skip the gym and try power vacuuming your house to disco for 30 minutes. Or walk an extra couple of blocks. Take the stairs if you work in a building with stairs or are just at the mall. Maybe even take them twice just for the hell of it. Do this 3-4 times a week, and you will have unlocked the powerful healing available for the exact parts of your brain most affected by childhood trauma.

It turns out that this level of increased physical exertion is enough to make the neurons in the hippocampus fire so much that, just like the rest of your muscles, the size of your hippocampus grows. Pop quiz question. Do you *remember* what the hippocampus does? I just gave you a hint! ......Right! Memory!

New hippocampus neurons mean it's easier to make new memories! We need to make new memories to replace all the shitty ones. We need both the experiences and a memory of the experience to show the amygdala the hard proof it needs to chill out.

That same level of physical exertion is also enough stimulation to build the prefrontal cortex. This means you'll have a better chance of accurately evaluating and responding appropriately to any situation. And I mean react appropriately biochemically, not just outwardly. You won't have to blow your entire wad of self-control for the day in one go.

With practice (LTP), your body will get better at sending a more appropriate amount of chemical signals into your blood to get you to do whatever it is it thinks you need to do.

When you know your body responds appropriately, it frees you up to be authentic in the moment and to still have that self-control for later. Who doesn't want a less dramatic startle response? Go ahead, I'll wait.... And who doesn't want clearer thought processes and self-control?

If we don't have crazy startle responses we then suppress, and if we think more clearly, even while upset, I'd venture to say that you would struggle to describe yourself as broken.

Physical movement is the most powerful thing you can do for your brain's physical mal-formations today to have an immediate and lasting positive effect on your CSA brain.

MOVEMENT'S EFFECTS ON ALZHEIMER'S AND DEMENTIA

If you aren't already sold on movement, let me add something. You already know that the two areas of your brain discussed in this chapter, the PFC and Hippocampus, are negatively affected by early life stress and traumas. They are also the two regions of the brain most implicated in neurogenic diseases and aging. They are the areas most implicated in dementia and cognitive decline in old age.

Dementia is a horrible disease. Watching someone you love decline to a shell of them-selves causes incredible suffering and pain for the victim but especially for those that love them. Dementia is not curable as of yet, either. Once you have it, it's too late.

My grandfather was my father figure. In junior high, I wrote a paper called "The Definition of a Man." It was about him. He was strong, patient and kind. He was slow to anger, and he loved his family.

One of my favorite memories was sitting in the garage with him with the doors open as we watched a tornado go through town. He taught me to watch for the color of the sky as it turned green, and he told me that the thunder was the angels bowling. When the tornados got too close, I was reluctant but eventually was sent to the basement for my safety.

My grandfather declined very quickly after his retirement. He went from "Big Guy," his nickname due to his stature and presence, to a 98lb sack of bones in just a few short months. The effect it had on my family remains beyond my ability to describe. It was very tough for everyone to manage. But it was hardest on my Grandma.

My grandmother, who spent 50+ years married to him, will probably never recover from that loss. Watching one of the strongest men I've known collapse into something so pathetic shook me to my core. He was strong my whole life, and then suddenly he was just gone in a few short years. I knew from then on that if there was anything that I could do to prevent my loved ones from having to watch me decline like my grandfather did, I would do it. Whatever it was, no matter how annoying or uncool, I would do it.

It turns out there is. It's movement. These neurogenic diseases are not curable, *but they are preventable!* And exercise is the #1 way to prevent it.

That brain-derived neurotrophic factor released during that 30 min of aerobic exercise gets concentrated in both the hippocampus and the prefrontal cortex and protects them! It goes straight to those brain regions and keeps them safe from degeneration of various kinds, which, as a group, are called, get this... "cellular insults." I love that! I couldn't make it up. Occasionally, scientists nail the naming of things.

Now you know the minimum level of exercise you need to get the benefits. Although it technically varies from person to person and among age groups, as a rule, 30 -35 min of aerobic exercise is best. How aerobic?

If whatever movement or exercise you are doing causes you to struggle a little to hold a conversation while doing it, you're doing it right! If you can still carry on a conversation, but it's hard? That enough! It's literally that simple.

WHICH EXERCISES OR FORMS OF MOVEMENT SHOULD I DO?

Like so many other things in this book, the answer is it depends! But to give you the gist, let me tell you a story of one of my favorite studies on the effects of exercise in mice. It went like this.

Mice were put on running wheels - It's important to know that mice typically enjoy their running wheel. It gives them a chance to stretch their legs and de-stress. They put two mice on two running wheels in two different cages, but the wheels were attached. When one wheel turned, so did the other.

Mouse B was stuck on a running wheel that would spin anytime mouse A would run on *his* wheel. Which means both mice were getting the same amount of "exercise." Both mice ran the same distance at the same speed. The only difference was that mouse A ran willingly- and the other – mouse B - was forced into it since the wheels were attached.

The mouse whose exercise was *on their terms* got all the benefits! While the mouse who was forced to run, mouse B, got none. Mouse A got *all* the health benefits, and mouse B, whose exercise was *forced* on them, had <u>worse</u> health outcomes!! Not just no health benefits, but had worse outcomes! How crazy is that?! It's still mice and not people, so obviously, it's not an exact correlation, but Geez! That was wild to me.

The moral of this story is that we probably can't or shouldn't do things we *actively hate* and expect to feel better as a result. Hard things? Absolutely, but not hated things. I know a lot of us CSA folks do it occasionally anyway because it is contrary to the general CSA attitude of "just push through it."

We've learned through life that - pushing through it - is the only way to get things done. We've had to push through our trauma responses, push through the abuse, push through our screwups and our breakdowns. When we try working out, CSA folks tend to go super hard because we "Go hard or go home."

The general - fuck your feelings - vibe and intensity often resonate with the life we've lived. But if we genuinely hate whatever exercise we are doing while we are doing it? <u>We won't get the results that we want.</u> Then we use that "failure" as evidence that exercise "doesn't help." Except it does. Exercise does and will help you. It's the *hate* that hurts us.

So, remember this when you're choosing your preferred movements or exercises. It's paramount that **you pick something you can enjoy doing!!** And no, you'll want to do it only some of the time. Somedays, you'll wish you had motivation. That's normal. A lack of motivation is something we can safely choose to push through. But pushing through to the point of hating the time we spend moving our bodies is a terrible, horrible, no good, very bad idea.

I can dance for 30 min 3 days a week easily. And I will enjoy every minute of it! That's why I have such an impressive sound system in my van. So, I can have my own private dance party anytime I want! You might prefer weightlifting instead. Other people might love their power walks or group exercises at the community center or local YMCA. I also love acro-yoga as a movement practice too because it feels good, is novel, and it forces me to interact with people.

Whatever movement you can do and enjoy that gets your heart rate up high enough to struggle a little but still hold a conversation, 30 min at a time, will give the greatest returns with the least effort.

Isn't that the goal? Getting the most bang for our buck is always a goal. Don't overcomplicate it!

That's it. That's all the "exercise" you need to change the structure of your physical brain to make new memories, give you better self-control, and prevent suffering some of the most terrible diseases known to man. It's as simple as... Enjoyable varied movement makes for a better longer healthier life.

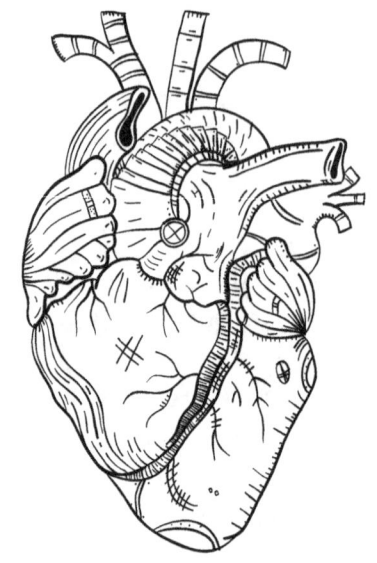

CHAPTER 22

TAKE GOOD NOTES

So far, you have been presented with a ton of information. We've covered microbiology, anatomy and physiology, psychology, life and trauma, love, family, boundaries and relationships. We've covered a lot in our time together and we're nearly finished. At this point, you're probably starting to feel saturated with information. If you're feeling saturated, now is probably a good time to introduce you to a way to keep track of the helpful stuff you've learned, as well as your wins, slip-ups and challenges.

As I said earlier, our biology makes it so we can make only a few changes at a time. It's designed to prevent too many changes from happening at once. So, how in the world do I expect you to keep whatever helpful information you've gotten so far straight in your head? Well, you have to - *take good notes*.

I find language stodgy, unwieldy and severely lacking in nuance. I prefer other forms of expression like dance, music, singing, art, and laughter to words—especially the words of the English language. But as a monolingual American, it's the best I've got.

Although I'm admittedly somewhat biased as the author of two books, I resisted writing for years despite prodding from friends. I was not a lover of words in that way. I always felt too stupid. I failed high school English. I didn't care for the subject and couldn't make the words do what I wanted them to. I do, however, love what words can do.

More than anything else, words shape our lives, from the words of a politician or legislator forming the rule of law of an entire country to the language we use to describe our lives affecting our RAS. Words carve the world around us. The words we choose when we speak or write are rich with implications for our inner world.

If you look closely at any sentence of a paragraph, you can determine so much more than what the words reveal. There is tone, undertone, and the words between the lines. There are the things purposefully left unsaid and questions skillfully avoided, while some that need no explanation can take up pages. All of this information can tell you far more than the words that were written even do. This is why I love writing now, even when I don't like what I write.

Life inside the brain of a CSA person is often a chaotic playhouse. We're full of strange memories and ideas that only make sense in our heads. And this is the key! Inside our heads, the things we think, feel and believe are all jumbled up and mixed in with everything else in our heads.

I use an analogy to describe what writing does for me. It's like I have a giant tangled ball of yarn for a brain. A ball of yarn always has one or more loose ends to pull from. Putting pen to paper pins down the free end, and each word I write untangles the ball a tiny bit.

Putting my thoughts outside of myself, however jagged, nonsensical and imperfect on paper, makes my mind slightly less crowded. Each time I write, I take another free end of that tangled yarn ball and untangle it, little by little. Each word brings me a tiny piece of peace.

It powerfully clarifies my thoughts. I have learned through this that if you know what you want to say but don't know how to say it, _you don't actually know what you want to say._ You just think you do. I sure thought I did. Writing, no matter how bad I am at it, helps me get from the ambiguous word soup in my head to a concise understanding of what I'm thinking so that I can say it.

I love communicating, and I've gotten pretty good at it with practice. But there are times when I cannot use my brain to communicate. I will have an idea or thought I want to share with a friend, and before I can finish the first sentence, the entire concept has been ripped from my head. "What was I saying?" It gets replaced with confusion, embarassment, and a mild sense of shame.

That mostly happens when I havent been writing. When I don't write, and I need to, I've learned that for me, there is a physical sensation that tells me I need to write.

I get a tingling in my legs that works its way up my whole body, which starts to feel alive, but not with clean energy. Inside, it feels more like static and sludge had a baby, and that baby is my blood. When I feel like this, there is no other remedy that can do as much as writing.

It is one of the most fundamental parts of my mental health maintenance. But it's the times that my yarn ball brain and static & sludge body feel overwhelmed that my brain won't work right. This is when the power of writing becomes apparent and paramount.

CSA folks are intelligent folks. We integrate information very quickly. But then that information needs to go someplace. Non-CSA folks have an automated filing system. Most CSA people's are analog. Which means we have to do something with the information we integrate. It has to get filed somewhere. If we don't file things away manually, there's a good chance that it just adds to the giant ball of yarn in my head that makes me feel anxious and stupid. Then I'll have to write it all out again later anyway.

The real issue with the ball of yarn in my brain is that it contains all of the unorganized information in the world, but none of the story that makes the data make sense. When there is information inside your head in a yarn ball, if we try to describe what we know, we fail to describe it with sufficient clarity, which pisses us off.

We know that we know the info, but we can't recall the info in a way that makes sense in words. Does this happen to you? How many times have you thought to yourself, "I know this! It's on the tip of my tongue." Those things get stuck on the inside because we haven't practiced making our thoughts tangible outside of our heads.

Writing is how I externalize and make sense of my inner world. Which is something I've learned I have to do to make sense of anything. If you are trying to understand a thing by observation, you are the observer, and the thing you are trying to understand is the observed. If both of those things are you, then you cannot understand the mystery because you are both the observer and observed, both subject and object. It never ends well.

That strategy makes about as much sense as having the
police investigate the police for police brutality.

It's idiotic, and it will never end in understanding or justice for the victim. In this case, the victim is you. Getting your thoughts outside yourself is the first step to objectively observing all the complexities inside you. This is why that sensation I get that tells me it's time to write is unpleasant. The unpleasantness is more and more data being dumped into my yarn ball, swelling it without it being useful. By writing things out, I connect dots, and then the information makes more sense, making the info more valuable.

When I write - each letter I write in those moments of dysregulation is a tiny piece of freedom. And I mean each letter because it doesn't matter what I write. I need to take whatever's in me and get it out. So, I write.

After writing it out, I can choose to trash it or not. So can you. You don't have to keep the notes. The point is only sometimes the words you write. It's more often the sense of peace and clarity gained by writing.

Pro tip: Keep as much of your writing as you can stand. I keep most of mine now, but I didn't always. I wish I had some of my trashed journals to watch my progress from those days. I wish I had kept more journals, too, which brings me to why taking good notes is so useful.

KEEPING A PAPER TRAIL & TAKING GOOD NOTES.

A paper trail is a concept that was beaten into my head in the Air Force too - especially the Air Force Honor Guard. It was a high-profile fancy pants job, and the military likes its procedures. The USAF Honor Guard is as on top of their procedures as any group could be. The most essential part of procedures is tracking what happened, what didn't, and when.

Stoics back in the day believed that daily reflection on one's life was a necessary part of self-development and self-growth. The reason is **continuity & accountability**. We all need help with these things. All humans exist under the constant flux of our biology.

For CSA people, it's that much more challenging because we experience things more intensely and for longer. Since we know that when we feel threatened, our PFC stops talking to the amygdala because she's busy screaming and can't hear the PFC anyway. It's important that we take good notes we can refer back to when we are less dysregulated to see if our actions align with our goals.

How far can you trust yourself? Do you often wish you had an accountability buddy for the hard stuff you want to do in your life? Do you have so many trust issues that you actually don't want an accountability buddy? Are you the type of person that, if you had an accountability buddy, you might think about lying to them on occasion because you subconsciously, conveniently assume they might also lie to you?

Well, guess what?! You can avoid every single one of these problems by not outsourcing your accountability partner. This process is all about learning to trust and believe in **yourself**. You can avoid trusting other people by only talking to yourself about it. By writing! But you *will* have to learn to trust yourself. You can reach your goals, and you can do it all with only a pen and paper.

Human existence is one big, messy experiment in consciousness that's been going on for a few million years. In the last 100 years or so, science has been very useful, and do you know why? Do you know what makes any given scientist a good scientist? What makes their shoulders so easy and useful to stand on? I bet you can guess. It's timely, detailed and accurate notes!

A good scientist knows that if she wants to know anything for sure, she needs to run experiments and take very detailed notes about each step of the process. The journey you and I are on is no different. I told you you need to become your own hero. It helps to become a scientist too. If you want to live the best life you can, then while experimenting with changes in your life, take good notes.

When you meditate, take notes. When you get angry at someone, take notes. When you feel twisted and can't seem to communicate, take notes! With good notes, it's easy to see the patterns we have and make adjustments we think are appropriate. That's a lot harder if all you have is a giant ball of yarn in your head.

Are you convinced yet? Are you convinced to start a journaling/good note-taking practice? For all of the reasons covered in this chapter, journaling, writing, note-taking, or whatever you want to call it that allows you to do it is mandatory on the road of rethinking broken.

Journaling and writing are how we track and evaluate whether or not what we are doing is working. We know we can only trust ourselves to remember everything accurately for a short time. Reflecting on your day while taking notes is a mandatory habit if you want to achieve maximum change in your life. Regular writing is that important.

It clarifies the things we feel we already know but struggle to describe. Until you ask yourself how you did today and then answer yourself outside the confines of your mind, you won't notice enough of the details, and the devil is always in the details, just like in the story with Ren.

Remember that your RAS is running on years of influence. It takes concentration and effort to shift the needle where we want it to be. Each letter that you write out about how your day went, what went well and what went poorly, who pissed you off, where you were, and why you feel some type of way is one letter closer to peace, self-understanding, and growth. So, write!

You don't even have to read it back now. Just take notes, be somewhat detailed and future you will greatly appreciate your past efforts. It makes all the difference in the world to see how our inner world has changed in black and white. In the future, you will read the words you didn't say. In the future, you will read between the lines and glean fantastic, insightful information that you can use to their benefit. So, take good notes!

TAKE GOOD NOTES HABIT BUILDING:

Get yourself a journal. Make it a pretty one. The prettier or cooler you think it is, the more likely you will write in it. The same goes for the pen. I found some cheap fountain pens online, and now they are all I use. The feeling of writing on good paper with a fancy pen makes me want to write more. Set yourself up for success by doing your version. Use a gel pen or calligraphy if you like. Just make it enjoyable.

Daily writing suggestion:

Each day, at the end of the day, reflect on your day. A simple prompt I liked was What's your flower and what's your thorn for the day? In this exercise, you take 5 minutes in the afternoon/evening to reflect on what was pleasant about the day and what was painful. Just go with it. Any answer is good enough. If the only good thing that happened was a song while you stood in line, so be it. Please don't force it.

THE "NOPE" LIST

Pro-tip for those who tend to sell themselves short. Yes, I mean you. Keep an extra list of "nopes." When I'm not feeling great about myself, when I've had a hard week and haven't been at my best, I can get really down on myself. One way I combat this using good note-taking is I keep a list on my phone of things I said "nope" to.

Each *time I want to do something I know I shouldn't*, like drink or eat something sweet to calm my nervous system, and *I don't do it?* I write that down. When I do this, I'm consistently surprised at how many times I exercise willpower, something I have always felt I struggled with.

My *"nope" list* helps me not dismiss and forget the work I've already done and how many times I have said no in a day. If you struggle with willpower or with self-esteem when your willpower slips, try keeping a "nope" list. You'll see you're probably doing better than you think.

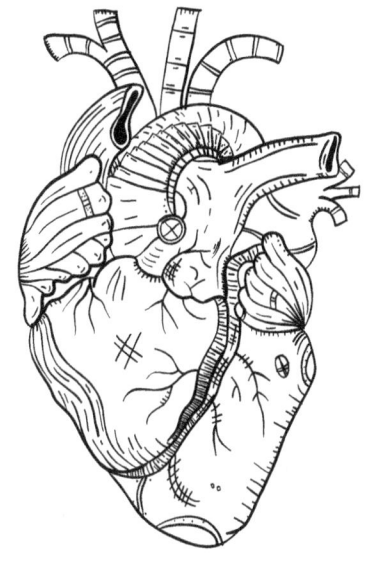

CHAPTER 23
SERVICE SERVES CSA

No matter your story, no matter whether you experienced outright violent abuse or the death-by-a-thousand-cuts kind, there is one more solution I find mandatory for us CSA people. You, I, and every single other CSA person eventually conclude that we do much better when we are regularly of service.

Service? I hear your hyper-independence recoiling. Yes, service, I know. But hear me out. After all the shit CSA people have survived, each one of us struggles with a deep emptiness inside. It's like by surviving the things we survived, we are living proof that the world is fucked up. We feel the evidence of the world's injustices in our very cells. We must be of service if we are going to balance that feeling to find peace in our lives.

The trauma we survive is imprinted in our brains and bodies. Hell, it's pretty safe to say that through epigenetics, the unluckiest of us have their trauma imprinted in our DNA.

The betrayal experienced by some CSA people is so profound that we feel and know the injustice of the world because it lives in our bones. We lived it firsthand. We lived it at a time in our lives when injustice had a significant role in the shaping of our personalities and perspectives.

So far in this book, you've learned ways to help you maintain stability when things get rocky. You've learned about boundaries and non-negotiables, the importance of movement and journaling. You've got some powerful tools on your side. Some of which are powerful enough that they have become non-negotiable habits for me. Due to their effectiveness in helping me keep a temperament and perspective I am proud of.

They help me be chill enough in any given moment to be able to think clearly and react appropriately to the environment I'm in. These valuable tools have been necessary for me at some point to maintain my sanity. Though necessary, they were insufficient.

NECESSARY YET INSUFFICIENT.

- You can and should do your 30 min of movement three times a week.
- You can and should write in your gratitude journal and be firm in your non-negotiables.
- You want to become skilled at placing, honoring, and when appropriate, adjusting your boundaries to accommodate your goals.

If you do everything we've explored up to, but not including service, you will live a pretty good life. You'll still have a new and more whole sense of self. You will be able to navigate relationships much more effortlessly. You might excel at work like you've never done before.

When you do the other things right, you will feel amazing. Your life will flourish like you didn't believe possible. If you instill all the habits we have discussed, you will feel way better than you ever have.

But once the newness of your newly free life wears off. Once your shoulders get used to not having a chip the size of a boulder on them. You will adjust to your freedom and newfound weightlessness. You will feel much better, but you will still feel a sense of "unfairness" deep inside you, you feel compelled to resolve.

You may say Nope, not me! I've always taken care of everyone else. I'm tired of it! It's time I take care of myself. And I say you're right! Take care of you, baby!

But taking care of others *is* taking care of yourself. I don't mean in the spiritual; *we are all one* kind of way. Being of service is directly beneficial to the CSA person.

The more trauma you experienced in your life, the more that trauma shaped you. The more it shapes you, the more it is a part of you. In a way, what that means is that *injustice could be a deep, deep part of you.* You feel its weight in the backdrop of your life every moment of every day. The weight of it can throw us off balance if we aren't careful. Carrying around the memories of trauma while actively trying to live a life that is focused on the things that bring peace and purpose is a dissonant task.

We always feel a desire to resolve that dissonance. But since we can't go back in time to stop the injustice from happening, we seek out injustice in the present moment and do what we can to counteract that.

Bringing justice to an unjust world is why the most CSA people find they love and need to be of service. It isn't about the other person. It doesn't have to be, anyway. Frame it however you need to to make it work for you. Just figure out in your own life a way to do something that balances those scales. I've learned the service lesson firsthand, at Standing Rock, in clinic and the physicist in Tijuana are only a few examples.

The more shaped you are by your trauma, the more service you will feel obliged to provide. The evidence of how much my trauma shaped me is this book. The greatest thing I have ever done for myself right next to getting sober was to write this book.

Trauma lies around in the background of the body and mind of a CSA person. This is why we practice mindfulness, to become aware of this energy in our lives and prevent it from screwing us over. But for myself and for most CSA persons I know, it's not enough to be aware of it.

Name it to tame it – just isn't strong enough for some of our more feral demons. I needed something more robust to drown out the feelings. Liquor worked until it didn't. Now that something is service.

It's like there is this part of me that is eternally, acutely aware of inequality, disparities, neglect and abuse. Even when the rest of the world is quiet, there is this sentry guard in my head, always looking for it, not just in my life but in the world. It's my conditioning. Being aware of that energy makes it tolerable, yes, but only *doing* something about it gets rid of it completely.

Even that only lasts for a short time. I must consistently be of service. While writing this book, my dog and best friend of 12 years died. I started a podcast, a non-profit educational website, and a trauma coaching business. These are the things that solidify and regulate me. They allow me to be of service. This book, too, allows me to be of service.

It cant be just any service for me, just like it can't be any service for you. Your unique strengthnesses are best utilized in ways that allow you to prevent the same type of abuse you suffered from happening to someone else. The crap that we survived should have never happened to us. That is the truth that no one was there to tell us when we needed to hear it.

There is a knowing I experience in my body that does not allow me to forget that at every moment of every day. There is a person out there somewhere who is *hating themselves*. A person out there who thinks they deserve all the worst things in the world to happen to them because they screwed up.

I can never forget that good people like me are suffering under the weight of that one horrible lie. "I am broken." I can't do shit about what happened to me. I can't do shit about what happened to you. But what I can do to right that wrong – what I can do to bring some balance to the world is bust my ass to make sure I help every single CSA person like me to stop with the senseless drama and the self-hate, realize they believe a lie and set them free.

I've spoken with many incredible humans who have devoted their lives to helping CSA people, even while they call them something else. Everyone agrees that we must be of service if we are to stick to our new path.

The trauma that we survived lives on inside us. It formed us. It gave us our strengthnesses, which, like a puppy, are ignored only to our detriment. Even with all the other pieces in place, the puzzle often eventually falls apart without acts of service. Service is the edge piece of the puzzle.

This is the last and final instruction in your Rethinking Broken manual. Many CSA people can never escape our traumatic pasts. Service is what allows us to counterbalance those shitty experiences.

No matter how jaded we are – it's easy to believe there's good in the world if we're the ones doing it.

CONCLUSION

Congratulations, you did it! You've taken your life into your own hands. You are no longer going to let the circumstances of your past rule your future! When you bought this book, you sought wholeness. Now you have it. Best of all, now you know that you never really lost it. It just sure as hell seemed like it.

Thank you for sticking with me till the end of this. There is a lot of information and challenges getting through this book, but you did it! I hope that you now understand that kids are blameless—even you. Kids aren't born shitty they're trained that way. Rarely, if ever, can a child be blamed for their action, thoughts, or behaviors.

You were a perfect specimen raised in an imperfect world by imperfect people. You, too, now are similarly imperfect. If we ever want this cycle of Chronic Stress Adapted parents raising Chronic Stress Adapted children, thinking they're broken to end, we have to start with ourselves.

Thank you for making that first step. There is so much more life coming your way after you close the cover of this book. If you forget every fact, quip, and story from this book, I hope you remember this one thing.

You adapted appropriately to inappropriate circumstances.

No matter how mad you get at yourself. No matter how *depressed* you feel, I hope that this truth is now planted so deep inside you that even in your darkest, most dysregulated moments, you remember that it's not that you're a failure or that you are weak.

You are a beautiful, strong, intelligent, whole person. **You are a highly trained specialist.** In your darkness, I hope the things you learned here can be a light shining compassion and empathy on those pieces of you that you were told were unacceptable or unlovable. You are lovable, and I accept you wholly and utterly. I hope you remember that. And I hope it brings you comfort.

We can't rewrite our past, but we can change how we see and tell our story. If the difference between a tragedy and a comedy is where the story ends - Consider this your invitation to begin writing your story. Keep a close eye on your assumptions and tweak them as necessary little by little until you assume the things you *want* to assume.

When I knee-jerk assume things, which I have no choice but to do, I want to assume compassionate narratives automatically. This is how I create the world I want for my friends' children and their children's children. Life is much better when our automatic assumptions become reasonable, rational, and accurate. It takes time to instill it, but now you know exactly how to.

The model you have now is almost my entire tool belt to help me deal with this chaotic world. It is the greatest gift I can bestow upon anyone. It helps me not get mad at myself for getting mad. It helps me not judge myself or others when something little upsets me. I hope that you use it to find compassion and empathy for yourself and the person your life created. Then, create the life you want. You deserve it.

It would <u>help tremendously if you were to leave a review</u> about your experience with this book. From the bottom of my heart, thank you for spending your time with me. Be Blessed.

Become a member of <u>www.rethinkingbroken.com</u> to join the Rethinking Broken book-club.

*For more from Owl, check out the <u>**Speak Plainly Podcast**</u>*

Available anywhere you get your podcasts.

BIBLIOGRAPHY

1. **International Journal of Research and Innovation in Social Science (IJRISS) |Volume IV, Issue II, February 2020|ISSN 2454-6186.** /journals. *rsisinternational.org.* [Online] feb 2020. https://www.rsisinternational.org/journals/ijriss/Digital-Library/volume-4-issue-2/174-175.pdf.

2. **World Health Organization.** [Online] https://www.who.int/news-room/questions-and-answers/item/stress.

3. **Medcircle.** [Online] https://medcircle.com/articles/types-of-trauma/.

4. **Websters.** [Online] https://www.merriam-webster.com/dictionary/trauma.

5. **theannainstitute.** Adverse Childhood Experience (ACE) Questionnaire. [Online] https://www.theannainstitute.org/Finding%20Your%20ACE%20Score.pdf.

6. **NPR.** living near your grandmother has evolutionary benefits. . *NPR.com.* [Online] https://www.npr.org/sections/goatsandsoda/2019/02/07/692088371/living-near-your-grandmother-has-evolutionary-benefits.

7. **National Child Trauma Stress Network.** *National Child Trauma Stress Network.* [Online] https://www.nctsn.org/what-is-child-trauma/trauma-types.

8. **Dana.org.** sapolsky-on-the-biology-of-good-and-evil. *dana.org.* [Online] https://www.dana.org/article/sapolsky-on-the-biology-of-good-and-evil/.

9. **stack exchange.** stack exchange psychology. [Online] 2017. https://psychology.stackexchange.com/questions/17182/basis-for-we-make-35-000-decisions-a-day-statistic.

10. **1in6.org.** The 1 in 6 Statistic. [Online] 2011. https://www.acesdv.org/wp-content/uploads/2014/06/1-in-6-factsheet.pdf.

11. **Govrnment of Wales.** Understanding why your child's brain is so amazing! [Online] https://www.gov.wales/parenting-give-it-time/your-childs-development/understanding-why-your-childs-brain-is-so-amazing.

12. **Momentous Institution.** What is attunement? *themomentousinstitute.org.* [Online] feb 7, 2017. https://momentousinstitute.org/blog/what-is-attunement.

13. **A. James Barkovich, William B. Dobyns, and Renzo Guerrini.** Malformations of Cortical Development and Epilepsy. [Online] https://www.ncbi.nlm.nih.gov/pmc/articles/PMC4448581/#A022392C68.

14. **Amy L Krain, F. Xavier, Castellanos.** Brain development and ADHD. [Online] https://www.sciencedirect.com/science/article/abs/pii/S0272735806000079.

15. **Arguinchona JH, Tadi P.** Neuroanatomy, Reticular Activating System. *https://www.ncbi.nlm.nih.gov/.* [Online] https://www.ncbi.nlm.nih.gov/books/NBK549835/.

16. **Aron, Elaine N.** *The Highly Sensitive Person.* New York : Three Rivers Press, 1998.

17. **Furman, Stephen W. Porges and Senta A.** The Early Development of the Autonomic Nervous System Provides a Neural Platform for Social Behavior: A Polyvagal Perspective. [Online] 2011. https://www.ncbi.nlm.nih.gov/pmc/articles/PMC3079208/.

18. **Gregory S. Berns, Samuel M. McClure, [...], and P. Read Montague.** NIH. [Online] https://www.ncbi.nlm.nih.gov/pmc/articles/PMC6762527/.

19. **Herman, James P.** Neural control of chronic stress adaptation. [Online] https://www.ncbi.nlm.nih.gov/pmc/articles/PMC3737713/.

20. **JoAnn Stevelos, MS, MPH, and Candace White, MEd., MS.** Sexual Abuse and Obesity – What's the link? *obesity in action.* [Online] https://www.obesityaction.org/resources/sexual-abuse-and-obesity-whats-the-link/.

21. **Johanna Hepp, Benjamin E. Hilbig, [...], and Inga Niedtfeld.** Borderline Personality and the Detection of Angry Faces. [Online] 2016. https://www.ncbi.nlm.nih.gov/pmc/articles/PMC4816443/.

22. **Kolk, Bessel Van Der.** *The Body Keeps score.* s.l. : Viking Press, 2014.

23. **Martin Kronbichler, Heinz Wimmer, [...], and Gunther Ladurner.** Developmental dyslexia: Gray matter abnormalities in the occipitotemporal cortex. [Online] https://www.ncbi.nlm.nih.gov/pmc/articles/PMC6871168/.

24. **McEwen, Bruce S.** Neurobiological and Systemic Effects of Chronic Stress. [Online] https://www.ncbi.nlm.nih.gov/pmc/articles/PMC5573220/.

25. **Radclif, Ian D. Duncan and Abigail B.** Inherited and acquired disorders of myelin: The underlying myelin pathology. [Online] 2016. https://www.ncbi.nlm.nih.gov/pmc/articles/PMC5010953/.

26. **Ramirez, Jan-Marino.** The Integrative Role of the Sigh in Psychology, Physiology, Pathology, and Neurobiology. [Online] https://www.ncbi.nlm.nih.gov/pmc/articles/PMC4427060/.

27. **S G Selevan, C A Kimmel, and P Mendola.** Identifying critical windows of exposure for children's health. [Online] https://www.ncbi.nlm.nih.gov/pmc/articles/PMC1637810/.

28. **Sapolsky, Robert.** *Behave.* s.l. : Penguin Press, 2017.

29. **Simpson, J. A. and Beckes, . Lane (Invalid Date).** Encyclopediabritannica.com . [Online] https://www.britannica.com/science/attachment-theory.

30. **Tasler, Nick.** whats your momentum factor. *psychologytoday.* [Online] https://www.psychologytoday.com/intl/blog/strategic-thinking/201208/what-is-your-momentum-factor.

31. **Ursina McCaskey, Michael von Aster, [...], and Karin Kucian.** Persistent Differences in Brain Structure in Developmental Dyscalculia: A Longitudinal Morphometry Study. [Online] https://www.ncbi.nlm.nih.gov/pmc/articles/PMC7379856/.

32. **Mate', Gabor.** *In the Realm of Hungry Ghosts.* s.l. : North Atlantic Books, 2010.

33. —. *The Myth of Normal.* s.l. : Avery, Sept 13 2022.

34. **Brown, Brene.** *The Power of Vulnerability.* s.l. : Sounds True, 2012.

35. **Spitz, V J Felliti RF Anda DF Williamson AM.** *Relationship of childhood abuse and household dysfunction to many of the leading causes of death in adults. The Adverse Childhood Experiences (ACE) Study.* s.l. : CDC; Kaiser Preminente.

ABOUT THE AUTHOR

Best Selling author, speaker, and behavioral biology expert, Owl C Medicine, reveals a path to healing in 'Rethinking Broken.' Owl shares his intimate battle with Complex-PTSD shaped by a tumultuous upbringing and military service marred with painful losses.

His unique system of Healing & Integration, meticulously derived from behavioral biology, psychology, and neuroanatomy, offers a beacon of hope for those grappling with Complex PTSD, personality disorders and trauma.

Owl's pragmatic system, which has empowered individuals from rural and war-torn regions to urban centers, is not just a method but a journey of self-discovery and affirmation that lead to one inevitable conclusion. You are not broken.

With a personal track record of global impact, personal and professional triumph, Owl's story and system display a practical roadmap to integration, resilience, and leading a truly inspiring life.

ACKNOWLEDGMENTS

To all my Patreon supporters, I couldn't have done this without you. Thank you from the bottom of my heart.

Patreon Supporters:

Elizabeth Lira
Jenni Feingold
Peaceful Piper
Salome Carvalho
Eboney Marie
Tammy Bergstrom
Chris Hill
Nic Harlan
Jacob Hall

Grassroots Editing team:

Eboney White
Jess Doenges
Stephanie Doenges
Tammy Bergstrom
Trevor Hanks

My Clan and Community who helped me re-regulate, and patiently listened to me work out this system for 3+ years.

Jenni Feingold
Eboney Marie
Thu Nguyen
Michael Kaffel
Stephanie Doenges
Jess Doenges

My "real" editor: Penelope Jackson

You are worth your weight in gold. Thank you for organizing that hot pile of garbage I sent you and turning into something sensible & inspiring.

A Special Thanks

to Katy Bowman who sent me Penelope's contact info.

Photography, image credits

Thank you to Wren Morrow for the headshots for the bio.

Cover Design

The Cover design was created by Owl Chrysalis Medicine. The incredible center piece is a photo I took of:

The Kinstugi Porcelain Heart Vase, Concept by SELETTI S.p.A. Italy; Design by Marcantonio "Kintsugi-Love in bloom.

ADDITIONAL
WORKBOOK RESOURCES

*Write out the included exercises here to rip them out when
you're done! Give the book to a friend so they can do the same
thing! Give it to 2! There are 3 complete sets included.*

Finding your strengthness Appendix pages:

Exercise 1, Strengths and Weaknesses; write strengths in the left column and weaknesses
on the right.

(Strengths list)   (Weakness list)

_____   _____

_____   _____

_____   _____

_____   _____

_____   _____

_____   _____

_____   _____

_____   _____

_____   _____

Exercise 2: Exploring Core Beliefs.

Write out some core beliefs you have here. Feel free to reference the core belief example list on page 160 if you want a place to start..

_____

_____

_____

_____

_____

_____

_____

_____

_____

_____

_____

_____

_____

_____

_____

_____

_____

Exercise 3: Finding Your Strengthness, The Good Stuff.

Write out the good stuff. Times when you were in the right place at the right time with the right skills here:

_____

_____

_____

_____

_____

_____

_____

_____

_____

_____

_____

_____

_____

_____

_____

_____

Finding your strengthness: Exercise 4, The Not-So-Great Stuff

Write out some of your less proud moments here. Times that your strengthnesses got the better of you.

_____

_____

_____

_____

_____

_____

_____

_____

_____

_____

_____

_____

_____

_____

_____

My Strengthnesses List

Exercise 1, Strengths and Weaknesses; write strengths in the left column and weaknesses on the right.

(Strengths list)   (Weakness list)

_____   _____

_____   _____

_____   _____

_____   _____

_____   _____

_____   _____

_____   _____

_____   _____

_____   _____

_____   _____

_____   _____

_____   _____

_____   _____

_____   _____

_____   _____

Exercise 2: Exploring Core Beliefs.

Write out some core beliefs you have here. Feel free to reference the core belief example list on page 160 if you want a place to start.

_____

_____

_____

_____

_____

_____

_____

_____

_____

_____

_____

_____

_____

_____

_____

_____

_____

_____

_____

Exercise 3: Finding Your Strengthness, The Good Stuff.

Write out the good stuff. Times when you were in the right place at the right time with the right skills here:

_____

_____

_____

_____

_____

_____

_____

_____

_____

_____

_____

_____

_____

_____

_____

Finding your strengthness: Exercise 4, The Not-So-Great Stuff

Write out some of your less proud moments here. Times that your strengthnesses got the better of you.

_____

_____

_____

_____

_____

_____

_____

_____

_____

_____

_____

_____

_____

_____

_____

_____

_____

_____

My Strengthnesses List

_____

_____

_____

_____

_____

_____

_____

_____

_____

_____

_____

_____

_____

_____

_____

_____

_____

Exercise 1, Strengths and Weaknesses; write strengths in the left column and weaknesses on the right.

(Strengths list)   (Weakness list)

_____   _____

_____   _____

_____   _____

_____   _____

_____   _____

_____   _____

_____   _____

_____   _____

_____   _____

_____   _____

_____   _____

_____   _____

_____   _____

_____   _____

_____   _____

_____   _____

Exercise 2: Exploring Core Beliefs.

Write out some core beliefs you have here. Feel free to reference the core belief example list on page 160 if you want a place to start..

_____

_____

_____

_____

_____

_____

_____

_____

_____

_____

_____

_____

_____

_____

_____

Exercise 3: Finding Your Strengthness, The Good Stuff.

Write out the good stuff. Times when you were in the right place at the right time with the right skills here:

_____

_____

_____

_____

_____

_____

_____

_____

_____

_____

_____

_____

_____

_____

Finding your strengthness: Exercise 4, The Not-So-Great Stuff

Write out some of your less proud moments here. Times that your strengthnesses got the better of you.

_____

_____

_____

_____

_____

_____

_____

_____

_____

_____

_____

_____

_____

_____

_____

_____

My Strengthnesses List